# WELCOME
# TO THE
# HYUNAM-DONG
# BOOKSHOP

# WELCOME TO THE HYUNAM-DONG BOOKSHOP

## HWANG BO-REUM

### Translated By Shanna Tan

BLOOMSBURY PUBLISHING
LONDON · OXFORD · NEW YORK · NEW DELHI · SYDNEY

BLOOMSBURY PUBLISHING
Bloomsbury Publishing Plc
50 Bedford Square, London, WC1B 3DP, UK
29 Earlsfort Terrace, Dublin 2, Ireland

BLOOMSBURY, BLOOMSBURY PUBLISHING and the Diana logo
are trademarks of Bloomsbury Publishing Plc

First published in 2022 in South Korea by Clay House
First published in Great Britain in 2023

어서 오세요, 휴남동 서점입니다
Welcome to the Hyunam-dong Bookshop
Copyright © Hwang Bo-reum, 2022

A catalogue record for this book is available from the British Library

ISBN: HB: 978-1-5266-6227-9; TPB: 978-1-5266-6226-2;
ANZ EDITION: 978-1-5266-6663-5; EBOOK: 978-1-5266-6230-9;
EPDF: 978-1-5266-6956-8

2 4 6 8 1 0 9 7 5 3 1

Typeset by Integra Software Services Pvt. Ltd.
Printed and bound in Great Britain by CPI Group (UK) Ltd, Croydon CR0 4YY

MIX
Paper | Supporting
responsible forestry
FSC® C171272

To find out more about our authors and books visit www.bloomsbury.com
and sign up for our newsletters

# CONTENTS

# What Makes a Good Bookshop?

A man was loitering outside the bookshop. Stooping slightly, he shaded his eyes and peered through the window. He'd mistaken the opening time and come too early. As she walked towards the bookshop, Yeongju recognised the man from behind. He was a regular customer who would drop by two or three evenings a week, always in a business suit.

'Hello.'

Startled, the man turned his head sharply. At the sight of Yeongju, he quickly lowered his hands and straightened up, grinning sheepishly.

'I usually come in the evenings. First time I'm here at this time,' he said.

Yeongju smiled at him.

'Well, not sure about other things, but I'm definitely envious that you start work at lunchtime,' he quipped.

She laughed. 'I get that a lot.'

At the beeps of the passcode being punched on the keypad, the man looked away and turned back only at the click of the door. His face relaxed upon glimpsing the interior through the crack.

Pushing the door wide open, she turned to him.

'It's going to smell a little – of the night air and books. If you don't mind, you're welcome inside.'

The man stepped back, waving his palms. 'No, no. I'm good. I'd hate to bother you, especially outside business hours. I'll come by again. Oh my, isn't it hot today?'

She smiled at his considerate gesture and didn't insist further. 'Only June and it's already scorching,' she said, the sun's rays prickling her arm.

Yeongju stood by the door and watched his retreating figure before turning into the bookshop. The moment she stepped inside, she relaxed, as if her body and senses basked in the comfort of returning to her workplace. In the past, she used to live by mantras like *passion* and *willpower*, as if by imprinting the words on her mind, they would somehow breathe meaning into her life. Then one day she realised it felt like she was driving herself into a corner, and she resolved never to let those words dictate her life again. Instead, she learnt to listen to her body, her feelings, and be in happy places. She would ask herself these questions: does this place make me feel positive? Can I be truly whole and uncompromisingly myself? Do I love and treasure myself here? For Yeongju, the bookshop checked all the boxes.

It was indeed a sweltering day, but before she could turn on the air-con, she needed to expel the stale air of yesterday and let fresh air in. *When will I escape from the past, or is that a futile task?* An unbreakable habit, the negativity reared its ugly head to drag her down, but she quickly pushed back with happier thoughts.

Warm humid air rushed in as she opened the windows one by one. Fanning herself with a hand, she surveyed the bookshop. Questions swirled in her mind. If this were her first visit, would she have faith in the staff's recommendations? How does a bookshop earn trust? What makes a good bookshop?

She imagined walking in for the first time. *I'd probably go starry-eyed at the wall over there*, she thought. The floor-to-ceiling shelves crammed with novels. No, wait. She caught herself in time. Not everyone, even if they're a book lover, enjoys fiction. It was something she learnt only after starting Hyunam-dong Bookshop. Those who didn't like the genre would probably give the wall a wide berth, she mused.

The wall of novels in the bookshop was her way of coming full circle to fulfil her childhood dream. In elementary school, little Yeongju pestered her dad to line all four walls in her room with storybooks. Each time, her dad would admonish her, saying that it wouldn't do for her to be so greedy – even when it came to books. She knew he wasn't angry and was just trying to break her habit of throwing tantrums to get what she wanted. But still, she would burst into tears at his stern demeanour and later, tired from crying, she would curl up and fall asleep in his embrace.

Shifting her weight away from the bookcase she'd been leaning against, Yeongju walked to the windows and closed them one by one, starting as usual from the rightmost. With the last window firmly shut, she switched on the air-con and put on her favourite album – Keane's *Hopes and Fears*. The album was released back in 2004, but she had only discovered the British band last year. It was love at first listen. Since then, she put it on almost every day. The languid and dreamy voice filled the air as a new day at Hyunam-dong Bookshop began.

## It's Okay to Stop Crying

Next to the counter, Yeongju sat down at her desk and checked her inbox for new online orders. The next thing to do was to run through the to-do list she'd prepared the night before. It was a habit from high school that carried well over to her adult life: to write down the tasks she needed to do the following day, starting with the most important one. Years later, she still maintained the habit, albeit with a different purpose. Her younger self had wanted to rule her day with an iron fist; now, Yeongju soothed herself with the lists. Running through the tasks she needed to work on gave her confidence that it would be another day well spent.

For the first few months after the bookshop's opening, she'd completely forgotten about lists and long-time habits. Each day passed by in a blur of struggles, as if time had slammed to a halt. Before she started the bookshop, it'd been even worse, as if something was siphoning her soul away. Or maybe it was more accurate to say she was not herself at all.

There was only one thing on her mind.

*I must open a bookshop.*

Clinging to the thought, she forcibly drove everything else out of her mind. Luckily, she was the type to hold herself together if she had something to focus on. It was the anchor she needed. She plunged headlong into the process. She settled on a location, found a suitable property; busied herself with the fittings and furnishings and bought in the stock. In between everything, she even got herself certified as a barista.

This was how Hyunam-dong Bookshop, nestled in the residential neighbourhood of the same name, came to be.

In the beginning, she left the front door open and did nothing else. People walking by strolled in, drawn by the seemingly gentle atmosphere. But in fact, the bookshop was like a wounded beast, wheezing feebly. The footfall soon trickled to a drop. It was the sight of Yeongju sitting on a chair, her face so ashen you'd wonder if she still had a drop of blood in her: stepping into the bookshop was like an intrusion of her private space. She welcomed everyone with a smile, but none of them returned it.

Mincheol's mother, a good-looking lady with a flashy sense of fashion, was among the rare few who felt the sincerity in her smile.

'Who would come into a shop like this? Bookselling is also a business. Here, look at you slumped in that chair! Do you think money will fall from the sky?'

Twice a week, Mincheol's mother attended drawing and Chinese classes at the neighbourhood community centre. After her classes, she made it a point to stop by the bookshop to check on Yeongju.

'Feeling alright today?' Mincheol's mother asked, a hint of worry in her voice.

'Always fine.' Yeongju smiled weakly.

'Aigoo. Everyone in the neighbourhood was so happy to have our own bookshop. But they see this lady nailed to her chair looking like she has a screw loose, as if she belongs in the hospital instead! Who would dare come in?' Mincheol's mother exclaimed as she fished out a sparkly wallet from her equally flashy bag.

'Just one loose screw? Hey, that's not too bad,' Yeongju exclaimed.

Mincheol's mother snorted with laughter. 'One iced Americano.'

'I'm trying to be less perfect, more human. Guess that backfired,' Yeongju deadpanned.

'Hrmmph. Did someone tell you I love a good sense of humour?'

Yeongju pressed her lips into a thin line and wiggled her eyebrows as if saying, 'Please draw your own conclusions,' to which the older lady returned an amused scowl. Leaning against the bar table, she watched Yeongju prepare her coffee.

'I've been through something similar too,' she said quietly, half to herself. 'My body shut down and I was completely drained. After giving birth to Mincheol, there was a period when I lived like a patient. Well, I was one. My body was in pain. But what I couldn't understand was why my mind was hurting too. Come to think of it, it was probably depression.'

'Your coffee is ready.'

Yeongju was about to put a lid on the cup when Mincheol's mother waved her hand away. She grabbed a straw and settled down at a table while Yeongju sat across from her.

'The worst thing was having to act like I was fine when I wasn't. I cried every night, feeling so sorry for myself for not being able to speak of my pain. I wonder if things would have turned out different, if I could have been like you, sitting there and letting go of everything else. The tears wouldn't stop, but you know, when we feel like crying, we should let it all out. Forcing them back only makes the wounds heal slower.'

At Yeongju's silence, Mincheol's mother paused and, in one go, drained the iced coffee.

'I envy you,' she added, 'to have the space to do that.'

For the first few months, Yeongju, too, had cried her heart out. She let the tears flow, but if customers walked in on her crying, she would dab her eyes dry and greet them as if nothing had happened. Nobody said anything about her tear-stained face. Nobody asked why she cried; they simply assumed there was a reason. Yeongju knew very well why she was crying. For a long time – perhaps her whole life – it would cast a shadow over her, making her cry.

Nothing had changed. The reason, stuck in the past, remained as it was. But one day, Yeongju realised that the tears had stopped. That moment – knowing that it was okay to stop crying – felt as if a heavy rock was lifted from her heart. The days of listlessly sitting in her chair dwindled as each morning felt a little more hopeful than the last. She didn't have enough energy yet to do more for the bookshop, but she started reading voraciously again.

It was as if she was back to the days of reading from morning to night, giggling as she piled on more books to the stack, scrunching up her face in concentration as she leafed through the pages. She was back to being little Yeongju, who turned a deaf ear to her mother's nagging as she read through mealtimes; back to basking in the joy of reading even as her eyes protested. *If I can experience that happiness once more, perhaps I'll be able to start afresh*, she thought.

Up till middle school, Yeongju had been an avid reader. Her parents, both perpetually busy, left her alone reading in a corner at home. Once she devoured all the books in her collection, she turned to the library. She loved books. Novels were her favourite, bringing her on expeditions across lands and seas in the comfort of her home. When she had to pull herself back to reality – cutting a sweet dream short – her heart sank. But she needn't feel sad for long. She only had to open the book to dive right into the adventures again.

Reading in the empty bookshop brought back memories of her childhood and she smiled. It occurred to her, as she rubbed her dry eyes with her palms, that she was past the age for a reading marathon. She blinked several times before returning to the page. As if trying her best to mend a broken friendship from her childhood, she immersed herself into the books, day and night, never leaving their side. It didn't take long for their treasured relationship to rekindle. The books welcomed her back with open arms without judging the person she'd become, and accepted her for who she was. Like a well-nourished person who ate three good meals a day, she grew stronger. One day, lifting her head from the pages, she found herself looking at the bookshop with clearer eyes and a sharper mind.

*I need to do better than this.*

Yeongju sought out book recommendations and worked hard to fill the half-empty shelves. For each book she read, she penned down her thoughts on memo paper which she wedged between the pages. The ones she hadn't read, she would put together the opinions of literary critics, book reviewers and readers she found online. When customers asked for an unfamiliar title, she made sure to look it up. All this she didn't do for the profits; her priority was to create a bookshop that looked and felt like one. Gradually, her efforts paid off. Residents nearby stopped throwing doubtful looks at the bookshop; the astute ones even noticed the changes. Each time they walked in, the bookshop seemed a little warmer, a little more inviting, casting a magnetic charm on passers-by. The biggest change was Yeongju. The bookshop lady who had flustered customers with her tear-stained face was no more.

The bookshop began seeing visitors from further neighbourhoods. Mincheol's mother was delighted to see unfamiliar faces browsing the shelves.

'Did they mention how they got to know of the bookshop?'

'Through our Instagram.'

'The bookshop's on *Instagram*?'

'Yes. You know the handwritten notes in between the books' pages? I post the photos online too.'

'Uh. And people travel all the way here because of that?'

'Well, not only that. I'm quite active on Instagram. I usually post a warm greeting during the morning rush hour. Or a book I'm reading. Sometimes, I share small grumbles in life. Oh, and another greeting during the evening commute.'

'What's in the brains of the young ones is beyond me. Why travel so far because of this? Well, anyway, great. I thought you were just sitting around like a mannequin, but it looks like you're doing something.'

There wasn't much to do when she couldn't be bothered, but once she started to care, the work was never-ending. From the time she punched in the passcode till she locked up for the day, her hands and feet never had an idle moment. When her limbs almost tied themselves into a knot as she bounced between the bookshop and the coffee orders piling up, she decided it was time to get some help. She put up hiring notices in the neighbourhood for a barista. Minjun walked in the very next day. The same day, after she had a sip of his coffee, she took down the notices. He started work the following day, around the first anniversary of the bookshop.

Since then, another year had passed. Minjun was set to arrive in five minutes. As usual, over a cup of his coffee, she would immerse herself in a novel until one o'clock, when the bookshop was ready to welcome its customers.

# What's the Coffee of the Day?

On his way to the bookshop, Minjun cast an envious glance at a man walking past him with a handheld fan. Calling the day hot was an understatement when his scalp tingled in the unrelenting heat. It hadn't been this insufferable last year, or had it? Thinking of the weather reminded him that it was this time a year ago when he'd come across the hiring notice.

*BARISTA WANTED.*

*8 hours a day, 5 days a week.*
*Renumeration to be discussed in person.*
*Anyone who makes good coffee is welcome to apply.*

Back then, Minjun was desperate for a job. He didn't care what it was. Making coffee was fine. So was moving bulky items, cleaning toilets, flipping burgers, delivering parcels, or scanning barcodes. To him, they were all the same. As long as it paid. So, he turned up at the bookshop.

It was about three in the afternoon when he pushed open the door. As expected, the bookshop was empty, save for a lady who appeared to be the owner. She was sitting at one of the square tables in the café section of the shop, busy scribbling on a notepad the size of her palms. At the sound of the door, she looked up and gave him a little nod of greeting. Her warm smile seemed to say: feel free to browse, I won't bother you.

When she returned to her work, Minjun thought he would take things slow and have a look around. The place was spacious – big, in fact – for an independent bookshop, and the couple of chairs nestled among the bookshelves seemed to welcome customers to take their time to browse. Fully stocked shelves reaching all the way to the ceiling took up one third of the wall to the right while display racks aligned to the height of the shop windows flanked both sides of the entrance. It wasn't quite clear, at first glance, how the books were organised. He randomly pulled a book out from the nearest shelf. A piece of paper peeked out from the top. Opening the book, he took out the note and read it.

*Every one of us is like an island; alone and lonely. It's not a bad thing. Solitude sets us free, just as loneliness brings depth to our lives. In the novels I like, the characters are like isolated islands. In the novels I love, the characters used to be like isolated islands, until their fates gradually intertwined; the kind of stories where you whisper, 'You were here?' and a voice answers, 'Yes, always.' You think to yourself,* I was a little lonely, but because of you, I'm less alone. *It's a wonderful feeling and the book in your hands gives me a taste of that joy.*

Minjun slid the note back and flipped to the title. *The Elegance of the Hedgehog.* He tried to imagine a prickly hedgehog ambling elegantly. A hedgehog? Solitude? Loneliness? Depth? He couldn't quite link them together. *Solitude sets us free, just as loneliness brings depth to our lives.* He had never given much thought – good or bad – to solitude or loneliness, and hence never tried to avoid either. In that sense, he was free. But did it add depth to his life? He wasn't sure.

It looked like the owner was working on a similar note right now. Did she handwrite these all by herself? He had always thought a bookshop simply stocks and sells books, but it seemed like there was more to it.

Ending his tour with a quick glance at the coffee machine, he approached the lady.

'Excuse me.'

Yeongju stood up. 'May I help you?'

'I saw the hiring notice. For a barista.'

'Ah! Yes! Please have a seat.'

Yeongju grinned at him, as though he was the person she'd been waiting for for the longest time. She walked over to her desk next to the counter and returned with two sheets of paper, which she placed on the table before taking the seat opposite.

'Do you live nearby?'

'Yes.'

'And you know how to make coffee?'

'Yes. I've worked part-time at several cafés.'

'Are you able to handle that coffee machine over there?'

He glanced in the direction she was pointing. 'I guess so.'

'Alright, would you make me some coffee?'

'Now?'

'Two cups. We'll chat over coffee.'

A while later, he returned with freshly made coffee. He kept his gazed fixed upon Yeongju as she took a sip from hers. Even with the sudden request, he wasn't at all nervous; he had no reason to be when serving up decent coffee was easy for him. But he tensed up when Yeongju took her time to savour the dark liquid, slowly tipping the cup back for a second sip before looking up.

'Why aren't you drinking? Drink up, it's good.'

'Okay.'

They chatted for the next twenty minutes, or rather, Yeongju did most of the talking while he listened. Praising his coffee, Yeongju asked if he was available immediately. Yes, he replied. As a barista, you'd focus on the coffee, she said, adding that her only request was for him to take over all the coffee-related tasks so that she could free up some bandwidth. When she followed with a question on whether he could also handle the selection and procurement of coffee beans, he wondered why such a nondescript task would warrant a separate mention, but out loud, he simply replied, 'Yes.'

'There's a roaster I work with. The boss is a good person.'

'Got it.'

'You and I, we'll keep to our own roles. But if either of us gets too busy, the other person can chip in.'

'Got it.'

'To make it clear, it's not only me who can ask for help. If you're swamped, I'll help too.'

'Got it.'

Yeongju pushed the documents to him. It was his contract. She handed him a pen to sign once he was agreeable to the terms and started to walk him through each clause.

'You'll be working five days a week; rest days are Sundays and Mondays. Work hours are from half past noon to eight thirty in the evening. Are you okay with this?'

'Got it.'

'The bookshop is open six days a week, so I only take a break on Sundays.'

'I see, got it.'

'In the event you have to work overtime, though I don't really see it happening, you'll be paid for the extra hours.'

'Got it.'

'Your hourly rate is twelve thousand won.'

'Twelve thousand?'

'You're working five days a week and putting in the hours equivalent to a full-time job. To be paid adequately, that's what you should get.'

Minjun couldn't help but look around the bookshop. Since the moment he had stepped in, there had been no customers. He wondered if the boss realised it. She seemed to have no idea what the market rate was, as if it was her first time hiring for a casual position. The offhand way she was handling the process gave him pause. Even though he knew that he was overstepping boundaries, he couldn't resist telling her.

'The pay is usually lower.'

Yeongju glanced up with a knowing look before looking back down at the contract.

'For sure, it's going to be tough with the expensive rent . . . But Minjun, it's fine. You don't have to worry about this.'

She looked up into his eyes; they were impassive but warm. She liked that. The kind of eyes that were hard to read at first sight, but something in there compelled her to slowly get to know him. She was also pleased with how he didn't put up a façade, nor try to get on her good side, but remained polite throughout their conversation.

'You need rest to work, and to rest, you need a certain level of income to live comfortably,' she said.

Minjun read his contract again. So, this boss, in order to ensure work-life balance, deliberately made it an eight-hour, five-days-a-week position and for the person to be adequately compensated, she did the calculations and ended up with the hourly pay of 12,000 won. Was this the righteousness of a first-time employer? Or was this book-shop doing better than it looked? Minjun had questions but he signed as he was told, followed by Yeongju.

He stood up with his copy in hand and nodded in greeting at Yeongju, who got up to see him to the door.

'By the way,' she called out. 'I may only be able to keep this bookshop running for two years. That alright with you?'

In this time and age, who would think of staying in a casual job for more than two years? Six months was his longest record. Truth be told, he wouldn't feel at all disappointed even if she suddenly told him next month that he was no longer needed. But to her, he simply said, 'Got it.'

Now, a year had passed since the day he said yes to the intriguing boss of Hyunam-dong Bookshop. In that time, they followed their agreement faithfully. Yeongju spent her time experimenting with new ideas and observed how the customers took to them, while Minjun, in his steadfast way, handled the selection and procurement of the coffee beans, and manned the coffee machine. True to her words, she didn't expect anything more from him beyond good coffee. When she caught him staring vacantly into space during a lull between customers, she'd chuckle. *Shouldn't bosses give you a dirty look when they catch you lazing?* At that thought, he couldn't help but laugh along too.

Swiping away beads of sweat gliding off his fringe, he pushed open the door and was immediately welcomed by the cool breeze from the air-conditioning.

'I'm here.'

Yeongju looked up from her book. 'Terribly hot out there, isn't it?'

'Yeah,' he said as he lifted the countertop and entered his workspace, which took up the other side of the counter.

'What's the coffee of the day?'

'Make a guess later.' He smiled as he washed and dried his hands.

After placing a cup of fresh coffee next to her book, he returned to the café counter, but his gaze remained fixed on her. He watched her take a sip, a thoughtful expression on her face.

'It's kind of similar to the one yesterday. But the fruitiness in this one seems stronger. Delicious.'

He nodded, pleased that she could tell the difference. As usual, they chatted a little more before naturally gravitating back to their own work. Yeongju had a habit of reading before opening, while Minjun would prepare the beans for the day, and in his spare time, he would help to tidy up the bookshop. He knew that she would have cleaned up the night before, but it was an area where he could help.

## Stories of People Who Walked Away

Before the bookshop opened for the day, Yeongju was usually absorbed in a novel. Immersing herself into the feelings of the characters provided a reprieve from her own. She grieved, suffered, and emerged stronger with them. As if sharing their experiences and emotions would, at the end of the book, allow her to understand anyone in the world.

Often, she read in search of something. However, she didn't always know exactly what she was looking for when she turned the first page. Sometimes she was several chapters in before she went, *Ah, so this is what I'm looking for.* There were also times she clearly knew – right from the beginning – what she sought. The novels she'd been devouring for the past year were mostly the latter. She wanted stories of people who walked away from their lives – whether it was for a few days, or forever. A myriad of reasons and backstories, but they had one thing in common: their lives changed from then on.

Back then, she was told, 'I don't understand you.' Sometimes, it was an accusation. 'Why do you only think of yourself?'

Just when Yeongju thought she was starting to forget those biting words, their voices would return as hallucinations to haunt her. Just when the memories were fading into the distance, they would surge and inundate her the next moment. Each time, she cracked a little deeper. Dreading a complete breakdown, she decided to bury herself in stories of people who'd left their old lives behind. She read ravenously, as if on a mission across the world to collect them all. Somewhere within her was an empty vessel; she poured into it – past its brim – their stories, reasons, emotions, and the courage they had to summon. She wanted to know all about their lives thereafter, their thoughts over time, their joy, suffering, happiness and sadness in life.

When the going got tough, she would retreat into herself, curling up next to them as she listened to their stories and sought comfort in their words and experiences.

She drowned the biting criticism – *I don't understand you! Why do you only think of yourself?* – with their voices. They gave her strength, and finally, she mustered the courage to tell herself, 'That was my only option back then.'

For the past few days, Yeongju had been absorbed in Monika Maron's *Animal Triste,* the story of a woman who – in the most complete sense of the word – leaves her husband and daughter. She has fallen in love with another man, but because nothing can be more important in life than true love, because the path ahead – the one and only – is so obvious, she feels no remorse. When the man later walks out of her life, she stops making new memories, for fear of erasing him and their shared time. She disengages completely from the world, living out the remainder of her life in solitude, for decades, until the ripe old age of ninety, or one hundred.

A good novel, to Yeongju, was one which would bring her to places beyond her expectations. In this book, her focus had initially been on the woman 'walking away', but later, she realised 'love' was what made everything possible. She mulled over how the woman starts to wear the glasses the man had left behind, even though it ruins her sight eventually – her final, desperate attempt to be close to him.

How does one love so unconditionally? Yeongju wondered. To live decades in isolation, cherishing a love affair forty or fifty years past. Did she not have regrets; what made her so certain he was the only love of her life? Yeongju didn't understand the woman, but for having lived so fiercely and intensely, she admired her.

Tearing her eyes from the pages, she ruminated on the woman's words: 'Of all life has to offer, only love is indispensable.' Was love the most important thing in life? Did nothing else compare? *Love is great*, she thought. But indispensable? No, she didn't agree. Just like how some thrive on love, it's also possible to live without it. *I'm doing quite well without love,* she thought.

While she was lost in her thoughts, Minjun was wiping the coffee cups dry with a tea towel. When the alarm rang at one o'clock, he returned the cloth to its position and walked to the door. The thud of the 'open' sign being turned shook her out of her reverie. As he walked back to the counter, she felt the urge to ask his opinion on love. But she thought better of it. She could already imagine his response. He would pause to think and answer, 'Well . . .' She wished she knew what was in his head in that moment of hesitation, but Minjun was never one to share his thoughts readily.

Looking at him pick up the same cup again, Yeongju thought she made the right decision not to ask. In any case, there was only one correct answer: the one she had in mind right now. Isn't that what life is about? Forging forward with the answer you have – stumbling along the way and picking yourself up – only to one day realise that the answer you've held on to for a long time is not the right one. When that happens, it's time to look for the next answer. That's how ordinary folks, like herself, live. Over our life span, the right answer will keep changing.

He was still drying the cups when she called out, 'Minjun, may today be a good one too.'

# Please Recommend Me a Good Book

Before running the bookshop, Yeongju had never considered whether she was suitable to be a bookseller. She thought, rather naively, that anyone who loves books could be one. It was only when she started her own bookshop that she realised she had a serious shortcoming. She fumbled questions such as 'Which book is good?' and 'What's an interesting book?' Once, she made a complete fool of herself when a man in his late forties sought her recommendation for a book.

'*The Catcher in the Rye* by J. D. Salinger is really interesting,' she enthused. 'Have you read it?'

The man hung his head. 'No, I haven't.'

'I've read it more than five times, I believe. It isn't that interesting, not in a generic sense. You know how some books make you throw your head back in laughter, or dizzy with anticipation? This book isn't interesting in *that* sort of way. I mean . . . it's beyond the generic *interesting*. There's no uh . . . climax or a central plot stitching the book together. The entire story follows a child's thoughts and takes place over the span of a few days. That said, I mean . . . I still find this book interesting,' she finished pathetically.

'What does the child think about?'

The man looked so serious Yeongju felt a stab of nerves as she tried to explain.

'It's about how a child sees the world, his thoughts about schools, teachers, friends, parents . . .'

The man furrowed his brows. 'Will I also like this book?'

She was stumped. *Will he find it interesting? Why, of all books, did I recommend this?* It must have shown on her face, for the man simply thanked her and walked away. Later, he approached the counter and bought *Insights of Eurasia*[1]. So that was what he liked. Historical non-fiction. Something he said before leaving the shop that day had remained on her mind ever since.

'I'm sorry I asked a difficult question when everyone has their own preferences.'

A customer saying 'I'm sorry' to a bookseller for seeking a recommendation when she should've been the one to apologise for her incompetence! It was an important lesson learnt: never to blindly recommend her own favourites to the customer. She wanted to do better. But how? In her spare moments at work, she brooded over it and came up with the following:

- **BE OBJECTIVE**

    Avoid personal biases. Instead of 'books I like', recommend 'books which the customers may enjoy'.

- **ASK QUESTIONS**

    Don't rush into a recommendation. Ask the following questions: what is a book you enjoyed reading recently? Which book left a deep impression on you? What genres do you like? What is on your mind recently? Who are your favourite authors?

[1]Lee Byeong-han, 유라시아 견문 *Yurasia Gyeonmun* (Seohae Munjib, 2016)

Despite developing a strategy, she still blanked occasionally at such requests.

'Is there a book that'll unclog a smothered heart?' Mincheol's mother asked as she ordered an iced Americano, adding that she'd skipped her classes because she wasn't in the mood for them.

A book to unclog a smothered heart? The request was too abstract but none of her prepared questions seemed at all appropriate. Desperate not to drag out the silence, she cast around for something to ask and landed on the innocuous, 'Something's bothering you?'

'It's been like this for the past few days, as if I'm stuffed with injeolmi rice cakes, stuck all the way up my throat.'

'What happened?'

At Yeongju's question, she suddenly stiffened, her eyelids trembling. She quickly gulped down half the iced Americano, but it didn't bring light back to her eyes.

'It's Mincheol.'

A family issue. Somehow, running a bookshop made Yeongju privy to the most private matters of her customers. She'd read somewhere that authors often get people opening up to them, as if being a wordsmith somehow meant that they would understand things that even the closest of friends couldn't. Apparently, people thought the same of booksellers, as if owning a bookshop was an accreditation of exceptional emotional intelligence.

'Something happened to him?' she asked.

She had seen the lanky high schooler on a few occasions. He'd inherited his mother's pale face and when he smiled, he looked pure and bright.

'Mincheol . . . he told me he sees no meaning in life.'

'No meaning in life?' Yeongju echoed.

'Yeah.'

'Why?'

'I have no idea. I don't think he really meant it, but since then, I haven't been able to focus on anything. My heart aches whenever I think of what he said.'

According to his mother, Mincheol said he had zero interest in anything – studying, games, hanging out with friends. While it wasn't like he completely stopped doing any of these – he still studied when exams were around the corner, played games when he was bored and met his friends occasionally – he was indifferent to them all, and on most days, he would return home straight after school, browse the Internet on his bed and drift off to sleep. At the age of eighteen, he was sick of life.

'Is there no book that'll help me?' Mincheol's mother poked her straw in between the ice cubes and sucked up the last drops of coffee.

For Mincheol, Yeongju could draw up a reading list. There were plenty of stories about fatigue or being lost in one's own world. What, though, could she suggest to a mother whose child was going through a teenage life crisis? No matter how hard she thought, she couldn't come up with anything suitable. She couldn't recall any novels about a mother and son, nor had she read a single parenting book. She was filled with dread. Not because she couldn't find a suitable book, but because it suddenly hit her that she was the limiting factor of the bookshop, the cause of its narrow worldview. Hyunam-dong Bookshop was tailored to her preferences as a reader, her interests, and her reading repertoire. How could such a place be helpful to others? She decided to be honest.

'I can't think of any book that'll help.'

'Don't worry about it.'

'Actually . . . wait. There's a novel I just thought of. *Amy and Isabelle*. It's about a mother and daughter living under the same roof who hate each other as much as they love each other. Being a parent and child doesn't mean they'll always understand and accommodate each other. Reading it made me think that, in some sense, even parents and their children should lead their own separate lives eventually.'

'This sounds intriguing,' said Mincheol's mother, 'I'll get it.' She declined Yeongju's offer to lend her the book first to see how she'd take to it. As Yeongju watched her leave with the book in hand, she thought about the power books held. *Is there a book that'll unclog a smothered heart? Will a book have that much power?*

Two weeks later, Mincheol's mother dropped by again.

'I have to run but I wanted to tell you how much I enjoyed the book. It reminded me of my own mother. We fought a lot, too, although not as much as Amy and Isabelle.'

She paused, as if her thoughts had drifted far away and when she spoke again, her eyes were slightly red.

'That last scene, where the mother kept calling out for her daughter . . . I bawled, thinking about how there'll come a time when I'll miss my child so much. I can't hold him in my arms forever and a day, I'll have to learn to let him fly, to let him live his own life. Thank you so much, Yeongju. Please recommend me more good books again. Alright, got to run!'

While it wasn't quite the story she was looking for, Mincheol's mother had enjoyed what Yeongju some-what hesitantly recommended. The heaviness in her heart remained, but the book brought back memories of her mother and nudged her to reflect on how to handle her relationship with her son. Could it count as a good recommendation? Despite falling short of expectations, could a book, if enjoyed, be considered a good read?

Is a good book always a good read?

Her recommendations might not be what the customers hoped for, but if they said, 'It's still good,' perhaps she had done a good job. Of course, suggesting a novel about a high school student – even if it's one of the best literary novels with social commentary – to a middle-aged ajusshi who enjoyed non-fiction history titles could still be a no go. But who knows? One day, he might feel like reading a novel. Or maybe, when he wanted to better understand his children, he might recall being recommended such a book and seek it out. If he did, he might even enjoy it. As with everything in life, reading is about the right timing.

That said, what counts as a good book? For the regular person, it's perhaps a book they enjoyed. But as a bookseller, Yeongju needed to think beyond that.

She tried coming up with a definition.

- *Books about life. Not something generic, but a deep and raw dive into life.*

Recalling Mincheol's mother's red-rimmed eyes, she tried to elaborate further.

- *Books by authors who understand life. Those who write about family, mother and child, about themselves, about the human condition. When authors delve deep into their understanding of life to touch the hearts of readers, helping them to navigate life, isn't that what a good book should be?*

# A Time for Silence, a Time for Conversations

The bookshop was a flurry of activity – customers needing assistance, non-stop coffee orders, inventory forms to be filled in – but when they next surfaced from the bustle, all was quiet again. No customers, no drink orders, and nothing that needed immediate attention. During these pockets of peace, Yeongju would insist that they take a break. Ignoring the mess on the shelves, she cut some fruit by the sink and as if on cue, Minjun would have fresh coffee ready when she passed a plate to him.

Silence settled comfortably between them. Yeongju enjoyed these quiet moments. She was glad to share space without needing to force a conversation. Small talk could be a considerate gesture, but most of the time, at your own expense. With nothing to say, squeezing the words dry leaves only an empty heart and a desire to escape.

Sharing space with Minjun taught her silence could also be a form of consideration, that it was possible to be comfortable without needing to fill the silence. Gradually, she learnt to get used to the natural quietude.

No matter how long the break lasted – ten, twenty or thirty minutes – Minjun always did the same few things.

For one, he never took out his phone. She knew he owned one; he'd written his number in the résumé although she had never needed to call him. Sometimes he read, even though he didn't seem to particularly enjoy it. Most of the time, he was like a lab researcher, fiddling with the coffee beans. Initially, she thought he was doing it to while away time, but as the aroma and flavour of his coffee deepened, it became clear that they were purposeful experiments.

There was someone with whom she could discuss the topic 'How Quiet Minjun Is' at length – Jimi, the owner of the roaster supplying their beans, who also taught her everything she knows about coffee. They complemented each other well; Yeongju loved cracking jokes and Jimi was a great listener. Their ten-year age gap didn't bother them one bit.

At first, Jimi used to come over to the bookshop, but in no time at all, Yeongju's apartment became their hideout. Sometimes she would return home from work to find Jimi squatting by her door, who would, upon seeing her, dust her bottom and stand up. Each time, she would bring bags of food and drinks. They became fast friends who could talk about anything under the sun. Even with the most random topics, their conversations flowed easily. If the conversation trailed off, they would easily pick it up again. Neither was more dominant than the other; the banter moved to and fro quickly, like a game of table tennis.

Once, over beer at her place, they had a whole discussion about 'How Little Minjun Talks'.

'He's really a man of few words. At first, I thought he's just a bot. You know, he greets you, and that's it.' Jimi paused to chew on a strand of dried squid. 'But he's good at responding to what you say.'

The dried squid dangling from Yeongju's mouth bobbed along as she nodded vigorously. 'He answers well when spoken to. Aha! So that's why I've never felt frustrated talking to him.'

'Come to think of it, Minjun isn't the only silent one,' Jimi said as she chewed on her squid. 'All men are the same, their tongues tied after marriage, as if silence is their wordless protest.'

For a moment, Yeongju's thoughts were carried away to married men and their silent protests, before she pulled herself back and confessed what she'd made of Minjun's silence. 'I thought he didn't like me. I thought I was the problem.'

'What's with the victim mentality? Did you grow up being disliked?'

'It's not that . . . It's like I don't have the capacity to get close to people. I was always alone, my heels clicking furiously as I kept trying to move ahead of others, farther and farther. But when I finally paused to turn around one day, everyone passed me by as if I were invisible. No one came up to me to ask, "Would you like to try this? It's really delicious!" Does this count as being disliked?'

'Yep.'

'I knew it!' Yeongju sighed dramatically just as Jimi pulled out the strand of squid from her mouth and exclaimed, 'Is this it?'

'Huh?'

'Maybe Minjun doesn't talk to us because he sees us as ajummas!'

'Come on! Minjun and I are barely a few years apart!' Yeongju pouted, stretching out her palms close to Jimi's face and folding both thumbs in, to emphasise the number. 'Only eight years!'

Jimi laughed. 'Is Minjun in his thirties?'

'He was already thirty when he first started working here.'

'I see. Well, if it's only an eight-year difference, I don't think he'll see you as an ajumma. Say, don't you think Minjun has changed a little though?'

'What?'

'He's talking a little more these days.'

'Really?'

'He's asking questions every now and then.'

'Is that so?'

'He laughs and chats with my staff too.'

'Seriously?'

'It's cute.'

'You think he's cute?'

'Don't you think so? That quiet, focused look on his face when he's completely absorbed in a task.'

'You mean when he's absorbed in—'

'It can be anything. I just find people who give their utmost to a pursuit cute. It makes me want to treat them well.'

When Yeongju started offering Minjun fruit every day, he was slightly thrown off, but he grew to accept it politely, treating it as Yeongju's idea of an employee benefit – like pantry snacks. Despite never liking fruit much, he'd gotten so used to it that skipping a day of fruit felt odd enough that he would go out of his way on his rest days to buy some for himself. And that is how habits are formed.

For Yeongju, preparing fruit for Minjun was her way of telling him to take a break. Sometimes she would finish cutting the fruit only to be called away – before she could grab a slice – by something or someone demanding her attention. Then, there were days like today where they'd already enjoyed twenty minutes of uninterrupted rest. On such days, she would savour the fruit slowly and select a book from her stack. Tucking stray strands of her shoulder-length hair behind her ear, she immersed herself in the printed word, occasionally looking up with unfocused eyes as if her thoughts were still elsewhere. It looked as if she was staring into empty space but suddenly, she would toss a question at Minjun.

'Minjun, do you think we should abandon a boring life?' Her chin was propped on her palms, but she wasn't looking at him. When she did this, he used to keep quiet, thinking that she was talking to herself. But now he knew better.

'There are people who, one day, decide to leave behind their old life and start afresh elsewhere. Do you think they'll be happy with their new life?' She turned to him.

It was a difficult question. Minjun wondered why Yeongju liked to ask these questions. Thinking a prolonged silence would be rude, he decided to buy some time. 'Well . . .'

This, or some variation of an affirmative answer, was how Minjun usually answered her questions. He couldn't help it. He wouldn't know whether those people were happy with their new life or not, would he?

'I'm reading this novel,' Yeongju said, 'where the protagonist meets a woman by chance on a bridge. She's somewhat enigmatic and because of their chance encounter, the man, who lives in Switzerland, leaves for Portugal on a train one day. It's not a holiday; he buys a one-way ticket. I wonder why he chooses to leave. He's bored of his life, but it isn't as if he has a hard time. He's one of those quiet, talented types; not world-famous, but still held in esteem in his circle. He could have easily enjoyed a good life in Switzerland, but he leaves the country as if he'd been waiting for this moment his whole life. What do you think he hopes to find in Portugal? Will he truly be happy there?'

Yeongju was usually a pragmatic person but when she was deeply engrossed in a story, she was like a person trying to grasp at moving clouds. Minjun found the juxtaposition interesting, as if she had one eye on reality while the other gazed at some faraway dreamland. Just the other day, she'd asked him another question about life.

'Do you think there's any meaning to life?'

'Huh?'

'I don't think there is.' Her proclamation was met with silence. 'That's why people try to make sense of their own. In the end, everyone's life is different, according to the meaning they find.'

'. . . I see.'

'But I don't think I can find it.'

'Find what?'

'Meaning. Where can you find meaning? In love? Friendship, books, bookshops? It's not easy.'

Minjun didn't know what to say.

'Even if you want to search for it, it's not going to be quick and easy. What do you think?' Unruffled by his silence, she continued. 'It's obviously not going to be easy. After all, it's the meaning of *life*. Well, I still want to try. But if I fail, does it mean that my life has no meaning?'

Minjun found it hard to keep up with her stream of thoughts.

'Well . . .'

It seemed to him that instead of seeking his answer, Yeongju was throwing out questions to make sense of the swirling thoughts in her head. Hence, despite him giving a non-committal response most of the time, she was never reproachful. Slowly, he started to understand how shuttling between the two worlds – floating among her clouds of thoughts and grounding herself in reality – enriched her life.

Yeongju's ways started to rub off on him. Something seemed to lie at the end of his stretch of thoughts.

Something vast, like a dream. Not the kind synonymous with goals or aspirations, but something more nebulous; like what motivated the man in the story to take a train to Portugal and never return. He wasn't sure if the man would find happiness or suffering at his destination, but he was sure that life was going to change completely for him. Wasn't this sufficient? To live a life completely different from the present. For those who dream of a brand-new tomorrow, the man's future is a dream come true.

# Book Talks Hosted by the Bookseller

If independent bookshops sprouting up on street corners and in alleyways was a trend, then the same could be said of such bookshops turning into cultural spaces. For the latter, it wasn't like booksellers were jumping on the bandwagon just because it was the trendy thing to do. Hosting events was a business strategy – they had to attract a crowd to boost sales; bookshops couldn't survive just by selling books.

At the start, Yeongju only wanted to sell books, but she quickly realised that the bookshop would never see profits if she were to rely solely on book sales to make ends meet. When she started hiring – albeit just Minjun – it became even more imperative to escape the red to be a responsible employer. She decided to make their space available for bookings on Friday evenings. Book talks, performances, or exhibitions were all welcomed. As the bookshop would only be providing the use of space, there wasn't much extra work for them. They only helped to promote the event by putting up a poster on the display stand outside the bookshop or posting the sign-up link on social media.

At first, she worried about the noise inconveniencing customers who came in for some quiet reading time, but it turned out to be the opposite. Many of the walk-in customers asked if they could stay for an author reading or a live band, so it was decided that with a purchase of a book or a beverage, anyone could join the event of the day by paying an additional 5,000 won on the spot.

Book talks were held every second Wednesday of the month and the book club met on the last Wednesday of each month. For the first six months, Yeongju led the book club meetings but as more things landed on her plate, everyone readily agreed to her suggestion that a couple of regular members take turns as leaders.

Yeongju continued to host the book talks. She had challenged herself to take up the role, knowing that there would be no better opportunity to meet authors and ask all the questions she wanted. At the same time, she thought 'book talks hosted by the bookseller' could become the Hyunam-dong Bookshop niche. She went the extra mile to record the talks and transcribe them, and the authors were pleased to see extracts of their talks shared on the bookshop's blog and social media.

Currently, special events were only held on Wednesdays and Fridays. She hadn't quite decided what to do in the long run. Too much of something – no matter how enjoyable – turns it into a chore. Or if it was something she dreaded in the first place, torture. The amount of fun in work is very much tied to workload, so she was careful not to let her work and Minjun's cross that threshold. Hence, Minjun was only asked to stay an extra half hour on book talk and book club Wednesdays.

Despite having done it several times, Yeongju was always nervous when preparing for book talks. A few days ahead of the event, she would question her decision to pile on more work for herself and stew in regret, thinking about how much she hated being in the spotlight and what a terrible host she made. But once she was in action, she had so much fun that all misgivings were thrown out of the window. She could never give up hosting book talks. That would mean missing out on the opportunity to talk to the authors and gush over the parts she loved.

When she was young, little Yeongju thought authors didn't even go for bathroom breaks, as if they were too far removed from the likes of ordinary beings who need three meals a day. She imagined that at night, the raindrops would trickle down from their shoulders as vines of lone-liness sprouted from the nape of their necks, twisting and wrapping themselves over their bodies down to their toes. To little Yeongju, authors were all somewhat eccentric and she should try to understand them. After all, those steeped in loneliness could sometimes appear gruff and unfriendly. She imagined authors to be enlightened about the workings of the world, thereby being drawn by fate to spend their lives with the written word. Was there anything authors didn't know? Probably not. Even now she still hung on to the image.

However, the authors she met during book talks were a lot more personable and ordinary than what she'd imagined. They were regular people who struggled with imposter syndrome. She met authors who'd never touched alcohol, those who led more routine lives than company workers and those who went for daily runs to train their stamina – an essential skill for writers, she was told. An author who wrote seven hours a day to become a full-time writer once told her after a book talk: 'Writing was something I wanted to try. So, instead of worrying whether I had the talent or not, I told myself to start writing, to just do it. I wanted to live like this at least once in my life.'

Yeongju also met authors shyer than herself who dared not meet her eyes. Once, there was an author who said that he ended up writing because he was no good at expressing himself verbally. He drew laughter from the audience when he joked that his brain lacked the processing power to speak faster. She felt strangely comforted by authors who spoke at their own bumbling pace and not in a rapid-fire style, as if they were telling her that it was okay to show her vulnerabilities as she traversed the journey of life, one careful step at a time.

Tomorrow, the bookshop would hold their next book talk, 'Fifty-two Stories to Get Closer to Books', with Lee Ahreum, the author of *Every Day I Read*. Halfway through reading it, she already knew that she wanted to meet the author. When she finished the book, she jumped straight into making a list of questions. In no time, the list grew to twenty – a sure sign that she had plenty to ask the author.

### Q&A WITH AUTHOR
(Uploaded to the blog at 10:30 p.m. An extract was uploaded to Instagram at 10:41 p.m.)

YJ: I love your book. It makes me feel like I'm successful by virtue of reading and I like this feeling. (laughs) It's totally my kind of book.

AR: Yes, absolutely. (laughs) Reading makes you see with clearer eyes and understand the world better. When you can do that, you become stronger – the feeling you associate with success. But at the same time, it gives you pain. Within the pages, there's much suffering, beyond what we've gone through in our finite experience of life. You'll read about suffering you didn't know existed. Having experienced their pain through words, it becomes a lot harder to focus on pursuing individual happiness and success. Reading makes you deviate further from the textbook definition of success because books don't make us go ahead of or above anyone else; they guide us to stand alongside others.

YJ: I like that line – to stand alongside others.

AR: We become successful in other ways.

YJ: How so?

AR: We become more compassionate. To read is to see things from someone else's perspective, and that naturally leads you to stop and look out for other people, rather than chase after success in the rat race. If more people read, I think the world would become a better place.

YJ: It's common to hear people say that they have no time to read but I believe you read a lot?

AR: Not really, about one book every two or three days.

YR: I call that *reading a lot*. (laughs)

AR: Really? (laughs) Being so busy, we're usually left with only small pockets of time to read – perhaps in the morning, during lunch, in the evening after work and before we go to bed. But these pockets of time can add up to become something substantial.

YJ: You mentioned that you usually read a few books at any one time.

AR: Yeah, I have a short attention span. I get bored and distracted easily, even if the book is interesting. So, when I start to feel restless, I'll switch to reading something else. I've been told that I'll mix up the plots, but so far, that has never happened.

YJ: I feel like I'll forget what I've read earlier by the time I return to the previous book.

AR: Hmm . . . when I read, I don't obsess over the need to remember every detail. Of course, I'll need to remember the earlier bits to a certain extent, but that said, it's also unlikely that you have zero recollection of what happened. I usually recall most of it, but if my memory is a little hazy, I'll reread the bits I've underlined in pencil before I move on.

YJ: Yes, I remember you mentioned in your book that there's no need to obsess over the details. But is it really okay? (laughs)

AR: (laughs) It's perfectly fine. Books are not meant to remain in your mind, but in your heart. Maybe they exist in your mind too, but as something more than memories. At a crossroads in life, a forgotten sentence or a story from years ago can come back to offer an invisible hand and guide you to a decision. Personally, I feel like the books I've read led me to make the choices I've made in life. While I may not remember all the details, the stories continue to exert a quiet influence on me.

YJ: That's very comforting to know. To be honest, I can't even recall much from the books I read just a month ago.

AR: Same for me, and I think most people will agree too.

YJ: Some say we're in an era where people no longer read. What do you think?

AR: While I was writing this book, I used Instagram for the first time. I was so pleasantly surprised by what I saw that I started to question who dreamt up the notion that people don't read these days? There are so many people on the app who are devouring books at an incredible pace, and it convinced me that readers aren't an extinct breed. That said, I know these Instagram readers are not representative of the average person and are probably a niche bunch. Some time back, I read this article claiming that half the adults in Korea don't even finish one book in a year. But when people don't read, you can't just call it a problem. It's not that straightforward. There're so many reasons: being busy, having no emotional bandwidth or time. It's because we're living in such a suffocating society.

YJ: Does that mean that until we create a more liveable society, it's going to be hard for people to read?

AR: Hmm . . . we can't just sit and wait for society to get better. If more people start to read, they'll be able to empathise with the pain of others and the world will become a better place sooner.

YJ: What can we do?

AR: It's not an issue I can solve. (laughs) But I believe that people still have an appetite for reading, and that they feel it's important to read. What about the people who want to read, but can't, for one reason or another?

YJ: . . .

AR: As the age-old saying goes, the first step is always the hardest. (laughs) How do we start? Oh, is this the point where I should say I wrote the book with this group in mind? (laughs)

YJ: That's it? Not even a teaser? Come on, share something with us. How about the bit about using timers on days when you can't concentrate?

AR: Of course, I was just kidding. On days when you can't concentrate, ask yourself what's been on your mind recently. Humans are naturally motivated to be curious about things we're interested in. For example, many of us want to quit our jobs. If you're thinking of quitting, read books written by people who've quit. There are many such books. If you want to emigrate, read stories about people who've moved across lands and oceans. If you're struggling with low self-esteem, have lost touch with a good friend or feel depressed, seek out books about that. But if you haven't read for a long while, it might be hard to concentrate, and you may get distracted easily. When I feel this way, I set a timer on my phone for twenty minutes. Until the timer rings, I'll focus on the book. Setting small restrictions like this adds a little tension that'll help us concentrate. Once the twenty minutes are up, we have the choice to stop reading, or if we want to go on a little longer, we can set a timer for another twenty minutes. If we do it three times, we have read for an hour already. Let's try to set the timer three times and complete an hour of reading every day.

# Coffee and Goats

When Minjun first started out at the bookshop, he used to arrange for the coffee beans to be delivered twice a week. To preserve the aroma and flavour, he would then repack the beans into small vacuum-sealed bags. These days, he had taken to visiting Goat Beans every other day before work to pick up his order and to discuss the beans he wanted to try next with Jimi.

Goat Beans was the first and only roaster the bookshop worked with. Yeongju had looked around for recommendations and had been lucky to find a reputable roaster with quality beans in their neighbourhood. The boss, Jimi, was so passionate about her beans that when the bookshop was still a one-man show, she would come down personally once a week to do a spot check on Yeongju's coffee. While the quality of the beans is important, the barista's skills also make a huge difference in the taste of the coffee. And so, sometimes Jimi even stepped in to make the coffee.

When Yeongju hired Minjun, Jimi was the first person who came running to the bookshop. She pretended to be a customer and paid for a coffee, not just once, but several times. Each time, she'd give Yeongju her feedback right after leaving the bookshop.

'He's much better than you. I can finally put my mind at rest.'

'Eonnie. I'm not that bad, right?'

'You're that bad.'

On the fourth visit as an undercover customer, she approached Minjun.

'Minjun, you have no idea who I am, right?'

He stared at her, as if unsure how to respond to a customer whom he'd never spoken to, who was hinting that he should know her.

'I'm the one who roasted the beans you're holding right now.'

'You're from Goat Beans?'

'Bingo. Minjun, doing anything tomorrow at eleven?'

He kept quiet as he considered her words.

'Come to our shop,' Jimi continued. 'As a barista, you should know where your beans are from and how they're roasted.'

The next day, skipping the yoga class which he'd never once been late for, Minjun headed for Goat Beans. The door opened on to a small café; through the back door was where the beans were roasted.

Seeing the roasting machines, he was reminded of a pencil sharpener. It was as if the small device with the handle had grown to a human size and started roasting beans instead. There were three employees in the room – each one tending to a roasting machine – while Jimi sat at the table picking at a pile of beans. She waved him over.

'These are raw beans, I'm taking out the rotten ones,' Jimi started to explain even before he sat down. 'We call this handpicking.' Her hands continued to be busy as she spoke. 'Look at this. It's a lot darker compared to the rest, right? This is what you get from a rotten fruit. And this one is brown, which means it has gone bad. Try smelling it. Do you detect a sourish tinge? The rotten ones must be removed before we roast the beans.'

He followed her example and helped to pick out the blackish, brownish, or shrivelled beans. Even as her hands were busy, she kept an eye on his progress.

'You know what *goteu* refers to?'

'A goat – the animal – right?'

'Do you know why we call ourselves Goat Beans?'

'Is there a link between goats and how coffee was discovered?'

'Oooh. You're fast. Excellent!' Suddenly, Jimi stood up. 'That's enough,' she said, and led him to the roasting machine on the far left. An employee was handpicking the freshly roasted beans. 'We get better quality coffee if we do another round of handpicking after roasting,' she explained. 'These are the beans you'll be taking after they're ground.'

Jimi and the employee moved to the grinder, with Minjun tagging behind.

'We can do a coarse or fine grind by adjusting the settings accordingly. The way to extract the coffee will differ, of course,' Jimi said. She glanced at Minjun, who was listening quietly. 'You make good coffee but it's over-extracted, which makes it a little bitter. When I realised that, I gave you beans that were more coarsely ground and it removed the bitterness. Did you notice the difference?'

Minjun thought for a moment. 'I thought that was because I tried to shorten the extraction time, but I guess not.'

'Aha! You were working on it too!'

While the beans were being ground, she gave him a lesson on coffee. According to legend, coffee was discovered thanks to a herd of goats. When they ate a small round red fruit, they were very energetic and began to prance about, leading the goat herder to discover the coffee fruit and its properties.

'That's why we called ourselves Goat Beans. It's too much hassle to think of something else.'

Shaking her head, she told Minjun he would be hardpressed to find a person with a lower caffeine tolerance than her. But because she really loved coffee, she still insisted on drinking a few cups a day. He privately wondered if she could sleep at night, to which Jimi added, as if she'd heard his thoughts, 'That's why I adhere strictly to drinking my last cup before 5 p.m.' She paused. 'But if I really can't sleep, it's nothing a few glasses of beer can't solve.'

'The coffee tree is an evergreen shrub,' she said, 'and the seeds of its fruit are what we know as coffee beans. There are broadly two types of beans: arabica and robusta, with the ones at Goat Beans mainly the former. The taste is better,' she added, before asking if he knew what the deciding factor of coffee aroma was. He said he didn't.

'Altitude,' said Jimi. 'Coffee beans from trees cultivated at a low altitude have a lower acidity and the flavour is often mild and bland. High-altitude beans tend to be more acidic, resulting in a stronger fruity or floral scent and a more complex flavour.' When she first helped Yeongju select the coffee beans for the bookshop, Jimi noticed that she enjoyed a fruity flavour and from then on she made an effort to choose beans with a similar profile for the bookshop.

Minjun started to visit Goat Beans once a week and as his visits became more frequent, he decided that it was easier to change the time of his yoga classes. Slowly, he became attuned to the vibes at Goat Beans. A frosty atmosphere meant that Jimi must be extremely angry that day. And there was only one reason – her husband. Minjun had wondered if her husband was a unicorn, especially after her staff whispered that they'd never seen him – not even once – at the roaster. It was as if the husband lived only in her imagination and the reason for his existence was to bear the brunt of all her anger and swearing.

Minjun's suspicions cleared only after he saw a photo by chance. In the photo, a younger Jimi, in her thirties, stood next to a man and they were smiling happily at the camera. Jimi told him that it was taken barely a year into their marriage and despite her trying countless times to tear it up, she was a fool not to be able to. Talking about her husband set her off on a tirade. When she went on about how her husband turned their house into a landfill and left food rotting in the fridge, she ranted for ten minutes. Twenty minutes about the time her husband went to a funeral and drank the night away with his friends or when she found out that he was having a good time laughing and flirting with a young woman at a café while she was at work. Thirty minutes on days when she felt like he saw her as nothing more than a money-making machine. Minjun was almost late for work for the first time when Jimi had one of her thirty-minute episodes.

Today was a ten-minute rant.

'I was the one who fell for that man. Basically shot myself in the foot.'

Jimi always referred to her husband as 'that man'.

'I was smitten with his carefree ways, as if he was a hitchhiker travelling the world. My family gets very high-strung when shit happens. They basically go off in all directions – like popcorn in an uncovered pan. But that man was the most laid-back person I've ever met. When the boss yelled at him, or when the customers cursed and jabbed their fingers at him, he didn't even twitch an eyebrow.'

Jimi said they met while working part-time at a pub together. 'I made the first move because he was so cool. I was also the one who nudged him into marriage after we had dated for a few years. Before meeting him, I was planning to stay single for life. What do people these days call it? Anti-marriage? When I was a kid, I saw too many women – my mother, aunts, aunties outside of the family – suffering because of their marriages. They kept pounding their chests in regret, to the extent they bruised the skin over their hearts. But I was head over heels for him. I told him I'll buy the house and he just needs to put a ring on me. So here we are. I go home to a doghouse. Dirty dishes in the sink, clothes strewn everywhere, bathroom drain clogged with hair. You know what's worse? I was dying of hunger yesterday but there was nothing remotely edible in the fridge. That man said he finished the last two packets of ramyeon – one for breakfast, one for lunch – along with all the side dishes I bought on the weekend. I don't even make noise when that man doesn't have a job. But at the very least, shouldn't there be some consideration for people living under the same roof? Does that man think I don't have to eat? If he ate the ramyeon, he should buy more. Or fine, even if he didn't want to, the least he could do was tell me to buy more! When I pointedly told him this, he just went back to his room. He was so pissed off that even as

I left home this morning, he was still giving me the cold shoulder.'

Jimi downed a glass of water.

'Sorry to be like this every time. If I don't let it out, it'll get clogged up in my chest. I'm sorry to put you through this. You must hate it.'

Minjun didn't hate it. In fact, he found himself wanting to listen to her for a couple more hours after work, over a beer or something. As to why he would feel this way, he thought about it and concluded that perhaps if he was able to listen to someone rant for a few hours, he would also eventually be able to articulate his own struggles. For the first time, he was acutely aware of how lonely he'd been for a long time.

'I don't hate it. You can tell me more.'

'Nah, I feel even more sorry when you say that. I'll keep it short next time.'

'. . .'

'Alright, like I told you previously, today we're using a Colombia blend. Forty per cent Colombia beans, thirty per cent Brazil, twenty per cent Ethiopia and ten per cent Guatemala. The Colombian beans give balance to the coffee. What about the Brazilian beans?'

Minjun kept quiet.

'It's okay to get it wrong. Stop thinking too much.'

'Um . . . sweetness.'

'Spot on. Ethiopia?'

'Hmm . . . acidity?'

'Okay, the last one! Guatemala?'

'Erm . . . the bitterness?'

'Correct!'

As he stepped out of Goat Beans, Minjun felt the passing of time. The baking heat of the summer had abated, replaced by the first hint of crisp autumn. All summer, he had been taking the bus from Goat Beans to the bookshop. Soon, it would be cool enough to walk again.

His simple life – yoga, work, movies, sleep – was starting to feel like a well-put-together routine. Perhaps life was enough as it was.

## Buttons without Holes

Back when Minjun found out that he'd gained admission into the university of his choice, a sense of relief washed over him. He'd hated it when his parents reminded him of the Korean saying – 'Life's off to a good start after you do up the first button' – as they encouraged him to hang in there a little more. But with the acceptance letter in his hands, the first thing he thought was, *I've done up the first button properly.* According to the older folks, life is smooth sailing once you get into a good university; there're no obstacles an elite university can't break through. But Minjun and his friends soon came to realise that a prestigious university was no guarantee of a stable future. Throughout university, and even up till now, the rat race continued without reprieve.

To prepare for university life, he left his parents' home to move to Seoul alone. Even before the matriculation ceremony, he'd already come up with his four-year plan for university: GPA, internships, certifications, volunteer work and English. His friends had similar plans, too. While the speed and ease with which university students can achieve a glowing résumé was dependent on their parents' wealth, there were still things that even coming from money couldn't help. Minjun planned each semester down to the smallest detail, coming up with a timetable reminiscent of his summer break schedule in elementary school. He followed his timetable religiously. He was motivated, and passionate. Throughout the four years in university, he and his family were like one team; they worked seamlessly with him so that he could score the goals when it came to tuition fees, rent and living expenses.

For Minjun, university life was a series of part-time jobs, with any free time spent studying. Juggling work and his degree at the same time was no mean feat, but he saw it as a rite of passage. *I just need to grit my teeth and things will be better,* he thought. He strongly believed in working hard in life. Because he was permanently exhausted, the rare days that he got to sleep in felt extra blissful. He was able to stay positive because his hard work was always rewarded, giving him the unwavering conviction that hard work would always lead to the results he wanted. Throughout the four years, he maintained a steady GPA at 4.0. His résumé was coming together nicely, and he was confident he was doing well. However, he failed to get a job upon graduation.

'Does it make sense that we can't get a job? You. Me. What are we lacking?' Sungchul demanded as he knocked back a shot of soju at the drinking place near their university. Sungchul was his university classmate from the same faculty. They had met at the orientation camp and basically stuck together during the four years.

'It's not because we're lacking that we can't find a job.' Minjun's face darkened as he downed his shot too.

'So, what's the problem?' This was the question that Sungchul had asked him tens – no, hundreds – of times; the question that also plagued him constantly.

'Because the hole is small. Or maybe there isn't a hole in the first place,' Minjun said as he poured Sungchul another shot.

'What hole? The hole of job seekers?'

'Nah, the buttonhole.'

The two of them emptied their glasses.

'In high school, my mum used to say that if the first button is done up properly, the rest of the buttons will line up neatly, and just like that, life will be smooth sailing. The first button, she said, is getting into a good university. I was so relieved when I got my acceptance letter. If I continued at this pace, it seemed that I could easily do up the second, third and the rest of the buttons too. Was I foolish to think so? No. I'm good at studying. I'm smart. You'll have to agree I have better brains than you. What's more, I work super hard. How dare society turn its back on me?'

Minjun jerked forward suddenly, as if the alcohol was getting to him. He looked up again.

'I worked so hard to make the buttons during those four years. Well, not just me. You did too. I made those buttons so beautifully. Better than you. Nah, you were a big help actually, so thank you, Sungchul.'

He patted Sungchul's shoulders, who, looking mighty pleased, chuckled softly.

'I, the one with the more colourful buttons, convey my appreciation to you too,' Sungchul slurred.

The corner of Minjun's lips twitched as he looked up at his friend with bloodshot eyes. 'But Sungchul . . .'

'Yeah?'

'Recently, I've been starting to think that we spent all our energies making the buttons, but there's something we forgot.'

'And that is?'

Sungchul squinted his eyes to stay awake.

'There were no holes in the first place. Imagine a shirt lined with expensive and beautiful buttons on one side. But there are no holes. Why? Because nobody cut them open for us. What a ridiculous sight – a shirt with only the first button fastened and a row of dangling buttons.'

In his drunken stupor, Sungchul looked down. There was a neat row of buttons on his shirt, but none were fastened. Alarmed, he curled forward and clumsily tried to do up the buttons quickly, his bleary eyes straining to focus. As he finally pushed the last button through the hole, he thought: *was this why I couldn't get a job? Because my shirt was open the whole time?* Ignoring Sungchul, Minjun stared at the shot glass in his hand, as if seeing it for the first time.

'How silly. We could have just worn a buttonless shirt instead. But now, we're stuck with a shirt fastened at the top and a trail of useless buttons. This is not a shirt, it's a joke. The shirt is a joke, and wearing it makes me a joke. Isn't it hilarious? I worked so hard only to look like a joke. My life's a tragic comedy.'

'Hey, it's not that bad.' Sungchul tugged at his collar, straining against the suffocating tightness at his neck.

'What's not that bad?'

'It wasn't all tragic.'

Minjun stared at him vacantly and prodded at his forehead.

'Is that so! Tell me what's good about it? What's not bad about it?'

'Damn it. What's your problem?'

'The power of positive thinking, huh! Positive thinking, positive life! For real!'

As Minjun got louder and more incomprehensible, Sungchul lunged forward to cover his mouth. Slapping his hands away, Minjun raised his voice.

'So tragically hilarious!'

'Our tragically funny lives,' they said at the same time and burst out laughing. With Minjun holding an empty soju glass and a soju bottle in Sungchul's hands, they continued to chuckle over how there was at least something to laugh about amid the misery. Still hiccupping with laughter, Minjun called for another bottle of soju while Sungchul said he was in the mood for an egg roll and army stew. Looking at the unopened bottle of soju, they fell into the same thought – *I wish someone would appear and cut buttonholes in my shirt. Just to prove that I'm not a joke and I can fasten the second and the third buttons too. And while you're here, cut the holes for my friends too. Make enough holes for everyone, big holes that can fit even the biggest of buttons.*

After that drunken night, Minjun and Sungchul lost contact over the next few months. Minjun couldn't quite remember when they went radio silent completely, but he was sure that more than two years had passed since then. Perhaps Sungchul had already found a job. Minjun thought he would understand if Sungchul had cut contact because he was sorry to be the only one to find a job. If Sungchul stopped contacting him because he hadn't found a job, he would be even more understanding. It was the same for him. He had cut off contact with most of his friends from university. He didn't pick up when they called, and ignored their texts. If he ran into them by chance at one of those study groups for job seekers, he kept their interactions short. At that time, Minjun was in two study groups which focused on preparing for job interviews. He had no problems passing the document screening, and the aptitude and personality assessments, but he was always rejected at interviews. Several times a day, he would stare into the mirror. Was it because of his looks? Minjun wasn't handsome, but he wasn't ugly either. He was the average guy on the street – he had the type of face that probably existed in every company. He didn't think he looked any different from his interviewers. Was that why he failed? Because he looked too ordinary?

He worked as hard for the mock interviews as if they were the real thing. He made sure that his expression exuded confidence – with just the right dash of humility – as he answered the questions from his fellow study group members. He attempted to improve on his body language so as to come across as someone who could easily come up with better and more innovative ideas than others, while not being too experimental. Adopting an attitude that was neither too pushy nor meek, he acted like the reason he couldn't find a job two years after graduation was because companies didn't recognise his talents, and no, there wasn't anything wrong with him.

And yet, he was slapped with another rejection.

The company at which he'd progressed to the final round of interviews notified him of the rejection over text. He read it once and deleted it, standing still as he struggled to make sense of his feelings. Was it disappointment? Anger? Embarrassment? Did he want to die? No. He was relieved. Before getting the results, he'd already had a feeling that this was going to be the last one. His final attempt. It wasn't a conscious decision, but at some point, he simply stopped trying. Up till now, he'd dutifully shown up whenever he was called up for an aptitude test or an interview. It'd become a habit – this sense of duty to keep trying, along with the gnawing anxiety each time. It would end here. He'd worked hard enough. He was truly, truly relieved.

'Mum, I'm fine. Don't worry. I can get by with tutoring. I'll take a break first before I try again.'

Minjun sat on the floor in his rented room, his back leaning against the wall as he called his mum. 'Are you really alright?' His mum's voice sounded unnaturally bright, and he, too, found himself trying to match her tone. It was a lie, though. He'd no plans to tutor, nor did he want to continue looking for a job. He hated the label of a 'job seeker'. He wanted to stop seeking or preparing for things. He hated the feeling of walking on a road with no end in sight or trying to push against a solid wall that wouldn't budge.

He wanted to rest. From the time he'd entered middle school till now, he had never felt well-rested. Once he became a top student, he was expected to continue being one, and to work hard consistently. He didn't hate working hard, but if all his efforts only amounted to this, he thought he might have been better off slacking. He didn't want to regret his past efforts, but he thought he would also end up with regrets if he continued to live like this. He checked his bank account balance. There was enough to tide him over for a few months. That moment, he decided. He was going to rest until the balance hit zero. Until then, he would do nothing. *Alright, let's do this. What next though? What next . . .*

Next? There was no next.

At the tail end of winter, Minjun started his unemployed life. To avoid any form of disturbance, he decided to only check his phone before bedtime. That was if he even remembered. Before he forgot, he called up the telecom provider and downgraded his mobile plan to the most basic one. He didn't see himself making any more calls.

Now that he'd freed himself from the things he was expected to do, Minjun mulled over how he would spend his days. He hoped to naturally ease into a routine, although he wasn't sure how he could do that without a plan. He also hoped to completely free himself from morning alarms, the judgemental eyes of society, his parents' disappointment, the rat race, the competition and comparison, and the fear of the future.

He lazed in bed every morning, only getting up to eat when the hunger was unbearable. After feeding himself, he crawled back under the sheets. Save for the occasional street noise – of traffic, footsteps, and chatter – filtering through the window, he was enveloped in silence. The lack of sounds amplified his thoughts before they, too, faded away. His mood was like a rollercoaster: one moment depressed, then overflowing with optimism. He started talking to himself.

'Everything I've done . . .' Minjun spoke to the ceiling, and finished the sentence as a thought.

*. . . is only for the purpose of getting a job.*

He thought back to the time in kindergarten when he'd received full marks in a dictation test. In big red letters, his teacher wrote '100' on the paper, and patted his bum affectionally. 'Minjunie, well done!' He was a little embarrassed; nevertheless, he swelled with pride. That day, when he ran home and showed the test to his parents, they picked him up, asking what he wanted to eat as a special treat.

'Was that where it began?' Minjun wondered aloud as he took two eggs from the fridge. Everything he learnt in elementary, middle and high school. Everything he did at university. Everything he achieved. Once he gave up finding a job, everything lost relevance.

*No, I can't think like this. I mean . . . being able to speak English is helpful. Saves me lots of headaches when I go overseas. Wait, that's a silly thought. How many times can I travel a year? Well, I guess I can also give directions to foreigners on the street. Okay, whatever. Let's just say it's useful. What about the other stuff? Being exam-savvy? Knowing how to make PowerPoint presentations? My butt getting heavier from all the time I spent sitting? Testing the limits of how long humans can endure fatigue? Have all these become useless?*

He thought about *himself* – the person he was and the accumulation of his achievements. Sure, he was the loser getting rejected all the time, but he didn't hate himself. Actually, he'd never thought of himself as a loser. Someone once told him it wasn't enough to work hard, you needed to excel at it. But who determines what is 'excellent'? He thought about his buttons – the ones he sacrificed his sleep to make. His colourful and carefully crafted buttons. He never once doubted that they were 'excellent'.

But those buttons were tailored for the sole purpose of seeking employment and that made him upset. He didn't want to think that it had all been a waste of time. *Somewhere in me, in my heart, there must have been a time I enjoyed what I did, right? Or is my whole life a mistake?*

He soon settled into a routine as an unemployed person. After those early days of lying in, he learnt that he slept little by nature. Sleeping too much made him ache all over. He started to get up at eight without an alarm and he would tidy up his room before making himself a good breakfast. As he'd told himself not to worry about money until his bank balance hit zero, he ate well three times a day. Breakfast was usually toast with a side of eggs sunny side up, or sometimes scrambled eggs. Lunch would be rice with an assortment of vegetables, and for dinner, he ate whatever he craved that day.

At nine thirty, he would take a twenty-minute walk to the yoga studio, treating it as a leisurely morning stroll. He started yoga to relieve his body aches and found that he enjoyed the classes. At first, yoga made him ache in places he didn't even know muscles existed, but now he felt refreshed and light after classes. The quiet moments after class, lying flat on his back on the yoga mat, were his favourite. He was surprised how lying down on a mat seemed to drain the anxiety from his mind and body. Sometimes, he dozed off. When the yoga instructor softly called out, 'Everyone, please sit up,' he would awake with a shiver, slightly dazed. As he walked back home feeling a little lighter, he thought he had done something good for himself. That moment, he was happy.

But a fleeting moment of happiness was always followed by unhappiness. He was munching on a vegetable ssam back in his room when a thought barged into his head:

*Can I really live like this?*

The ssam was delicious, but the thought left a bitter aftertaste. He made another wrap – there wasn't anything delicious food couldn't cure – and stuffed it in his mouth. The moment of unhappiness was swallowed along with the ssam, returning him to a state of equilibrium.

Minjun usually spent his afternoons watching movies. Or sometimes, TV shows that came highly recommended by people as 'the best drama they'd seen in their lives'. He finally watched the 2007 hit series *Behind the White Tower* and cried over Jang Joonhyuk's death in the show. When he saw *Stranger*, he was constantly on edge. *Wow, our country is producing such high-quality dramas these days*, he thought. To find the next show, he usually browsed professional movie or drama review sites. Twice a month, he would visit the arthouse cinema. Sungchul would have been mighty pleased with the Minjun now.

Sungchul was a movie fanatic. He often went for late-night screenings, even during exam periods. And with sunken eyes, he would glare at Minjun and nag him for only watching action movies with all those fist fights.

Each time Sungchul put on a know-it-all air and said, 'You should watch movies you like, not blindly follow the crowd,' Minjun would try to shut Sungchul's mouth, literally, but Sungchul never shut up. When Minjun watched a movie because it was a box-office hit, Sungchul would even resort to personal attacks, and scoffed at him: 'That's only for the likes of you.'

'A good movie can become a mega box-office hit, but not all mega box-office hits are good movies. Don't you understand? A movie becomes a ten-million hit precisely because it was already a three-million hit.'

Minjun ignored him but Sungchul was unperturbed.

'What I'm saying is that millions of cinemagoers are slaves to the marketing. Once a movie crosses the three-million mark, the production company will use it to further promote the movie and that's how it will sell the four millionth ticket. Then, the company will say something like, this movie has captivated more than four million viewers. And people will say, "Ooh I heard this film has attracted more than four million viewers already, shall we watch it too?" And this is how it climbs to five million, six, seven . . .'

'Shut up.' Minjun tried to cut him off. 'That's just sophistry.'

'And why are you being pedantic?'

'Well, that's what you're trying to say, right? That having three million viewers is equivalent to having a free pass to becoming a ten-million movie. Are you trying to say that the target of production companies is three million moviegoers? As long as they hit that, the movie will auto-matically become a ten-million hit?'

'Forget it, you peabrain. Why are you taking this so literally? My point is that a ten-million hit doesn't mean that a movie is so amazing that ten million people love it. So, instead of watching something because of the label, as movie lovers, we should pick the ones we enjoy.'

'If I don't watch it, how would I know whether I'll like it or not?' Minjun asked as he busied himself with notetaking.

'You'll know just by looking at the director! The poster! The synopsis! Think about it. Do you really think that there are more than ten million Koreans who love those action movies pitting gangsters against prosecutors? Or tear-jerkers? Is everyone really a Marvel fan? Most people watch a movie because everyone else is watching it!'

Minjun didn't understand why Sungchul was so impas-sioned when talking about movies, but he was sure he was the only one who knew how to douse that fire. He paused and looked up at Sungchul.

'Sungchul, I get it now.'

'Right?'

'I absolutely get it. I was wrong. Thanks for telling me. It's very useful information.' Minjun stood up and grabbed him in an exaggerated hug. Sungchul remained oblivious to the theatrics and hugged him back tightly.

'Friend, I'm also thankful. Thank you for understanding me.'

Sungchul was right on one count. Minjun didn't watch action movies because he liked them. He only watched them because he didn't know what he liked, so he followed what other people were watching. He'd never regretted watching them though. What was there to regret? If he enjoyed it at that moment, surely it was enough.

Now that he had time on his hands, he could slowly figure out the movies he enjoyed. He wanted to tell Sungchul that to know what he liked, he first needed the energy and bandwidth to begin exploring. To understand profound and abstract films outside of the mainstream offerings, he needed the concentration that could only be possible if he had time. *I should also ask him how he managed to watch so many movies when he was so busy*, Minjun thought. How did Sungchul keep up with a hobby? He was curious.

After a movie, Minjun would mull it over for a long time. There were times a whole day passed like this. It seemed so extravagant, to spend the entire day thinking about a film. He'd never spent that much time on something that didn't serve a concrete purpose. Never did he have the luxury of taking all the time he wanted. In the process of figuring out his preferences, he had a vague realisation that, perhaps, spending time on a single thing was like looking deep into himself.

# The Regular Customers

As he wiped the table with his right hand, Minjun's eyes were fixed on the middle-aged man who had just walked in. It had been a few weeks since the customer started coming in on the dot, at half past one every single day, using the bookshop as if it were a library. According to Yeongju, the man spent the first few days combing the shelves to find a book he was interested in. When he'd zeroed in on his target, he started coming in for 'after-lunch reading' and had never missed a day since. 'He owns the real estate agency a five-minute walk away,' she added, 'the one that opened two months ago.'

The book that had caught his fancy was the thick and heavy *Moral Tribes*. Having spent about twenty to thirty minutes each day on it – reading or thumbing through its pages – he appeared to be about halfway through. Done with his lunchtime reading, he would return the book to the shelf and walk out looking serene, or, perhaps, basking in his excellent literary taste. A few days ago, the two of them had discussed how best to handle the situation – to impress upon him that this was a bookshop, not a library.

'Let's wait and see what he'll do after finishing the book,' said Yeongju, who was writing on a small memo pad at the table. Across from her, Minjun was making more copies by hand.

'You know,' he paused and looked up, pen still in hand, 'it's funny that the customer is reading *Moral Tribes* while doing something immoral.'

Yeongju didn't look up. 'Even if you read, it's not easy to self-reflect.'

'In that case, what's the point of reading?' Minjun bent down and returned to his task.

'Hmm.' For a moment, she looked out the window. 'It's difficult, not impossible,' she said, turning back to him. 'Those who can self-reflect are able to change a little just by reading one book. Even those who can't – I believe that if they keep stimulating themselves by reading, one day, they'll be able to reflect on themselves.'

'Is that so?'

'I know I'm the latter, which is why I read voraciously in the hope that I'll become a better person one day.'

Minjun nodded in understanding.

'Do you know why that customer chose to open an estate agency here?' Yeongju's tone indicated that she knew the answer.

'Are the real estate prices here increasing?'

'Not yet, but the customer believes that there'll be demand in the next few years. The neighbourhoods within a twenty- to thirty-minute walk are all affected by gentri-fication. Where do you think the people will end up? He believes it's here in Hyunam-dong. He predicts that there'll be a real estate boom here in a couple of years' time.'

Minjun glanced at the customer who was back for his daily reading. *If the time comes for the customer to thank the gods for his good fortune, that would be the day I have to leave this neighbourhood,* Minjun thought. The current rent was still somewhat within his means, but a property boom in the neighbourhood would probably double it. It was part of the balance of life – a person's dream coming true could mean the collapse of someone else's life. He was sure that he and the real estate agent would never stand on the same side of destiny.

Having worked at Hyunam-dong Bookshop for more than a year, Minjun was on speaking terms with the regulars. They were usually the ones who initiated a conversation; only occasionally would Minjun be the one who greeted them first. He knew most of the nearby residents, including Mincheol's mother, who came almost every day. He also recognised those who came at least once a week, in particular the book club members who came regularly and stayed the longest. And there were those who, on their own initiative, gave him feedback on his coffee – he remembered them even if they only came once.

He'd also spoken several times with a customer who appeared to be an office employee. He came two or three times a week and would stay to read until closing. On some days, the customer would rush in while Minjun was already tidying up. Still panting, he would sit at the table and read, even if it was just a few pages. Once he'd come at noon, before opening time, and that was when he'd first spoken to Yeongju. Apparently, they were now friendly enough to crack jokes with each other; Minjun had even heard them call each other by their first name. His name was Choi Wooshik. When she heard it, Yeongju had clapped her hands in delight and gushed over what a nice name it was. Minjun had thought that it was uncharacteristic of Yeongju, who normally didn't get excited easily, but later he found out that she couldn't help it as the customer shared the exact same name as her favourite actor.

The customer Wooshik had his own routine in the bookshop. On days when he bought a book from the shop, he would read in the café without buying a drink; on the days he didn't, he ordered coffee, of which he drank only a few sips. Occasionally, he would disappear for more than a week. He was usually exuberant when he returned as he explained to Yeongju the reason for his absence.

'We just launched new products at our travel agency, so we went around the branches to brief the staff. I really wanted to squeeze in a few moments to come here and read, but I had no time at all. When I finally did, it was already after closing time, and it reminded me of the sadness I felt when I had to walk past the arcade because I was scared of getting scolded by my mum.'

Was it because he enjoyed reading novels? Minjun thought Wooshik was a sensitive soul. Or was it the other way round – that he was a sensitive soul and hence preferred novels? Or maybe there was no link. One day, when Minjun was wiping the table, Wooshik came up to him.

'Sorry for not introducing myself before now. I'm Choi Wooshik.'

'Ah. I'm Kim Minjun.'

'I feel so bad when I come here.' Wooshik looked apologetically at Minjun.

'Why?' he said, looking alarmed.

'The coffee. I feel bad that I always leave most of it untouched. I get heart palpitations from the caffeine, but I still like to enjoy a few sips.'

'It's not something you need to apologise for.'

'Really? I guess I'm being sensitive again.' He chuckled. 'I don't really know coffee but even an amateur like me can tell that you make a good cuppa.'

Minjun recalled how Yeongju felt a sense of camaraderie for Wooshik just because he shared the same name as her favourite actor. Do people with the same name also give off a similar vibe? Minjun stared at him, as if he'd found a precious thing that he didn't even realise he'd lost.

'Thank you for your kind words.'

While Yeongju and Minjun noticed all their regulars, there was someone who, for the past two months, had had their full attention. The customer sitting right there at the table. When the weather first warmed up, she had started appearing from time to time, and by the peak of summer she had become a regular face. On weekdays she would spend five or six hours a day at the café. She stood out among the rest of the customers who were either reading or typing away. She did neither. Nor was she doing anything else. She simply sat there.

At first, when she came in once a week to sit and stare straight ahead for about an hour or two, neither Yeongju nor Minjun paid her much attention. Even when she came up to Yeongju to ask a question, Yeongju only thought she was kind of unique.

'How long can I stay here if I order a cup of coffee?'

'We don't set a time limit here,' Yeongju replied.

'Oh. But that makes me uncomfortable. It can't be good for the bookshop if I hog the table for the whole day with only one cup of coffee, right?'

'That's true, but we haven't had such customers yet.'

'Perhaps you should start thinking about it now. Because I might be the first one.'

True to her words, the woman stayed longer each time; her longest record was six hours. As Yeongju hadn't given her an answer about the time limit policy of the bookshop, she seemed to have set one for herself and ordered a new beverage every three hours. Minjun only knew about it after she told him herself. One day, she approached the counter to order a fresh cup of coffee, saying, 'Three hours have passed so I'm getting another coffee. If I do this, I won't be a nuisance to the bookshop, right?'

For days, she sat with only her phone and a notepad on the table. While she scribbled on the notepad sometimes, she spent most of the time sitting up straight with her eyes closed. Sometimes, her head would bob gently after a while, as if she was falling asleep. It was only later that Yeongju and Minjun found out that she'd been meditating, and the bobbing of the head was really because she dozed off halfway.

As the winds started to get chillier, the woman, who usually dressed in a loose short-sleeved t-shirt and wide-leg shorts, started to appear in a long-sleeved shirt and boyfriend jeans. It seemed like a casually put-together outfit, but she looked effortlessly chic. Her sense of fashion seemed to exude comfort. Around the same time, she stopped going to her usual seat and instead sat down at a table in the corner to crochet. She must be the kind of person who hated inconveniencing others because she sought Yeongju's permission beforehand. 'Is it alright if I crochet in the bookshop? I'll work quietly. I won't be a nuisance, right?'

Yeongju's number one rule was never to stare at customers and make them uncomfortable, but she found it hard to keep to the rule when it came to that customer. Damn that crocheting! She couldn't tear her eyes away, as if she'd lost her soul in the hand movements of the lady. A palm-sized crochet scrubby could be completed in a day, or even in a couple of hours. She also found out the woman's name: Jungsuh.

In between crocheting, Jungsuh would close her eyes for a while and sit still. Again, they later found out that she'd been meditating. Among her crochet scrubbies of different patterns, the loaf of bread – with brown yarn for the crust and a vanilla one for the bread – was Yeongju's favourite. It was a gorgeous combination and if she looked at it from a distance, it was as if a freshly baked loaf sat on the table. Jungsuh worked in silence, not forgetting to order a cup of coffee every three hours.

About a month after she started crocheting at the bookshop, Yeongju was brimming with curiosity. How many had she made so far? She imagined Jungsuh's home to be full of her crochets, the delicious-looking bread crust peeking out from the pile. However, Yeongju didn't ask her anything, and likewise, Jungsuh continued to crochet in silence, until one day, she brought along a bulging paper bag and went up to Yeongju.

'I'd like to donate my creations to the bookshop.'

# The Crochet Giveaway

The bag of crochet scrubbies was placed on the table and the three of them sat down for a short discussion. Yeongju thought that it was very kind of Jungsuh to donate her hard work without seeking payment, and decided that the bookshop shouldn't profit from it either. There wasn't much to deliberate over; they unanimously agreed to hold a crochet giveaway at the bookshop.

*Tuesday, 6:30 p.m. | Instagram*
*Our bookshop will hold a giveaway this Friday. Every visitor can take home a crochet scrubby! We have handmade scrubbies of many shapes and patterns – hearts, flowers, fish, loaves of bread, and more! Limited quantities so they'll be given out on a first come, first served basis. To avoid disappointment, check out this space for updates on the numbers left. Come spend your Friday with us and receive a crochet. ☺*
*#hyunamdongbookshop #neighbourhoodbook-shop #independentbookshop #bookshopgiveaway #everyonelikescrochetscrubbies #specialcrochetevent #guesswhomadethecrochetscrubbies #cantwaitforfriday*

*Friday, 1:04 p.m. | Instagram*
*Visitors to the bookshop today will get a crochet scrubby*
*for free. Everyone is welcome. We only have seventy.* ☺
*#hyunamdongbookshop #neighbourhoodbookshop*
*#independentbookshop #independentbookshopevent*
*#comeandgetoneofthe70 #noneedtobuyabook*

*Friday, 5:02 p.m. | Instagram*
*Wow! We didn't expect the crochet scrubbies to be so popu-*
*lar. There are only 33 remaining.* ☺
*#hyunamdongbookshop #neighbourhoodbookshop*
*#independentbookshop #independentbookshopevent*
*#TGIFcrochetscrubby*

The event was more well received than expected. Just like
Yeongju had been entranced by Jungsuh's crocheting,
customers were attracted to the cute patterns and shapes.
That day, she received more questions about the scrubbies
than about books. Many told her they'd previously bought
such scrubbies, but never thought of making them by hand.
She got a lot of questions on how to make one, so she told
them what Jungsuh had shared with her.

Yeongju learnt that customers respond well to interesting and unique ideas, and perhaps buoyed by the
happiness of receiving such a cute, small gift, many of
them also purchased something from the bookshop.
Compared to those who came in wanting a book and
received a scrubby as well, there were many more who came
to get a scrubby but ended up buying a book. *What if I hold
more of these giveaways?* she wondered. Surely the novelty
would fizz out in no time. She ought to focus instead on
building a good bookshop, spicing things up with novelty
events occasionally.

In the late afternoon, with only about five customers reading quietly in the bookshop, Yeongju finally had a brief respite. She walked towards the table by the window where Mincheol sat. Staring out of the window with his chin resting on his right palm, he looked like a bird imprisoned in his cage. Who had kept this child locked up? Did he know that the door could be opened from the inside? What she was about to attempt needed all the sensitivity she could muster. She'd try to help the child free himself from the cage. To nudge him to move.

In front of him was the book she had given him last week: *The Catcher in the Rye*. Yeongju had an inkling, from the way he straightened up as she approached, that she'd failed with her recommendation again. *I should stop suggesting books narrated by high school students struggling to fit into society*, she thought wryly.

'I'm guessing you didn't read this. Not a good story?' Yeongju asked as she sat down opposite him.

'It's not that. I know it's a good book,' Mincheol replied politely.

She touched the book. 'Is it difficult?'

'Yeongju imo, do you know when the first line of dialogue appears in the book?'

Last week, Mincheol had decided to address her as the bookshop aunt.

'When?' Yeongju asked, leafing through the book.

'The seventh page of the first chapter,' Mincheol replied matter-of-factly, as though he was just commenting that a rainy day meant wet weather. But she detected a trace of grumpiness in his voice. Mincheol must have realised she had caught on, for he haltingly added, 'I'm sorry. Because I haven't read a book like this. I barely touch my textbooks.'

Last week, Mincheol had come to see her at the book-shop. She knew that the boy and his mother had reached an agreement. If he dropped by the bookshop once a week and read the books she recommended, he would be spared from after-school cram classes. His mother also promised not to nag him for lying in bed for hours on end. When Yeongju first heard about the agreement, she put up a strong protest. It was too heavy a responsibility for her to take on. How could she step in to educate someone else's child, when she had neither children nor nephews? She'd apologised and said she wasn't up for the task, but Mincheol's mother took her hands.

'I know you're feeling burdened.'

Letting go, Mincheol's mother sucked up the iced Americano through the straw.

'How about simply treating my boy as any other customer and recommending him a few books? I don't expect more. Yes, I know I'm the one forcing him to come, but just think of him as a high school student who visits the bookshop once a week. And we'll do this just for a month. Four visits. Recommend him a book each time he's here. He just doesn't listen to us at all. Parents these days are useless, we can't get our children to do anything.'

Yeongju changed her mind the following day and agreed to speak to Mincheol. She'd thought about it. If there was a high school student who visited the bookshop once a week, it wouldn't be a burden, but a huge source of joy for her.

Flipping carelessly through *The Catcher in the Rye*, Yeongju was trying to dig into her mental depository for another suitable book for high schoolers when he pointed at the book and asked, 'Yeongju imo, do you think I must read this no matter what?'

'Huh?'

'I'll try my best for a week. I'll probably find it difficult because I'm not used to reading.'

Yeongju looked at him. This child could express himself properly. Perhaps it wasn't right to treat him as a hatchling in captivity.

'Well, possibly. Do you think you can do it?'

'What?' Mincheol's eyes widened as if unsure what she meant.

'Put in effort to read.'

'If I try, I'll probably be able to.'

'Hmm . . . it's not good to try too hard.'

'If I don't try, I can't hope for the results I want.'

'For someone who understands this logic, why aren't you doing anything?'

Yeongju glanced at him, as if she knew what he was going to say.

'Understanding it is different from actually doing it.' He shrugged indifferently.

Yeongju had liked the child ever since she'd first met him. He reminded her of her younger self – always frustrated, but never knowing the reason. She had tried to work through the frustration by pushing herself to extremes in her studies, whereas he did the opposite and let himself go. He was probably the smarter one, knowing how to pause to recalibrate and find a new direction – something she was finally doing, many years later.

Yeongju chatted intermittently with the boy as she did her work. He continued staring out the window, only turning around if she spoke to him. He didn't avoid her questions and answered them as best as he could. He was smart and frank; a hint of cheekiness belied his careful attitude. Yeongju decided to change her approach. She leaned forward, closing the distance between them, and whispered, 'Let's come up with a strategy.'

'What kind of strategy?' Startled by her sudden movement, he leaned back slightly.

'You're not going to read. Instead, come down once a week and have a chat with me. Your mother has given me some money for the books. I'll return that to her when the month's up, so in the meantime, let's keep this between us.'

'I don't have to read?'

This was the happiest she'd seen him today.

*Friday, 8:30 p.m. | Instagram*
*For those who've taken a crochet scrubby, have you started using it? We're left with four, so we're going to keep them for ourselves and use them in our kitchens. Thank you to everyone who visited us today. ☺*
*#hyunamdongbookshop #neighbourhoodbookshop*
*#independentbookshop #independentbookshopevent*
*#crocheteventends #goodnight #havearestfulnight*

Minjun was done for the day, but he continued to hang around at the bookshop. He held on to the tea towel, stealing glances at Yeongju as he picked up a cup to dry it again, before wiping the coffee machine for the second time. She seemed to be working late today. If he could also help out on busy days, then both of them could go home earlier. By now, he was familiar with most of the routine tasks in the bookshop. But with a boss like Yeongju who dutifully paid him for any extra hours put in, it wasn't like he could just volunteer to work overtime. It was equivalent to asking her for a higher wage. In the end, he reached for his bag, pausing a beat before he lifted the countertop and approached her.

'Boss, are you working late tonight?'

'Ah yes. I'll stay a little longer.' Yeongju tore her eyes away from the laptop. 'Why?'

'I'm happy to help if there's a lot to do. I'm not trying to ask for more pay. I just don't feel like going home yet.'

'Oh! Me too. I'm staying because I don't want to go back.'

'Really?'

'Just kidding.' She flashed him a mischievous grin. 'Don't worry, I don't have that much to do. I'll leave soon. Jimi eonnie is coming over to my place later so I'll only stay an hour more.'

When she put it like this, it was impossible for him to volunteer to stay behind with her. He gave a little nod. 'Alright, I'll head home first.'

'See you tomorrow, Minjun.'

*Friday, 9:47 p.m. | Instagram*
*There's a saying that men are more melancholic in autumn, and women in spring. Our hormones wax and wane along with the seasons. How are our men doing these days? Autumn is also the season of feasting. I get so hungry by the time I finish work. Since it's no good to eat too much, I've started to consume novels about food as if I was binge-ing cooking videos. I'm now reading Laura Esquivel's* Like Water for Chocolate. *I recommend that you watch the movie first before reading the novel.* ☺
*#hyunamdongbookshop #neighbourhoodbookshop*
*#independentbookshop #foodnovelsforhungrydays*
*#lauraesquivel #likewaterforchocolate #imfinishingwork-nowafterreading #seeyoutomorrow*

On her way home, Yeongju thought about how Minjun seemed to have changed a little. Before she realised it, she was already at her doorstep, with Jimi squatting next to her door. In her right hand was a six-pack of beer; in her left, a paper bag that seemed to contain an assortment of cheese.

'Eonnie!' Yeongju called out to her. Jimi grunted as she stood up, looking like a weightlifter with two barbells. Yeongju quickly helped her with a bag.

'That's a lot of food.'

'How's that a lot? In any case, I'm the one eating most of it.'

'Are you really okay to stay the night?'

'Of course. That man will only come back at dawn. I don't really care anymore.'

Yeongju and Jimi plated the cheese nicely and set it down on the floor before lying down comfortably on either side of it. Occasionally, they sat up for a mouthful of beer. When Yeongju had done up the interior, she had spent the most effort on the lighting. The lamps cast a warm glow on the two women stretched out comfortably on the floor.

'The only good thing in your house is the lighting,' Jimi said.

'And the many books,' Yeongju shot back.

'Only you like the books.'

'The owner is pretty great too.'

'Only you would say that about yourself.'

Yeongju suddenly sat up. 'Eonnie, I think so too,' she said, gulping down some beer.

'What're you talking about?' Jimi gave Yeongju a sideways glance, her expression seeming to say, *Alright, here you go again, being all serious. Stop being so serious.*

'I've been mulling this over recently. That my existence is good only for me but does absolutely nothing for others. Maybe not even good, just bearable.'

'You think too much.' Jimi propped herself up. 'Who in the world doesn't feel the same way? Do I look like I'm a good person? As much as I can't stand that man, that man also can't stand me. We're even. And that is how I have endured things till now.'

Peeling the wrapper off a thumb-sized cheese, Yeongju asked, 'Don't you think there'll be someone out there who knows how to love themself and yet not hurt others?'

'Is there even someone like this in the novels you love so much? Are you sure they aren't hiding wings?' Jimi replied tartly as she lay back down and stared at the ceiling. 'You were the one who told me that characters in novels are a little imperfect and that's how they lend their voice to the average person. Because we're imperfect, we knock into each other, and hurt each other in the process. You're just another ordinary person.'

Jimi continued her monologue.

'We're all the same. Of course, sometimes we do good.'

'You're right.' Yeongju lay down next to her. 'But . . . eonnie.'

'Yeah?'

'Do you remember the customer I told you about? The one who reads at the bookshop during lunch?'

'Oh yeah. What about him?'

'He stopped coming for a while. But a few days ago, he reappeared and continued reading from when he'd left off.'

'What a character.'

'Yesterday, just as he was about to leave, I went up to him.'

'What did you say?'

'I told him if he's going to read the whole book – not just a few pages – there's bound to be damage to the book, and we wouldn't be able to sell it.'

'What did he say to that?'

'He turned crimson and left without a word.'

'See. He's also being a nuisance to other people.'

'Today he came by again.'

'Did he kick up a fuss?'

'No. He picked out more than ten books, including the one he'd been reading, and bought them all. He didn't even look at me once the whole time.'

'He probably reflected at home. And realised, "Ah, I've been a nuisance."'

Yeongju chuckled at her tone. 'Oh yeah, eonnie. I brought a crochet scrubby for you.'

'What's with the scrubby?'

'It's handmade and in the shape of a loaf of bread. Super cute. I'd like you to have it.'

'Who gave it to you?'

'A regular at the bookshop. We had a crochet giveaway event today and I thought you, Minjun and I could take the leftover pieces.'

'Does he cook at home?'

'I don't know.'

'He looks quite smart, so he probably cooks at home too.'

'How's that even related?'

'He looks like the kind who can take care of himself, someone you don't need to babysit.'

After dinner, Minjun washed the dishes and selected a movie for the evening. He turned on his phone and checked his messages. Nothing much. Just as he was about to turn it off, the phone rang. It was his mum, whom he'd been avoiding. Pausing the movie, he tried to rearrange his expression before picking up the call.

'Hi, Mum.'

'Why is it so hard to reach you? Why is your phone always turned off?'

He let out a little sigh at the barrage of questions.

'I told you it's hard to take calls at work and I forget to turn it back on when I'm home.'

'Had your dinner?'

'Yes.'

'Good.' There was a pause. 'How's work?'

'Well, fine.'

'When are you going to stop doing those part-time jobs? Your dad has been asking.'

Minjun got up and sank down on the floor, leaning his weight against the wall. He shot back, irritated, 'I'm not the one who gets to decide.'

'If not you, who else?'

He raised his voice. 'The country? Society? The companies?'

'Are you going to take this tone with me? If you're going to work part-time, you might as well come straight home! I told you to come back and rest, why can't you listen? Get some proper rest, so you're ready to push on and find a job!'

He leaned his head back and said nothing.

'Why aren't you answering me?'

'Mum.'

'What?'

'Do I really have to push myself?' he mumbled under his breath.

'What?'

'I'm okay with how things are right now.'

'What's *okay* about this? I've been so upset I haven't had a good night's sleep since . . . When I think of you being like this, I'm so—Do you know how much I regret not being able to provide you with the environment to focus on your studies? You kept saying you were fine, so I thought you really were okay!' His mum's voice was choked.

Minjun squirmed. This was the reason why he couldn't quite bring himself to tell her that what he regretted was not lacking the environment to focus on his studies, but that he hadn't been smart enough to think about whether studying would truly give him a good life or if it was the right path for him, that he wasn't smart enough to consider the other paths out there.

'Don't worry, I'm fine.'

'Aigoo. I have faith in you, but I just feel bad.'

'I know.'

'Do you have enough money?'

'Yes.'

'If you're running out of money, do call. Don't be afraid.'

'I'm fine.'

'Okay, I'll not disturb you anymore. But keep your phone on, alright?'

'Yeah.'

Long after the call ended, he remained in the same position.

## Occasionally, a Good Person

Ever since the conversation with Jimi about hurting those around her, Yeongju had been dispirited. She tried stretching, but her body remained lethargic. There were moments – like now – where she would feel a little better, only for her past to crash down on her the next second. In a bid to escape her thoughts, she gave herself a slap on her cheeks, loitered outside the bookshop, or hummed a song under her breath, but the respite never lasted past the moment.

She screwed her eyes shut as her mother's harsh words screamed into the void of her head. Until the very end, her mother hadn't been on her side. She would come over to their place at dawn to make breakfast, not for her daughter, but for him. He would silently accept the food and looked on as his mother-in-law admonished his wife. Only when her mother left did he ask if she was alright. She didn't bother retorting that he shouldn't be asking her that. She simply nodded.

'Do you know how much wrong you've done to all of us?' her mother had yelled as she grabbed her shoulders. When she told her mother that she'd started divorce proceedings, her mother almost slapped her. From that day, Yeongju could no longer bring herself to see her.

'What did I do to her that was so terrible?'

Whenever she thought of how her mother had screamed at her, in her heart Yeongju wanted to lash out at her and demand to know what crime she had committed. No matter how she tried to expel the fury, the thorn remained stabbed in her heart, making it tender to the touch, as if full of bruises. Her mother always made her feel that there was no one in the entire world who was on her side. When the thoughts overwhelmed her, she forced herself to sit down, desperate to grasp at anything that would lift her out of the mire. It wasn't easy but she had no other choice.

Thankfully, Jungsuh was around today. Once she made sure there was nothing that needed her immediate attention, Yeongju sat opposite Jungsuh and watched her knit. After she had donated her crochets, Jungsuh continued to appear at the bookshop every day, mostly to zone out. However, a few days earlier, she had embarked on something new: knitting. When Yeongju asked if she was making a scarf, Jungsuh replied that she didn't like things that were too long, and instead wanted to 'make a short scarf that was just the right length to go two rounds around the neck'.

Yeongju absently ran her fingers over the grey wool, a colour neither too bright nor dark.

'The pattern is—'

'The most basic one. For the first-timer, always go for the basic. Once you've mastered it, the other patterns become much easier to learn.'

Yeongju nodded. She continued to fondle the scarf. 'It's a pretty colour, it'll fit any occasion.'

Jungsuh's hands moved rhythmically as she replied, her hands on the yarn. 'I like to start with a basic colour too. It goes well with all clothes.'

Yeongju nodded again. She let go of the half-done scarf and propped her chin on her palm as she stared at Jungsuh's fingers. The flow of the needle poking in, looping the thread, and pulling out again was as regular as a heartbeat. Until she was called away, Yeongju wanted to sit and watch Jungsuh knit. If possible, she didn't want to miss the moment the scarf was completed, as if by sharing the moment, she'd be able to escape the emptiness of being alone in the world.

### Thursday, 10:23 p.m. | Blog

*Sometimes, I despair that I'm worthless, especially when I bring misery to those who've showered me with care, concern and love. Does the weight of suffering you cause determine how unnecessary your existence is? Am I a person who'll only hurt others? Am I simply this kind of person? My heart numbs at these thoughts.*

*I'm just an ordinary human being. No matter how hard I try, I am nothing more than an ordinary person. Because I'm ordinary, I end up hurting others or making them sad. We smile at each other at the same time as we hurt each other.*

*Reading* The Guard of Light[2] *brings me comfort. A small act of kindness in the eyes of others could be heard as 'I'm your fan'. We're all inadequate, weak and ordinary beings. But because we're capable of being kind, for a moment – no matter how fleeting – we can be extraordinary.*

*In the novel, elementary school student Kwoneun has only one friend: a snow globe that snows for exactly*

[2]Cho Hae-jin, 빛의 호위 Bichui Howi (Changbi, 2017)

one minute and thirty seconds when you wind it up. An orphan, Kwoneun lives alone, perpetually hungry. Afraid of dreams, she's scared to sleep. For one minute and thirty seconds, she'll stare at the snow globe, and when the melody ends, she quickly buries herself under the blanket, praying for a dreamless night. Shaking in fear, the young child makes her wish.

'I beg for the clockwork in this room to freeze, and for my breath to stop.'
(Cho Hae-jin, The Guard of Light, *Changbi*, 2017, 27)

In the novel, 'I', the class representative – and the narrator of the book – approach Kwoneun. 'I' am apprehensive; Kwoneun's loneliness and poverty are alien to me, but 'I' feel guilty if 'I' ignore her existence. One day, 'I' steal a film camera from home and pass it on to her, telling her to sell it to buy some food. The camera, which 'I' meant her to sell, becomes a light for the child who had sought death.

'**Do you know what's the most amazing thing a person can do?**' she wrote to me in a letter. I shook my head as I read. '**Someone once told me,**' she wrote, '**that saving a person is an extraordinary act not anyone can accomplish. So . . . no matter what happens, remember this. The camera you gave me saved my life.**'
(Cho Hae-jin, The Guard of Light, *Changbi*, 2017, 27–28)

'I' am ordinary. Like the rest of us who look into the mirror asking, 'So, are you happy now?' but gets silence in return. As 'I' grow older, 'I' forget about Kwoneun. The next time 'I' meet her years later, 'I' cannot recognise her.

'I' had forgotten about having a poor student in our class, about how 'I' talked to her several times, or that 'I' gave her the camera. But what 'I' did remained etched in her mind. Thanks to me, she has the strength to live on and to her, 'I' am her life saviour, an extraordinary person.

As I close the book, I think to myself – I should stop labelling myself an inadequate person. I still have opportunities, don't I? Opportunities to act kindly, to speak with compassion. Even a disappointing human like myself can still be, occasionally, a good person. The idea gives me strength. And for the days ahead, hope.

## All Books are Equal

Yeongju hadn't seen her mother for several years but having to fight with her in her own head was exhausting enough. It took all her strength to suppress the waves of rage inside her. Her senses dulled, and she shuffled around the bookshop listlessly, oblivious to the fact that Minjun was also looking out of sorts. Wrapped in her own struggles, no matter how empathetic she might be, she didn't have eyes for anyone else's problems, even if they were right in front of her.

For the sake of the bookshop, she had to pull herself together again. The things she'd procrastinated on, thinking she still had time, became urgent tasks which she needed to complete today. At ten in the morning, she came in and checked the inventory orders, did the accounts she'd left aside for way too long, packed the book orders to be couriered and wrote the introduction notes for new book arrivals, all the while casting anxious glances at the book for this week's book club, which she'd yet to read.

The day was spent in a flurry of activity, without a moment of reprieve. She put her problem-solving skills to good use as she efficiently and methodically tackled the tasks at hand. If her ex-colleagues were to see her now, they probably would tease her. 'Yup, that's Yeongju for you. Leopards don't change their spots easily.' But none of the people from her past remained.

Meanwhile, Jungsuh sat at a table knitting a purple scarf. Mincheol, who was here for his weekly session with Yeongju, was staring at Jungsuh knit. Jungsuh thought it was cute that the teenager in school uniform was staring sullenly at her knitting a scarf. *Even if he had nothing to do, he would be better off watching YouTube or something else,* she thought.

'You like this kind of stuff?'

Jungsuh was the one who broke the silence.

Mincheol, who had been staring as if his soul was sucked in, quickly withdrew his arms from the table and repeated, 'This kind of stuff?'

'I was the one who asked the question, but I don't quite know what I mean either. I'm just asking why you're sitting here.'

'I have to come here once a week to have a chat with the bookshop aunt. Only then will my mum stop nagging me.'

'That must be Yeongju eonnie. I'll not ask why your mum is nagging you. Alright, if you like to watch, you're free to do so. If you want to try, tell me.'

'Knitting?'

'Yep, wanna try?' Jungsuh paused her hands.

Mincheol considered for a moment and shook his head. 'I'm good. I'll just watch you knit.'

'Alright, up to you.'

He rested his arms on the table once more and gazed at the purple scarf swaying rhythmically with the motions. To him, it looked like the scarf was dancing. Her hands maintained a constant tempo and his eyes darted along too. He was surprised that it had such a calming effect on him. He remembered watching a twenty-minute cooking video on YouTube where the YouTuber picked fresh ingredients from the wild, fermented them for a month, and after a very complicated preparation and cooking process, whipped up a delectable-looking dish. He was so amazed that he rewatched the clip several times. In the same way, he found himself wanting to watch her knit.

Her rhythmic knitting had a mesmerising effect on him, like a pendulum swaying back and forth, drawing his soul out with it. He could almost hear the hypnotist whisper, *It's alright, everything will be fine.*

Soon after, his eyelids felt a little heavy. Just as the drowsiness was about to overwhelm him, he spoke with a sudden realisation.

'It's my first time seeing someone do this.'

'What?'

'Knitting.'

'That's quite normal these days.'

He watched her in silence for a while before he spoke again.

'Imo.'

'Am I also your aunt?'

'If not, how should I address you?'

Jungsuh paused as she pondered the question. 'We're not blood-related, so technically you shouldn't call me imo. I don't like being called noona either. Ajumma is even worse. This is the problem with our country. We have so many second-person pronouns, but none that're appropriate for the two of us.'

'. . .'

'Well . . . since you call Yeongju eonnie *imo* . . . come to think of it, who really cares whether we're related or not.

Koreans and the absurd importance we place on blood ties. Acting like there's nothing we won't do for the sake of our blood relations, even if it means turning into monsters! No sense of shame! Hmm . . . alright, call me imo then.'

'Okay . . .'

'So, what's up?'

'Can I come again to watch you knit?'

He looked at her solemnly, as if it was a very important question. It was cute, and Jungsuh glanced at him before nodding her head.

'Sure, but you'll have to fight for the seat.'

'Why?'

'Because you're taking your Yeongju imo's seat right now.'

While Yeongju was neck-deep in the tasks she'd procrastinated on, Minjun was restless, stopping short of letting it show. When there were no customers at the café, he approached Yeongju to offer his help, and when he finished what he could, he wiped down every corner of the bookshop as if he was spring-cleaning, before going back to the café to clean the espresso machine, dry the cups for a second time, shift the tables at the café and go to the shelves to make sure that the books were arranged neatly in order. Yeongju took in everything he did but didn't think much of it.

Having put out all the major fires, she was finally left with only a few non-urgent tasks. She passed some cut fruit to Minjun, Jungsuh and Mincheol before finally sitting down. As she munched on the apple slices, she thought about how many copies of Jawaharlal Nehru's *Glimpses of World History* to order. Because Yeongju tried her best not to return books to her suppliers, it was all the more important to think carefully before placing any new orders. For books like this one where she didn't have a past record of sales figures, she had to hazard a guess as to how much longer customers would continue to look for it.

Today, she had received a call right when the bookshop opened for the day. The person on the other end had asked if the bookshop carried a copy of *Glimpses of World History*. When she said yes, the caller left his name and contact number, saying that he would drop by after work to collect it. Right after putting down the phone, she pulled out a copy of the book and placed it on the shelf with the rest of the reserved titles. For the first time since the title was brought in two years ago, a copy had been sold!

Once she made a sale, she would start to think of ordering more copies. For this book, she didn't need to think much; it was a book she would want to order again. Just as she was making an internal note to put in an order once the customer came to collect it, she received yet another call asking for the same book. How could a book that had not sold a single copy in two years sell two copies in a day? A thought flashed through her mind. She hurriedly sat down and searched the title on the Internet. Bingo. One of the hits was a recent article about a variety show making mention of the book.

Occasionally, a book would appear in dramas, or be referenced by a famous personality on variety shows, or feature on a celebrity's social media. When a book entered the limelight this way, there would be more customers looking for it, sometimes even turning these titles into overnight bestsellers. It was true that books needed to be 'discovered', and Yeongju thought that it was a good thing if those watching television could discover a new book this way and read it, no matter what it was about.

However, such books pose a difficulty for booksellers. She couldn't bring in every random book just because it was featured in a drama, or because some famous person liked it. To help her decide which books to stock, she used the following criteria:

1. Is it a good book?
2. Do I want to sell it here?
3. Does this book fit our bookshop?

The criteria might appear to be subjective, and some might even summarise them as 'the boss's whims and fancies'. However, they were important to her; having this set of guidelines allowed her to enjoy the work at the bookshop.

Following these criteria, she usually did not have to consider too long before deciding, because it was, like they said, 'her whims and fancies'. However, when it came to bestsellers or books that shot to fame – like this one – things were different. She had considered hesitantly (telling herself each time it was just for once) adding a fourth criterion:

4. Is this book going to sell well?

However, there were times she wanted to stock books despite the fact that they were unlikely to sell well. That said, the temptation of adding the fourth criterion was strong. When the bookshop first opened, she'd given in to the temptation. There was a period when she had stocked books based on the bestseller lists but, like a person carried by strong waves, she didn't know where she, or the book-shop, was heading.

'Do you have this title?'

'Nope, we don't stock this.'

There had been times when, tired of repeating 'we don't have it', she would order the book and, as expected, it sold well. However, there was a problem – Yeongju. Each time she saw the book, she would get upset, as if she was forced to eat something she did not enjoy, and thus ended up dislik-ing the dish, and likewise, the book. She decided to stick to her principles. Even if she had to repeat tens, no, hundreds of times, 'we don't have it here', she told herself never to take the easy way out. At the same time, she worked hard to bring in good books to help customers 'discover' good reads they'd never been exposed to.

Even if a book was a huge bestseller, if she didn't like it, she would no longer place an order. When she did, she would not deliberately place it at a more visible spot on the shelf. She believed that there was a rightful position for each book, and it was her responsibility to find it. She might not be able to be fair when choosing the books to bring in, but all books in her shop were equal in her eyes. She wanted to give them all a fair opportunity to be seen and sold. There were times a book which hadn't sold well got a surprising uptick in the number of sales when she moved it to another shelf. Curation was everything in an independent bookshop.

She needed to think carefully. How many copies of *Glimpses of World History* should she order? Maybe two for now, to be placed on the same shelf. She thought she could curate a collection. Instead of taking a Eurocentric view, *Glimpses of World History* examines world history from the non-Western point of view, and if she could pull out a couple of other books that see history from different perspectives, perhaps it would be well-received by customers. She thought the third shelf on the second row would be the perfect spot for the books. It was where she had placed similarly dense books when she showcased other collections in the past.

# Harmony and Dissonance

After the conversation with his mum, Minjun lost his passion and zeal for life. He lay in bed listlessly. His yoga form was bad. The only part of the day when he held himself together – even barely – was when he stood in front of the coffee machine. An overwhelming sense of guilt weighed him down. When he thought about how he'd been nothing but a disappointment to his parents, waves of misery swept over him. To his ears, his mother had sounded reproachful, as if she was reprimanding him for living his life wrong. No, it couldn't be. *Mum isn't this kind of person*, Minjun tried to reassure himself.

He was surprised how he'd managed to hold on for so long when it was so easy to crumble in an instant. It hadn't been bad thus far – he earned modestly and spent modestly. He was a little lonely, but ever since he started work at the bookshop and had someone to talk to, the loneliness was manageable, never overpowering him. He thought he could understand Yeongju's childhood dream of wanting to be surrounded by books all the time. He, too, was enveloped by a sense of peace each time he stepped into his workplace. Yeongju was a good employer, although she felt so much like a next-door noona that sometimes he forgot he was at work.

He did his job well, even creatively. As Jimi had told him, the sky was the limit when it comes to coffee blends. Beans that were grown in the same place and with the same method could still differ in taste, and coffee that was brewed from the same batch of beans could also taste different. A cup of coffee was simultaneously a work of nature and of the maker. He thought coffee brewing was, in some ways, similar to reading: anyone can do it, and the more time you spend on it, the deeper you want to dig. Once you fall into the rabbit hole, it is hard to get out. You start paying more attention to the fine details, eventually being attuned to the nuances of things. In the end, you love everything about it, be it reading or coffee. He loved his work. But . . .

It had been ten days since he last visited Goat Beans. Using every excuse he could think of, he got the beans delivered to the bookshop instead. One of the roasters even came down personally with his order and stayed for a short chat. When the roaster was about to leave, he quipped, 'Because you're not around, we have to be the ones listening to Boss complain about her husband. Sounds like the husband did something to upset her again.'

Minjun smiled but did not reply.

'Oh yeah, Boss blended some beans the way you like them. Do come over to test it.'

There was a pause before he replied, 'Okay.'

Minjun thought he was better off when he had thought all his efforts had gone down the drain. At least, back then, he could give up without any lingering regrets. If there was a critical point for hard work, he'd gone beyond that. He used to think about how, if he had worked a little harder, perhaps tried one more time . . . What if he was already at the 99 per cent mark? Then it struck him that what he needed to go from a ninety-nine to a hundred was not more effort, but luck. Without luck, he would be stuck there, always a hairbreadth away from success.

Watching a multitude of movies, he came to realise something simple – the characters are always at a crossroads. What moved the plot forward were their choices, their decisions. Wasn't it the same in life? What propels life forward are decisions. It came to him that what he needed to do was not to give up, but to make a decision – to step away from the path he'd been walking on.

When he was watching the documentary film *Seymour: An Introduction*, he kneaded the thought further. Seymour Bernstein did not give up his life as a pianist; he simply chose to do something different. No one around him could understand why the famed pianist had decided to teach rather than perform, but he was unperturbed. Even in his eighties, he said that he had never regretted his decision. When he was watching the documentary, Minjun had resolved to be like Seymour – to not regret his decision. But what he needed was not resolve. He needed courage. The courage not to waver in the face of disappointment from others, the courage to stick to his beliefs and choices.

From the day he told Yeongju he wasn't in the mood to go home, he started to dread being at home. The restlessness was worse when he was alone. Today, too, he dragged his feet finishing up and continued to stay past his working hours. Yeongju, who was frowning at something on her laptop, hadn't realised that Minjun was still around. He did some light stretching – rotating his shoulders, twisting his waist to the left and right – as he loitered around the bookshop, stealing occasional glances at her. Now and then, he drummed his fingers on the café tables, and even opened the front door for no reason. When the crisp autumn air whooshed in and he quickly shut the door again, the noise finally made her look up. She checked the time.

'Minjun, why are you not leaving?'

He walked towards her.

'I'm done for the day. I've knocked off and I'm browsing the neighbourhood bookshop right now.'

Yeongju laughed. *These days, Minjun seems to be saying less of his usual 'wells' or 'maybes'*, she thought.

'I think that the neighbourhood bookshop would have closed for the day by this time,' she said as she lifted her fingers from the keyboard. 'You shouldn't linger in a closed shop.'

Drumming a rhythm on the back of a chair, he seemed to come to a decision and pulled the chair over to her.

'Am I disturbing you?' he asked.

'Don't feel like going home again?' She patted the seat lightly, inviting him to join her.

'Yeah, I've been like this recently.'

He sat down and glanced at her screen.

'You have a lot to do?'

'I'm coming up with the list of questions for next week's book talk, but I'm kind of stuck.'

'What's the issue?' He peered at the document on the screen.

'I've been thinking about how I should stop letting my personal biases colour the decision of who to invite for book talks. I should be more objective, and make the evaluation based on the book and its contents.'

He turned his gaze towards her.

'What do you mean?'

'I approached a publisher to propose a book talk even before I read the book. I only started to read it after the author agreed to do the talk. Now, I realise that I don't know anything about writing. How can I ask about something I don't even know? I tried my best and only managed to squeeze out twelve questions so far.'

He glanced at the number 12 on the screen she was pointing to before shifting his gaze to the open book placed face down next to her laptop. The title, written in plain letters, read: *How to Write Well*.

'Why did you invite the author of a book you hadn't read?' he asked as he leafed through the pages.

'Um . . . because the author is charismatic?'

'As in, you mean he's good-looking?' He put down the book and reached into his pocket for his phone. He turned it on.

'It's just . . . his writing is razor-sharp, and he doesn't mince his words. That's why I like him.'

Minjun typed *Hyun Seungwoo* in the Internet browser.

'You're saying that you like him because he's honest?' he asked as he looked at the author's photo. Yeongju nodded slightly as she typed the number 13.

They settled into silence, each falling back into their own thoughts. As she returned to staring at the number (and berating herself), he wandered around the bookshop, grappling with the guilt that weighed heavily on his mind. After a long pause, she started typing. Finally, in between repeatedly pressing the backspace key, she added one more question to the list.

*13. How honest have you been in life?*

*Oh God. What am I asking!* She held the backspace key and watched the letters disappear. She rewrote it.

*13. I'm curious if you've spotted any mistakes in my writing?*

*He couldn't have read my writing before!* She reached for the backspace key again. Frustrated, she grabbed two bottles of sparkling water from the fridge and passed one to Minjun. He took it but continued staring out the window, a vacant look on his face.

Looking at him, she asked, 'Something happened?'

He twisted the cap open, and a few seconds passed before he spoke.

'I came over because I wanted to talk to you, but I don't know what to say.'

She took a sip. 'Aren't you the quiet type?'

'You and the boss from Goat Beans are the only two people who say I'm quiet.'

'Oh my! So, it's really true!'

Minjun startled at her sudden exclamation.

'Jimi eonnie and I talked about it before, that you don't talk to us much because we're ajummas. I was so sure it wasn't the case, but it turns out to be true!' Yeongju shot him a mischievous glance as she took another sip from her bottle.

'What, no.' He was flustered. 'And how are you an ajumma? We aren't that different in age.'

'You're telling the truth, right?'

'Of course . . .'

'Alright, I'll believe you. For my own sake.'

Seeing how she was joking, he relaxed and chuckled softly. He took a long sip and looked at her.

'Can I ask you a question? A personal one?'

'Shoot.'

'Where do your parents live?'

'My parents? In Seoul.'

Minjun's eyes widened. 'Really?'

'A little strange, right? Their daughter opens a bookshop, but they've never visited or called. It also doesn't seem like I meet them during my rest days. You probably thought they were overseas or somewhere far off in the countryside, but they turned out to be living in Seoul. "Ah, that's strange." You're thinking that, right?'

He gave an almost imperceptible nod, as though uncertain if it was an appropriate reaction.

'My parents told me they don't want to see me. Especially my mum.'

Minjun stared at Yeongju, a questioning look on his face.

'Growing up, I've never caused any trouble, but it took me just one shot to cause a lifetime's worth of trouble. If I knew things would come to this, I'd have shrugged off the obedient daughter complex a long time ago. I've been thinking it's my fault that I didn't help her build immunity.' Yeongju tried to relax her expression, which always hardened when she thought of her mother.

'Why did you ask about my parents?'

Minjun hesitated for a moment.

'My mum called me a few days ago. Because I always keep my phone turned off, it was the first time in a long while that we spoke.'

'Why did you do that?'

'Because I feel it's burdensome to be just a call or text away?'

'Aha. I see. What did you talk about with your mum?'

'Nothing much. She was fussing over me, so I told her not to worry. Then she told me to find a proper job soon, so I said I'd take charge of my own life.'

'Aha. I see.'

When Minjun saw her glancing at him, he hurriedly added, 'It's just her way of speaking. She's not trying to say that the job here is not proper.'

'I know.'

'She doesn't even know what I do now.'

'You don't have to explain yourself.'

Seeing her smile, he continued. 'In the past few days, I learnt something about myself.'

'What is it?'

'I've been pretending to be an adult when I'm not. I'm all shrivelled up because of what my mother said. It's as if I've tripped and fallen over an invisible obstacle. The problem is, I can simply brush myself off and get up. But I wonder if it's okay to do so. I'm afraid my parents will be disappointed in me, and that I'll never make them happy again. The guilt is eating away at me. I don't know if it's okay to get up coolly and just move on like this.'

'You're thinking that the life you're living now isn't what your parents wanted for you, right?' Yeongju asked softly. She could relate to that.

'Yes . . . I'm too weak-willed to live independently. And this makes me disappointed in myself.'

'You want to be an independent person?'

'It was kind of my childhood dream. I don't know why, but I've never aimed for a specific occupation. I was just not interested in becoming a doctor, or lawyer, or anything else. Neither did I want to be successful or famous. I just wanted a stable life. I mean, if I can be acknowledged for my skills in something, that'd be great, but that's about it. I just wanted to be an independent person.'

'That's a cool dream.'

'Not at all. It's as if I don't even know how to have proper dreams.'

Yeongju tapped the bottle absently and nestled more comfortably in her chair.

'My dream is to own a bookshop.'

'Well, you've achieved it.'

'I have a bookshop, but it doesn't feel like I've achieved my dream.'

'Why?'

Taking a deep breath, Yeongju looked out the window. 'I'm satisfied, but . . . it just feels like dreams aren't everything. I'm not saying that dreams are unimportant, or that there's something else above them, but life is too complicated. Just because you've achieved your dreams doesn't mean you'll always be happy. Well, something like that.'

Minjun stared at the pointed tips of his shoes and nodded. He chewed over her words. Perhaps he was miserable precisely because he was trying to simplify a life that was meant to remain complex.

As they chatted, with Minjun asking her questions every now and then, Yeongju reached the fifteenth question on her list.

'Boss. Do you happen to know the documentary film *Seymour: An Introduction*? It's not very famous, so you might not have heard of it.'

Tearing her eyes from the list (now at 16), she looked up thoughtfully.

'Ah. About Seymour Bernstein?' Yeongju pronounced it as *Si-mour*.

'Oh, is *Se-yi-mour* the same person as *Si-mour*?'

She nodded. 'There's a book about Seymour. In the translated Korean title, his name in Hangeul is written as *Si-mour*. Ah! Right. I heard the book is meant to continue his story from where it left off in the documentary. Guess you're talking about that documentary. Nope, I haven't watched it, but I want to. Why?'

'That grandpa . . .'

'You mean Seymour?'

'Yeah. In the documentary, he said . . .'

Minjun looked down, seemingly lost in thought, before he glanced up again at Yeongju.

'Dissonance before moments of harmony makes the harmony sound beautiful. Just as harmony and dissonance exist side by side in music, life is the same. Because harmony is preceded by dissonance, that's why we think life is beautiful.'

'That's a beautiful way to put it.'

Minjun lowered his head again. 'I've been thinking about it today.'

'What is it?'

'Is there a way that will accurately tell us whether the current moment we're living in is harmony or dissonance? How do I tell what state I'm in now?'

'Hmm, you won't quite know while you're in the moment. It's only when you look back that the answer is clear.'

'Yeah, I know what you're trying to say, but I'm just curious. About my life right now.'

'How does it feel to you?'

Minjun looked conflicted. 'I think it's harmony, but everyone else seems to see it as dissonance.'

Yeongju, who had been observing his expression, smiled softly.

'Am I seeing the harmonious side of Minjun's life right now?'

He grimaced. 'Well, if I'm even right.'

'You are. I'm sure you are. I guarantee that.'

He chuckled softly.

The two of them gazed out the window. The lights from the bookshop cast a soft glow on the alleyway, and on the people walking past in the narrow street. Some were in a rush, but they still gave the bookshop a curious glance as they walked past. Yeongju broke the silence.

'When it comes to parents . . . I think it's more comfortable to live a life that you want instead of a life that would not disappoint them. Of course, it's a pity that the closest people to you are the ones disappointed in you. But there's no way to live your whole life according to your parents' wishes. I used to stew in regrets, thinking how I shouldn't have acted the way I did, that I should have listened to what I was told. But there's nothing one can do about the regrets, because even if I could turn back time, I would have done the same things all over again.'

Yeongju kept her gaze on the alleyway.

'I'm living like this because that's the way I am. I ought to just accept it. Stop blaming myself. Don't be sad. Be confident. I've been telling myself this for the past few years – a form of mental training.'

The corner of his mouth lifted slightly at her words. 'I should try that. The mental training.'

'Do it. We should learn to think well of ourselves.'

'Alright, I won't bother you further,' Minjun said. He got up and returned the chair. As he walked to the door, he hesitantly told Yeongju not to stay too late. She drew a big O in the air, thanking him for his concern. Walking out, he mulled over what she said. *Learn to think well of ourselves.* He turned around. The warm glow of the lights seemed to envelop the bookshop like a protective presence. Yeongju had once shared with him five reasons every neighbourhood should have an independent bookshop. That moment, he thought he was looking at the sixth. Gazing at the bookshop from the outside made him happy.

# How Similar are You to Your Writing?

Yeongju arrived at the bookshop half an hour earlier than usual. She wasn't even done with half the questions for the book talk. Whether it was a sentence, or a long essay, writing didn't come easily to her. She only knew how to write business plans. Ever since she'd started the bookshop, she had to write several short posts a day for social media, and every other day, she needed to write a longer piece, like a book synopsis or a book review. Each time, it was difficult.

She would blank out suddenly, as if all the words were swimming away from her. At times, she started to write, only to realise the next moment that she barely knew anything about the topic. Or she might have an idea in mind, but somehow the thoughts wouldn't crystallise into words.

Staring at number 18 on her list, she wondered what it was this time. Was it that she didn't know anything about the author and his book? Or that she found it difficult to organise her thoughts? She rested her fingers on the keyboard, typed out a sentence, inserted a question mark, and reread what she'd written. *How would he answer this?* she wondered. Was this a good question?

*18. What do you focus on when you're reading or writing? Is it the sentences?*

It was through the boss of a one-man publishing house that she heard of the author Hyun Seungwoo. The boss told her about an incident that had spread like wildfire across the publishing industry and sent her a few links to blog posts. Beyond the first post, the rest read like a series of rebuttals, and rebuttals against rebuttals. The start of it appeared to be a blogger who, despite writing about a rather dry topic, had more than 10,000 followers. His blog was dedicated to the craft of writing, devoid of anything to do with his day-to-day life. His first blog post four years ago was titled: Korean Phonology 1. There were four categories: All About Korean Grammar; This is a Bad Sentence; This is a Good Sentence; Let Me Edit Your Sentences. What triggered the incident was a post under the category: This is a Bad Sentence.

The blogger had already amassed hundreds of posts quoting examples of bad sentences from newspapers and books, when he came across a translated book. Putting together a post quoting more than ten bad sentences from the work, he detailed what was bad about it beneath each sentence. The controversy brewed when the post was brought to the attention of the CEO of the publishing house that put out the book. On their official blog, the CEO wrote a post to shoot down the blogger's claims, setting off a chain of rebuttals. In the CEO's first post, he made a jab at the blogger by criticising his 'lack of manners stemming from ignorance', innocently adding that the 'ignorance' in question was how the publishing industry worked, not his grasp of Korean grammar.

In his rebuttal to the rebuttal, the blogger wrote: *While it is unfortunate that the publishing industry is facing strong headwinds, this is no excuse for readers to put up with poorly written sentences.*

The CEO then shot back: *Is there ever a perfect book with not a single poorly written sentence? If such a book exists, please enlighten me.*

The barbed language further exacerbated the tension. Soon after the CEO's post, the blogger uploaded a new post to the 'This is a Bad Sentence' category, as if he had been waiting to pounce.

In the new post, he picked out twenty more poorly written sentences from the same book, categorising them into: small mistakes people make in writing; big mistakes in the subject-predicate agreement; grammatically correct but I don't know what the sentence is saying. According to the post, he had methodically collected these twenty and more sentences from within five pages of a random page he had turned to. He didn't stop there. Taking an out-of-print book, he used the same method and came up with only six sentences – all belonging to the category of 'the small mistakes people make in writing'. He added the following explanation:

*Even though I am a blogger who is passionate about the written word, I often find myself wondering what constitutes a perfect sentence. That said, when a book is filled with awkward or poorly worded sentences, it sours the reading experience. On the question whether there exists a book with perfect sentences, I decline to respond. First of all, this is not the question that should be asked. Just because it may be impossible for a book to be made up of only perfect sentences, I do not think that it is right for a publisher to stop striving towards perfection, and to do so in such an entitled manner.*

The heated exchange spread like wildfire on social media among those in the industry, as well as anyone who was interested in books. The majority sided with the blogger. The CEO's posts were peppered with jeers and snarky remarks, which increased as time passed. As if angered by the public reaction, he started calling for the blogger to take down his posts or he'd sue, carelessly tossing out words like 'defamation suit' and 'damage to reputation'.

The blogger calmly responded that if he were in the wrong, he would gladly accept responsibility. Just when it seemed like the situation was going to escalate further, the CEO suddenly backed down. 'I'm sorry for being emotional and for failing to reflect on my behaviour,' he wrote in a blog post. 'I'll work harder to make better books in the future.' Those following the saga from the sidelines were disappointed that it ended so abruptly, but in their own ways, they found closure by virtually giving the CEO a pat on the shoulder and raising the blogger's hand in victory. It was a clear win for the blogger.

If things had ended there, it would have just blown over as a memorable incident. But the CEO was no average person. Since he'd admitted defeat openly, it seemed like he wanted to go to the extreme in conceding defeat thoroughly. You could also say he had business acumen. He uploaded a post to the publishing house's official blog – their previous battleground – with a formal and respectful invitation to the blogger. 'Please edit our book.' Four months later, they released the newly edited edition of the translation, which sold out its first print run immediately. Less than a month later, they were already on their third print run.

'An intense marketing stunt if it was one', was how the publishing industry saw this episode. Sending Yeongju a photo of the new book, the publisher who'd sent her the links told her, 'My brain knows the blogger is right, but my heart is rooting for the publisher.'

Since then, Yeongju occasionally searched for the blogger's name: Hyun Seungwoo. There were only infrequent and sparse updates on him, mostly vague, bare-bone details. Contrary to expectations, he was an ordinary company employee, though it seemed like his followers thought it interesting that he'd majored in engineering. They were impressed that the wealth of knowledge he had accumulated on writing was a result of self-study. Six months earlier, he'd started writing a fortnightly column for a newspaper, titled: *What We Do Not Know About Writing*. Since then, Yeongju had been encountering him – through his writing – once every two weeks.

His writing was calm, but sharp. Yeongju liked it when authors were sharp – which was why she enjoyed essays written by authors from outside of Korea. Korean authors who had started out with an edge in their writing usually mellowed with time, but foreign writers seemed to care little about how they were viewed. Most of the time, authors who (metaphorically) jab their fingers at humanity and cry out, 'You foolish people!' were, more often than not, not from Korea.

What set the two groups apart was that Koreans were raised in a culture where they were taught to be conscious of the eyes of others, which made them, Yeongju included, more self-conscious of how they were perceived. Perhaps this was what drew her to the writing of authors from abroad, to those who grew up in a different culture, and who were different in the way they thought, felt, and expressed themselves. As a reader though, she did not judge. Where characters in books were concerned, she accepted everything – their contradictions, inadequacies, malice, madness, and even violence.

She liked Hyun Seungwoo's writing style – neither exaggerated nor flamboyant. He wrote in deliberately plain language, although there was a hint of emotion peeking through his unadorned words. In an age and time where people laid themselves bare on the Internet, he revealed very little of his private life, adding to the mysterious aura. He focused solely on creating good content and seemed like the type who preferred to be judged on his abilities – in his case, writing. He probably wasn't even fixated on winning. Of course, this was all based on her imagination.

When Yeongju hosted book talks, she was not a bookseller; she was a reader who wanted to talk to the authors and to hear from them up close. When Seungwoo's book was published, she knew she had to act immediately. She'd already gotten wind of the news beforehand, so on the day of its launch, she immediately contacted the publishing house to invite him for a book talk. She received an affirmative reply within a few hours, along with a note from the publisher that it would be his first-ever book talk.

Yeongju cast a glance at Minjun, who'd just arrived, before typing the number 19. Resting her wrists lightly on the keyboard, she quickly typed out – her fingers dancing across the keys like a piano – the question at the forefront of her mind.

*19. How similar are you to your writing?*

# A Poor Sentence Weakens a Good Voice

Minjun thought the man with the tired-looking face and half-perm who'd just entered the bookshop looked familiar. Who was it? The man stood at the door, his eyes scanning the room before he stepped in. Putting down his backpack on a chair in the café, he took his time surveying the bookshop from the table.

Several coffee orders later, Minjun looked up to see the man perusing the menu in front of the counter. Now that he saw the man up close, Minjun realised who he was – the author whom Boss was a fan of. The star of today's book talk.

Seungwoo looked up, ready to order. 'A hot Americano, please.'

When Seungwoo passed him his credit card, Minjun waved his hand slightly to refuse it.

'You're the author Hyun Seungwoo, right?'

'What? Oh, I mean, yes.'

Seungwoo was flustered that someone recognised him.

'We offer a complimentary drink to the author doing the book talk of the day. Please wait a moment, I'll prepare your coffee.'

'Ah, I see. Thank you.' Seungwoo gave an awkward nod of thanks and stepped aside to wait for his drink.

Seungwoo looked exactly like his photo. Authors who came for book talks were usually excited or nervous. Seungwoo, however, was stoic, just like his profile photo. Minjun had thought that the expression he wore in the photo was part of the pose, but it seemed like that was how he really was. Seungwoo had a permanently tired look to him. Minjun thought he could hazard a good guess at the type of life the author led. He had looked exactly like that when he was running on a severe lack of sleep, juggling his studies and part-time jobs at university. Maybe it was more accurate to call it a lack-of-sleep look.

'Your coffee is ready.'

Seungwoo glanced at Minjun as he took the coffee. When Minjun directed his gaze past him, Seungwoo, too, turned his head. Yeongju was walking in their direction, carrying two chairs in her arms.

Keeping his eyes on her, Seungwoo asked, 'Is she the owner of the bookshop?'

'Yes, that's right.'

Minjun's gaze continued to follow her as she turned back. 'Is there anything else you need?'

When Seungwoo said no, Minjun left the counter to help Yeongju with the chairs. Seungwoo continued to stare as Minjun spoke to Yeongju. Seungwoo watched her turn around immediately and head in his direction. Her bright smile was approaching. Their eyes met. Seungwoo nodded his head in greeting.

'Hi. I'm Hyun—'

'The author Hyun Seungwoo, right?' Her gentle eyes sparkled. Seungwoo couldn't quite keep up with her enthusiasm, so he simply nodded.

'Hi, I'm Lee Yeongju, the founder of the bookshop. Really happy to meet you, and thank you for agreeing to do the book talk.'

Suddenly conscious of the radiating warmth from the coffee he was holding, Seungwoo replied, 'Nice to meet you. I'm the one who should thank you for the invitation.'

Yeongju's face lit up, as if he'd said something extremely touching.

'Thank you for saying that.'

Seungwoo was so flustered by her response that he couldn't even nod in reply. Yeongju thought he was a little stiff, but she attributed that to nerves before a talk and continued.

'The book talk is scheduled at 7:30 p.m., but we usually wait for ten minutes before starting. You'll be chatting with me for an hour before taking questions from the floor for twenty to thirty minutes. Feel free to sit in the café until the talk starts.'

'Alright,' Seungwoo said. He continued to stare at Yeongju. He wondered if it was rude, but because she was also looking at him as if that was the most normal thing to do, he couldn't tear his eyes away. Not privy to his internal thoughts, Yeongju maintained her gaze for a while before saying, 'I need to get some things done. See you later.' Only when she walked off did he turn to look out the window. His editor was heading towards the bookshop. Seungwoo stole another glance at her before going to the door to greet him.

*

'Alright, we'll begin the talk. Mr Hyun, would you introduce yourself, please.'

'Hi. I'm Hyun Seungwoo, the author of *How to Write Well*. I'm pleased to be here.'

There were more than fifty people in the audience, including some who hadn't preregistered. Everyone clapped enthusiastically. Yeongju had assembled all the chairs they owned, even her own work chair, and the two-seater sofa usually next to the bookcases. Seungwoo and Yeongju sat facing each other, about a metre away from the audience. As the chairs were arranged at an angle, there was no need for them to turn their heads to speak to each other.

Seungwoo appeared a little nervous at first, but he regained his composure in no time. He would pause a beat before answering a question, giving the impression that he was always trying to find the most appropriate word and checking whether he'd expressed himself clearly. He spoke slowly, but it wasn't boring. Yeongju looked on with interest at the way he spoke. He seemed to be very much like she'd imagined him to be based on his writing, as if his real-life personality blended seamlessly with his writer persona. That calm countenance, the stoic expression, the slight lift of the corners of his mouth when he smiled, the set of his lips that made him look considerate (although not to the extent that he would go out of his way to do something he disliked). Was it because of the set of his mouth?

Yeongju felt at ease throughout the talk, whether she was asking the questions, or listening to his answers. Even when faced with her challenging questions, he remained unflustered and gathered his thoughts calmly before answering slowly, just as he was doing now.

More than half of the audience were followers of his blog. One of them had had their sentences corrected by him (Seungwoo and his followers called it 'pruning the sentences'), and according to him, the experience was like an epiphany.

The audience chuckled. Yeongju added that she was a belated follower of his blog and had followed that 'incident' from the sidelines, which elicited another round of laughter. Choosing her words carefully, she tried to phrase the next question in a way that wouldn't make him feel too burdened.

'Can I ask you how you felt then? I think many of us here are curious.'

Seungwoo nodded.

'While I tried to be calm in my writing, I was, in fact, very flustered. I even considered shutting down my blog. It makes me uncomfortable to write, thinking about how my words can cause hurt to others.'

'Now that you mention it, I think you have barely updated the category of "This is a Bad Sentence" after that incident.'

'Yes. I did fewer of those posts.'

'Was it because you felt uncomfortable?'

'That too. I also didn't have time. I was writing this book.'

'When the CEO of that publishing house approached you to edit the translation, did you agree to it immediately?'

'No.' He tilted his head as if trying to recall the order of events. 'I'm not a professional editor.'

'You? The author who wrote a book on writing?' Yeongju laughed, and Seungwoo immediately corrected himself.

'I mean, it's not my profession. I've also never thought of editing a whole book. I deliberated for a long time and told myself, alright, I'll try it once. Also, because I was sorry for the CEO.'

'For ruthlessly criticising the book?'

'No. That book was published without sufficient effort, and I'm not sorry to point it out.'

Seungwoo's sharp tongue was more evident in speech than writing. Was it because of his tone, as if he was stating the obvious, or his aura?

'I felt like the way I handled it was like backing someone into a corner, and I'm sorry for that. It's a flaw of mine.' He looked at Yeongju as he spoke. 'It's a flaw I have difficulty overcoming. I'm always logical, and when the other person is emotional, I try to compensate by dialling up the logic, which can come across as rigid and unyielding. I'm aware of this fault of mine, and I try to be mindful of it. But sometimes, it's difficult.'

Yeongju looked on with interest at Seungwoo discussing his weakness during the talk. It was perhaps this honesty that made it far from boring, even though he was serious. She glanced at the time before continuing her questions.

'What is your focus when you're reading or writing? Is it the sentences?'

'No, although many would have thought so.'

'What is it then?'

'The voice. The author's voice. If the author has a strong voice, even when the sentences are a little clumsy, the writing will still come across as powerful. Well-crafted sentences can also enhance a strong voice, making it shine.'

'Can you elaborate?'

'Poorly written sentences can distract readers from an otherwise weak or unremarkable voice, making it seem more tolerable because their attention is focused on the sentences instead. In a sense, the unpolished sentences obscure the weakness in the voice, making it seem more palatable.'

'And the opposite is also true.'

'Yes, badly written sentences often obscure a strong voice, and when that happens, you just need to prune the sentences for the voice to shine through.'

'I get what you mean.' Yeongju nodded as she looked at Seungwoo, who glanced up at her too. As their eyes met, she asked, 'The next question is something that I really want to ask you. Mr Hyun, how similar are you to your writing?'

Her eyes were shining – just like when she had greeted him a while ago. *She is looking at me with the same sparkle in her eyes just now. Does it mean anything?* he thought. He was curious, but he tried to draw his focus back to answering the question.

'This is the hardest question tonight.'

'Really?'

'I'd like to challenge this question. Is there anyone who can know for sure? Even if I'm the person who wrote it, can I – or anyone – be sure whether a person is similar to their writing, or not?'

It dawned on her that the way she connected the writing and the author while reading might be something that was alien to others. When she thought about it, it was simply a bit of entertainment for her, nothing more, or less. It might even be construed as a rude or uncomfortable question, as if she was saying, 'You don't give off the same vibe as your writing.' But that was not her intention at all. She didn't want to embarrass the author.

'Hmmm . . . I believe it's possible.'

Seungwoo glanced up at Yeongju, brimming with curiosity. 'How?'

'When I read something by Nikos Kazantzakis, I form an image of him. For example, him sitting by the window on a train and staring solemnly out the window.'

'Why that image?'

'He loved travelling. And he's a writer who delves deep into life.'

Seungwoo held his gaze but didn't respond.

'I believe that he wasn't the chatty type who gossiped about people behind their backs.'

'What makes you think so?'

'His writing tells me that.'

*His writing* . . . He paused, blinking several times.

'Hmm . . . after hearing what you said, I think I can tell you this: I don't like to lie so I refrain from saying too much, and I try my best to write what I believe is the truth.'

'Could you elaborate on that?'

'While writing, it's possible to unintentionally include untruths. For example, let's say I haven't watched a single movie in the past year. One day, I might conclude that if I haven't watched any movies, I must not enjoy them. Later on, I might forget what really happened and simply believe that I don't like movies. In my writing, I might then subconsciously include the sentence "I don't enjoy movies". It's neither a lie, nor a mistake, because that's what I believe. The truth might be that I do enjoy movies, just that I'd been too busy. If I mull it over a little more, I might be able to tease out the truth; if not, I might unintentionally write an untruth.'

'In that case, the correct sentence should be . . .'

'I didn't watch a movie in the past year. Or couldn't.'

The conversation flowed smoothly, buoyed by their chemistry and an engaged audience. The audience stepped up during the Q&A session, and the questions ranged from 'Is your intelligence a result of nature or nurture?' to 'Are you pleased with your own writing?', and the person who asked the latter followed up by pointing out a mistake on page fifty-six in the twenty-fifth sentence. Seungwoo seemed particularly interested in the last comment and had a lengthy discussion with the questioner, ultimately concluding that they had different writing styles.

The audience were the first to leave after the event ended, followed by Seungwoo and his editor soon after. Minjun, who had hung around after his work hours yet again, helped Yeongju to tidy up. With everything largely back in place, she grabbed two bottled beers from the fridge. Sitting side by side in the empty bookshop, they drank in silence. Minjun gulped down the beer.

'How does it feel? Meeting your favourite author?'

'Great, of course.'

'Maybe I should look for an author I like too.'

'Good idea.'

As she drank her beer, Yeongju tried to recall if she'd made any slip-ups during the talk. She would enjoy transcribing it. She had to get the transcript ready for social media within the week, and then jump straight into the preparations for the next book talk. For today, at least, it didn't feel like a chore.

'That author seems perpetually tired.'

Yeongju laughed out loud. Chuckling to herself, she recalled his tired face. Serious. Honest. Attentive to every question. His sincere answers. *He was very much like his writing*, she thought.

## A Restful Sunday Evening

Yeongju was often advised to take Mondays off instead of Sundays. Bookselling is mainly a weekend business, the other booksellers told her. She'd briefly considered following their advice because it made sense from a business standpoint. But she also thought she ought to enjoy part of the weekend. Someday she hoped to have a five-day work week, once the bookshop had 'found its place' in the community, and then she could close Mondays.

What would it mean for the bookshop to 'find its place' though? Was it to provide a fair wage to her staff while also earning enough to feed herself? Or earn big profits, like any other business? No matter which one it was, a dreadful thought plagued her – that the bookshop might never establish itself in the community. In that case, what should she do? Should she close the bookshop, as she'd intended, or find another way to save the business?

Despite fretting over the future, Sundays still hit the sweet spot. She had the entire day to herself, from the moment she woke up till she went to bed. She was both an extrovert and an introvert; while she enjoyed her customers, a people-facing job drained her. There were moments at work when she was suddenly seized with the desire to hole up somewhere alone. On days when she had to spend the entire day interacting and socialising with people, she sometimes had insomnia at night. She needed her 'me time', even if it was to sit alone in silence for an hour. This was why Sundays were precious to her. At the very least, for one day, she had an escape from the anxiety of socialising.

On Sundays, she would get up at nine. After washing her face, she'd make herself a cup of coffee. As she sipped the coffee, she would think about how to spend the day, even though she knew that she wouldn't be doing much. When she got hungry, she would grab the first thing she saw in her fridge and sit down at the living room table for breakfast. After breakfast, still at the table, she would download a variety show and laugh her way through a couple of episodes over the next few hours, not budging from the living room until it was time for bed.

Yeongju's apartment was sparsely furnished. In her room was a bed and wardrobe; the other bedroom was lined with books. A mini-fridge fit for one stood in the kitchen, and in the living room was a huge desk, a chair, a side table, and a low, narrow bookcase. She'd briefly considered Jimi's suggestion to, at the very least, add a two-seater sofa, but decided that the room was fine the way it was.

She didn't see a need to fill the space. Emptiness was also a vibe. That said, there was something that her house had plenty of – lighting. There were three floor lamps in the living room alone: one next to the full-length windows opening out on to the balcony, one beside the desk, and one flanking her bedroom door. She liked how the lights cast a soft glow on everything they touched.

On the large desk was a laptop of the same model as the one she used in the bookshop. When she was home, she spent most of her time at the table. Today, like any other Sunday, she continued to sit there after breakfast to look for new variety shows to watch. She didn't like long-running shows, preferring shorter ones that were on air for a few months. When something she enjoyed watching ended, it felt like a reset of her emotions.

On days like today, where she couldn't find new shows to watch, Yeongju would go back to her old favourites. She particularly loved the variety shows produced by Na Yeong-seok PD. They were all about good people having great conversations in front of a beautiful landscape. Watching such sincere and warm-hearted content had a calming effect on her. Her favourite among the Na PD programmes was *Youth Over Flowers*, in particular the episodes where the cast went to Africa and Australia. She wasn't familiar with the celebrities but seeing their youthful and bright smiles made her feel warm and fuzzy.

Watching the show made her miss her younger days, a time when she must have been alive, but lacked the vigour of youth. She thought of youth as a fleeting moment, an unattainable utopia, like the clear skies of Australia, the charming smiles of young and good-looking idols as they came together for one unforgettable trip. Youth wasn't something you could hold on to. It amused her to think that she was longing for a time she'd never quite experienced.

She put on the first episode of the Africa trip. Even though it was her third time watching, she was mesmerised by the majestic landscape, and she smiled at the youthful idols having a great time as they laughed and bonded over activities. If she were there, she'd also want to climb up the sand dunes and sit on the peak. What would it be like to watch the sunrise or sunset from the peak? Would she cheer loudly? Or would loneliness creep in? Maybe she would start crying.

After the fourth episode, she looked out of the window. The sun was setting. She missed it more than her youth, this time of day with the last rays bowing out in the twilight. She wanted to take a walk under the dimming skies. Like youth, it was a fleeting moment, but there was no need to mourn, when it would come again tomorrow, and the next day. Wanting to get closer, she moved her chair to the window, wrapping her hands around her raised knees as she stared out at the dawn of a winter's night.

She'd gotten used to spending a whole day without talking. When she first lived alone, by evening time she would deliberately try to make some sounds like 'ahhhhh', before bursting into laughter at her ridiculous behaviour.

But now, she treated the silence as a day's rest for her voice and was perfectly at ease. When she wasn't talking, her inner voice grew louder. She wasn't talking, but she still spent the whole day thinking and feeling. Instead of sounds, she expressed herself through the written word. Sometimes, she even wrote three essays on a single Sunday. But these belonged solely to her, and were never shared with anyone else.

The living room was now pitch-black. She stood up, turned on all three lights and sat down again. A while later, she got up, walked to the bookcase in front of her side table, and pulled out two books. A few days ago, she'd started reading a story every night from each of the two short story collections: *Too Bright Outside for Love*[3] and *Shoko's Smile*. She alternated between the two books to start with, and today, it was *Too Bright Outside for Love*.

The sixth story in the collection was titled 'Waiting for Dog'. The story begins with a mother losing the family

[3]Kim Keum-hee, 너무 한낮의 연애 *Neomu Hannajui Yeonae* (Munhakdongne, 2016)

dog during a walk, and her daughter returns from abroad to look for it together. Unresolved past trauma – domestic violence and rape – forces the characters to confront their issues as they struggle with suspicions and, finally, a confession. Despite the heaviness of the story, the ending is hopeful. When Yeongju finished the last sentence, she flipped back to the previous page, and for the first time that day, spoke aloud to read a few sentences.

'Every possibility starts from something small – like the apple juice you drink every morning – but it can change everything.'[4]

Yeongju loved such stories. Stories of people going through hard times, taking one step at a time forward as they seek comfort from the flicker of light across the horizon; stories of people determined to live on despite their sufferings. Stories of hope – not the rash or innocent kind, but the last glimmer of hope in life.

She read the sentence aloud once and ran her eyes over it a few more times before heading to the kitchen. She turned on the light, took out two eggs from the fridge, and cracked them into a pan drizzled with olive oil. As the eggs sizzled, she scooped out some rice to fill half a soup bowl. She placed the two eggs sunny side-up on top of the rice, drizzling half a spoonful of soy sauce on them. Soy sauce egg rice – with two eggs – was her favourite. Two eggs were perfect. Just enough to coat each grain of rice with the runny egg yolk.

Yeongju turned off the kitchen lights and mixed the rice with a spoon as she walked back to the window and settled into the same position as five minutes ago. She ate her dinner as she gazed out the window. Then she picked up *Shoko's Smile*. Chewing a mouthful of egg and rice, her eyes

[4]Kim, *Neomu*, 177.

ran over the contents page and landed on the sixth story: 'Michaela'. It seemed like this was also a story of a mother and daughter. When she started to read the first line, she didn't expect to be bawling her eyes out by the end of the story.

Like any other day, she would fall asleep while reading. Spending a restful Sunday like this made her wish she could do the same for one more day a week, but she was comforted by the thought that she wouldn't be caught in the Monday morning rush hour and could go to work feeling happy. If life continued at this pace, or hopefully, a little more relaxed – if she enjoyed a little more freedom – Yeongju thought she could live out the rest of her days like this.

## You Look Terrible. What's Wrong?

Minjun chatted intermittently with the roasters at Goat Beans while his hands were busy picking out the bad beans. They told him to sit down and work comfortably, but he waved off the suggestion and continued to stand with his back bent forward.

'Jimi is late,' Minjun said to no one in particular.

'It happens once every few months,' one of them replied.

'Is there something going on?' he asked.

'Well, we don't know. On those days, she'll just call to say she's coming in late,' the roaster said as he pulled up a chair for Minjun.

'Oh, thank you.'

'Aren't you the one with something going on?'

'What do you mean?'

The roaster pointed at the mirror. 'Guess you haven't been looking at yourself in there?'

Minjun laughed, and the roaster chuckled too.

Minjun sat down and continued to sieve out the shrivelled and discoloured beans, which he threw into the dustbin. Beans that could no longer be used should be thrown away without hesitation. Once a bad bean – even if it's just one – was mixed with the rest, the coffee tasted somewhat disappointing. One bean was enough to make a difference. Just like bad beans, there were thoughts he should throw away, too. One bad thought was enough to cause his mental health to spiral. He picked up a shrivelled bean, curled up like a human, and stared. He wished he could unfurl the bean. He tried, but the bean didn't budge. He pressed hard again. When he was about to try for the third time, Jimi walked in.

'Oh! Finally. I thought I'd never see you here again.'

Minjun startled as Jimi approached. He tried not to show his surprise, but it probably made him stiffen up even more unnaturally. It was obvious she'd been crying. When she smiled, her eyes bent into puffy crescent moons.

'You were the one who told me to be here for the beans.' Minjun tried to maintain an even voice.

Jimi walked past him to see how her staff were doing. She checked each of the orders carefully, grabbed a fistful of the freshly roasted beans and put them close to her nose. When she walked to the roaster at the grinding machine, he nodded and said, 'Yup, it's this one.'

'How much longer?'

'Another ten minutes.'

Jimi signalled for the roaster to call her when the coffee was ready; he shrugged in response and pointed at the door to indicate he'd bring it to her instead. Signing an OK, Jimi waved Minjun over to her office. When they walked out of the roasting area, Jimi turned around and peered at his face in concern.

'You look terrible. What's wrong?'

'Ah.' Minjun rubbed his cheeks with his palm.

'The light's extinguished in your eyes. Why do you look so defeated?'

He stared worriedly at her instead.

'That's my question. Do you know that your eyes are really swollen right now?'

'Oh, right!' she said as she pressed her palms against her eyes. 'I've been doing that all morning. So silly of me! I forgot to look in the mirror before I came in. Is it obvious?'

He nodded.

'Do you think the rest of them saw it?'

Another nod.

'Ah whatever, I don't care anymore. Let's go.'

Goat Beans owned several coffee machines – the popular models used in cafés – so that clients could sample the beans before placing orders. The machines were also used for hands-on demonstrations to guide first-time café owners like Yeongju, who came in with zero knowledge of coffee-making and the various types of coffee. By going the extra mile, they formed a close relationship with their clients, which, once established, would not break up easily. This was why Goat Beans boasted many long-standing accounts.

Separated by a bar table, Minjun sat on the outside while Jimi stood on the other side. Looking at each other's faces, they chuckled, which made them feel a lot better.

'Don't like the work anymore?' she asked.

He smiled wanly.

'That's not it. I just feel lost.'

'Lost?' Jimi repeated.

'According to Boss, human beings wander for as long as we keep trying.'

'And where did she pick up this line from this time?'

'Goethe's *Faust*.'

'Aigoo. When is she getting rid of her know-it-all air? If she wasn't hanging out with me all the time, I would love to smack the ideas out of her.'

Both of them burst out laughing at the same time.

'So, what is it? You're making an effort and that's why you feel lost?'

'I was trying to change the topic but you're refusing to let it go.'

Jimi nodded. 'Yeah, there're times we just want to move on.'

'Do you feel the same way too?'

'About?'

'The reason you cried. Do you also want to move on from it?'

Just as Jimi was about to say something, the roaster came in holding two bags of vacuum-packed ground coffee – a 2 kg bag, and a 250 g one. Jimi pointed to the smaller bag.

'What's this one? You're giving it to Minjun?'

The roaster gestured a 'yes' and winked at Minjun before walking out.

'Is there something in his mouth? Why is he not talking?'

'Well, you didn't either.' Minjun mimicked her calling gesture.

'Whatever, nothing's going my way. That's his way of retaliating, huh.'

Jimi stood up and moved to the cupboard, from which she took paper filters, a dripper, a glass server and a goose-neck kettle. She filled the electric kettle with filtered water and turned it on, lifting the lid once the water boiled. As she waited for the water to cool slightly, she fit a paper filter on the dripper and set it on top of the server.

'Let's do a hand drip today.'

Pouring the hot water into the gooseneck kettle, she asked, 'Do you remember how to do this?'

'Yes.'

'You've tried it at home?'

'Often.'

'Good. It'll be the same as last time. I'm just going by gut feeling today but you should use a scale to be accurate. If you have any questions, just ask.'

Jimi poured the hot water through the coffee filter before adding the finely ground coffee powder on to the wetted filter. Holding the gooseneck kettle steady, she slowly poured some water to saturate the dry grounds as she murmured half to herself.

'Indeed, you get a richer flavour with a hand drip. Strange . . . when a machine is more accurate.'

Minjun observed carefully as she slowly poured the water in a clockwise motion, starting from the centre of the soaked grounds and moving outwards in circles. Finishing a round, she paused and said, 'Look, look at the bloom,' before continuing a second pour from the centre to the edge. Minjun listened to the coffee dripping slowly into the server.

'I always have trouble deciding when to stop the pours,' he said.

'When the rhythm slows, it's time to stop. If you like a more acidic flavour, then carry on a little longer.'

'I know the theory. But sometimes I wonder if anyone really knows when exactly coffee is the best.'

'Don't we all. Just trust your instincts. The only way is to do it often and drink it often. And drink the coffee other people brew.'

'Okay.'

'Believe your gut feeling. You have a pretty good sense.'

'Sometimes I wonder if I can believe you.'

Jimi chuckled as she took two cups from the shelves.

'What's there to think about? Just believe who you want to believe.'

She poured out the coffee and handed a cup to him before pouring some for herself.

'Drink this and you'll really want to believe me.'

Inhaling the aroma of the coffee, they took a sip and stared at each other in awe.

'This is really good,' he exclaimed as he set the cup down.

'Of course,' she said, looking like she'd anticipated his reaction. Over small sips of coffee, they made small talk; conversations that stayed in the moment, words that need not be remembered for a long time. For a while, there was silence before Jimi spoke, her gaze fixed on her cup.

'I wanted to move on.'

Minjun looked up and waited for her to continue.

'If only moving on from the topic could make it feel trivial. But it's not working the way I want it to. As long as it's about that man, it always cuts too deeply.'

'Something happened?'

'The same as usual. But this time, my reaction was too explosive. Even I thought so. I almost slapped him.'

Jimi tried to smile but her expression crumbled.

'What exactly is family? What is it about family that makes me lose control completely? Minjun, do you have plans for marriage?'

Despite being in his thirties, he had never seriously considered marriage. *Can I really get married?* Sometimes the thought would flash across his mind, but he'd never thought about it more deeply.

'I don't know.'

'You need to think carefully.'

'Of course.'

'I shouldn't have gotten married. I shouldn't have tied myself to that man and made him family. He was good as a lover. Or we could have just been acquaintances. He's not someone I would want to live with, although I wouldn't have known that before getting married.'

'That's true.'

'This coffee's still good even when lukewarm, right?'

'Oh yeah.'

There was a moment of silence before Minjun spoke.

'My parents have a good relationship. They've never fought. Or at least not in front of me.'

'Wow, that's a feat.'

'I didn't think much about it when I was younger, but I grew to realise how amazing that is. We lived like a team, like three teammates who were bound together for some competition.'

'Sounds like you have a harmonious family.'

'Yeah . . . but . . .'

'But what?'

Minjun tapped the handle of the cup and looked up.

'I've been thinking that it's not good for family to be so tight-knit, that there should be some distance. I don't know, for now, if it's the right way to think, but I'm going to hold on to the thought and see where it takes me.'

'Hold on to the thought?'

'It's something Boss told me. When you have thoughts, just hold on to them, see where they take you, and as time passes, you'll find out if you were right. Never decide right at the start if something is right or wrong. I think she's right. So, I'm going to hold on to it and act accordingly. It's not much, but I plan to keep a distance for a spell, and not to think of my parents for a while.'

Like Yeongju told him, Minjun decided to think well of himself for now.

They drained their cups. *How could lukewarm coffee still taste this good?* he wondered. There were only two possible answers: good beans, good skills. Jimi pushed the cups aside and got up.

'You should get going.'

Minjun stood up, putting the coffee in his bag. He nodded a farewell to her, but as he was about to leave, he turned back again. Jimi, who was clearing the table, looked up and raised her eyebrows.

'I don't know if it's my place to say this, but perhaps you should also think more carefully.'

'About?'

'About family. Becoming family doesn't mean you need to stay a family. If you're not happy, they are not the people to keep beside you.'

Jimi stayed quiet. She liked what Minjun had just said. He'd worked up the courage to tell her something that she had not dared to say out loud. She smiled and gestured OK. It wasn't quite his place to say that, but as Minjun left Goat Beans, he had no regrets. He'd wanted to tell her for a long time.

## How We View Work

In ones and twos, the book club members trickled into the bookshop. The nine of them, including Yeongju, formed a circle. Starting from the leader, Wooshik, and going anti-clockwise, everyone was given some time to 'talk about anything'. One by one, they shared something about their lives: I cut my hair. I started a diet. I fought with a friend and I'm not feeling great. I'm a little depressed because I'm feeling my age. The others would reply encouragingly: the new hairstyle suits you, you're looking great right now. There's no need to diet. It seems like your friend is in the wrong. We the younger ones are also depressed, so it's not your age.

That day, once again, Minjun didn't want to go home just yet. Once he made sure there were no customers who might order a coffee, he pulled up a chair and sat down quietly on the edge of the circle. Everyone automatically shifted a little to make room for him. Minjun waved his hands to indicate he was comfortable where he was, but when the rest of them gestured even more insistently, he pulled his chair forward and joined them. This evening, the book they were discussing was *The Refusal of Work: The Theory and Practice of Resistance to Work*.

'Let's get started. If you would like to speak, raise your hand and you may do so. As usual, you're welcome to jump in at appropriate junctures, but please refrain from cutting someone off in the middle of a sentence.'

Nobody spoke; everyone was waiting. In the book club, there was no pressure to speak. They spoke if they wanted to; if not, it was okay to listen. A moment later, a lady in her twenties – the one who had fought with her friend – put up her hand.

'It's predicted that there'll be fewer jobs in the future because of AI and automation, so I'm very worried. I can't spend my whole life doing casual jobs. I was pinning my hopes on the government doing their best to create more jobs. As to how to achieve that, they should be the ones to come up with a strategy. But here, on page thirteen, there's a passage that goes like this.'

Seeing everyone open their books as if on cue, Minjun quietly slipped to the bookshelves and returned with a copy. The lady read the passage aloud.

'"What is so great about work that sees society constantly trying to create more of it? Why, at the pinnacle of society's productive development, is there still thought to be a need for everybody to work for most of the time?"[5]

'Just the other day, someone here in the book club said that books are axes. When I read this sentence, I felt like I was hit on the head with one. Yeah, what's so amazing about work that we obsess over having a job? What we should be worried about is not work, but whether we can feed ourselves. I've been thinking that what the government

[5] David Frayne, *The Refusal of Work: The Theory and Practice of Resistance to Work* (Zed Books, 2015), 13.

should do is not create more jobs, but to find a way for the citizens to make a living.'

No one said anything. Minjun had gotten used to the moments of silence in between. After a moment, a man in his early forties (who was on a diet) spoke.

'You need to work to make a living. This is what society has ingrained in us, so I'm not able to immediately separate the two concepts. Reading the book makes me feel like making a living without a job is theoretically possible, but I still find it hard to embrace it – it's too idealistic. But the book does help me to better understand why I think of work in a certain way – why I think it's beneficial to humans, why I think skivers are lazy and useless people, and why I spent so much effort on finding a good job. Am I the only one who feels empty after reading this? It's like the book is telling us our present views and perspectives of work were arbitrarily shaped by people in the past, and here we are, accepting it as though it's a universal truth.'

'I feel empty too,' said the woman in her thirties who'd just gotten a haircut. 'The Puritan work ethic has also influenced the way we think about work – placing work on a moral pedestal. Those who work are contributing members of society; skivers are useless. It's ridiculous that the idea of hard work as a way of gaining salvation survived centuries, crossing time and space to be passed on to people like me – a non-religious person living in twenty-first-century Korea, precariously holding on to my job. Even as a kid, I was determined that I would work when I grew up. I told myself, I'm going to be an amazing career woman. I'll divorce any man who dares stand between me and my goal.'

The non-religious woman paused a beat and continued.

'The problem is that even the atheists have taken to becoming extremely passionate about work, imprinting all the wonderful things about it in our minds: work is good for me. I need to work hard. I'm so lucky to have a job. A life without work is the worst.'

'That's not a bad thing, right?' Wooshik commented.

'Well, reading this book makes me feel like I can't even say that.'

'Which part of the book is it? I can't remember where I read it,' said the woman in her fifties, who had lamented her age.

There was a rustle of pages. Minjun recalled what he'd learnt about Max Weber's work on the Protestant Ethic in an elective module at university. The Protestant Ethic has survived through time, extending its reach to not only the non-religious woman, but him, too. Like the Protestants, he was prepared to work diligently. While he didn't think of work as a vocation, Minjun, like the man in his forties, thought that everyone was born to work.

'Here it is. Page fifty-two. I'll read it out,' said the non-religious woman.

'"The problem here is not that the labour process presents no opportunities for expression and identification, but that the employer expects workers to become fully involved and invested in the job."'[6]

'I found something related at the end of page fifty-six as well,' said the university freshman who'd just shed the school uniform this year.

'"Workers are, in other words, transformed into 'company people'. In Hephaestus, identification with work was promoted via an organisational rhetoric around ideas

[6]Frayne, *Refusal*, 52.

138

like 'team' and 'family', designed to encourage workers to feel a sense of devotion and personal obligation. Ideas like 'team' and 'family' function to reframe the workplace as a field of ethical rather than economic obligation, binding workers more tightly to the goals of the organisation.'"[7]

The university freshman stopped there.

'Eonnie, I think you're what they call a "company person". Your whole identity and value are tied to the company, and you work as if you own the company. It says here that businesses use words like "team" and "family" to make an employee a company person. It reminds me of how my brother-in-law was recently promoted to team lead, and I congratulated him heartily then. But now, I'm scared of the word "team". I wonder if he's also being made into a company person.'

'But I think not everyone who works hard or likes their work is a company person. The book also doesn't take an entirely negative view on work. I think the joy of working, and the personal development it entails, can enrich our lives.'

Minjun glanced at Yeongju, who'd spoken for the first time.

'That said, the problem is that our society is too obsessed with work, and working takes away too many things from us. It's like we surface from the depths of work to get a breather, only to feel thoroughly spent. And when we return home after a long workday, we no longer have energy for leisure time or hobbies. I think many of us will agree with this sentence on page ninety-three.

'"When significant proportions of our time are spent working, recuperating from work, compensating for work,

---

[7]Frayne, *Refusal*, 56–57.

or doing the many things necessary in order to find, prepare for, and hold on to work, it becomes increasingly difficult to say how much of our time is truly our own."[8]

Yeongju continued. 'What it means is that we work too much. And when work eclipses life, work becomes a problem.'

Minjun thought back to their first meeting, when Yeongju had emphasised what his working hours were. She probably wasn't referring to this book; it was what she thought work should be. It shouldn't overwhelm a person; nobody can be happy living a life swamped by work.

'I agree,' Wooshik chimed in. 'I like my work. After a day of hard work, it makes me happy to enjoy a can of beer while playing a video game, or to drop by the bookshop to read a few pages of a book. But like Yeongju said, if the work becomes too much, you'll get thoroughly exhausted by it no matter how interesting it is. If I have to live like this, shuttling between home and the office – even if it's just for a week – I'll probably die.'

'If you have kids at home, it's worse,' the man next to Minjun added.

'Sorry to bring up kids when we're talking about work, but because of work, I can't even take care of my child. My wife has been talking about wanting to move to northern Europe. I can't remember if it's Sweden or Denmark, but apparently, they call them latte dads: dads who finish work early to enjoy a latte while spending time with their children. Both my wife and I finish work after nine. My mother-in-law is staying with us, but by the time we return home, she's so tired she immediately goes to bed. The book club is the

[8]Frayne, *Refusal*, 93.

only hobby I'm allowed to have. My once-a-month leisure activity. Life is tough.'

'Can't everything be solved by working less?' a woman in her twenties asked, trying to lighten the mood. There was a murmur, some in the circle smiling, others looking solemn.

'I'd love to work less. The problem is how to do it for the same pay.'

'Might be possible at the big corporations, but not the smaller enterprises.'

'And not those one-person companies that rely on casual workers.'

'Basically, almost nowhere.'

'In any case, getting paid less for doing less work is a no-no.'

'Definitely a no. Not in a world where every single cost is rising, and the only thing that's stagnant is our salaries. And the thought of getting even less . . .'

'It pisses me off that the old fogeys in the ivory tower are being paid astronomical sums, and here we are, earning a pittance. Honestly, aren't the worker ants like us the ones keeping the company running like clockwork?'

'About time to revolt.'

Sensing that the conversation was about to diverge, Wooshik put up his hand.

'To sum up, the reality is that work is the main contributing factor to our income. So, in order to make a living, we have to work.'

The man in his forties started to say how it was best to make a living from property gains, but sensing it would lead the conversation astray, he turned his focus back to the book.

'This is why the author wrote the book. Because our society is constructed in a way that it's only possible to make a living if you work. However, there are many people around the world who, for some reason, cannot find work. Those who work can't live a decent life because they're exhausted all the time; those who don't work also can't live a decent life because they have no money. The book posits that if people work less, we can then redistribute some of that work to those who don't have a job, and that it's theoretically possible.'

'Well, it's also possible in real life. The problem is those who aren't willing to give up part of their pie.' The non-religious woman pointed up as she spoke.

'Yet another problem.' Everyone chuckled.

The discussion had been going for more than an hour. The members, as if a little tired, started to chitchat. Seeing how Wooshik didn't try to intervene and even joined in the chatter, this was clearly part of the usual flow. The woman in her fifties spoke.

'When I was young, I thought that sacrificing myself and accommodating others was part of my duty. It's good to see the younger ones these days thinking differently.'

'Well, it's not that we see things differently, but at least we need to see a glimmer of hope at the end of that sacrifice. But these days, there's not even a shred of hope. So, we don't see a need to sacrifice anymore,' the younger ones chimed in.

The older lady was shocked.

'Is it that bad?' she asked, looking at them in turn, and they nodded. 'How sad that there's not even a glimmer of hope.' She sighed.

Minjun tuned out the conversations and turned his attention to the introductory chapter. In short, it was about how GDP growth per capita is a poor measure of one's happiness, about how the expansion of production and consumption doesn't automatically lead to a satisfactory life, about the rise of 'downshifters' who overturn the traditional concept of work to chase satisfaction rather than success. Downshifters . . . the book defined them as people who give up a high-paying job or give up working altogether. Just as Minjun was wondering if it was possible for them to make a living, a man who claimed to be a downshifter spoke.

'I'm in a downshift mode right now, so I absolutely relate to the book.'

The man cleared his throat and continued.

'It's been about a year since I quit my job of three years to help out at my friend's business to earn some pocket money. I had been depressed for the three years I was working. It was a job that I wanted, but despite getting it, I felt perpetually frustrated. I was putting in extra hours all the time too, and in the end, I quit. Because if I didn't, I thought I might go crazy. After I quit, I took on casual work for about four hours a day and I did that for four months. I was only happy in the first week. When my good friends asked me, "Hey, what have you been up to?" I stuttered and couldn't string together a proper answer. I like how this book doesn't just talk about the benefits of being a downshifter, but also the pain behind the choice. It gives me comfort, knowing that I'm not the only one feeling like an idiot. And it reminds me of my motto in life.'

'You have a life motto?' The non-religious lady looked amused.

'My motto is "There's good and bad to everything". No matter what it is, there's always two sides to things, so I tell myself, don't go on an emotional rollercoaster.'

'Well, then, isn't it more straightforward to define your motto as "Don't be too emotional"?' the woman teased.

'Aha! You're right.' The man acted like he was hit with a revelation. 'In any case, what I'm trying to say is that being a downshifter has its ups and downs too. It's great to have more free time to yourself, but on the other hand, you don't earn much, and this creates a lot of frustration. You can't even afford to go anywhere nice. Not to mention, you aren't getting any recognition from society.'

'It's true some people do feel this way . . . but most people who choose the downshift life don't care much about taking vacations or getting acknowledged by society. The book also mentions this,' said the man next to Minjun. Everyone else nodded in agreement.

'But being a downshifter may not be a personal choice.' Yeongju raised her hand and spoke. 'Many people quit not because they want to. Maybe they are unwell or suffering emotionally. There're many people who have depression or anxiety issues. The book talks about how it's terrible of society to criticise and judge those who can't work because they aren't well – physically or mentally. Like the book says, there are parents who keep badgering their children, asking when they plan to get a job.'

'We just have blind faith when it comes to how we view work,' said the man next to Minjun. 'From youth, we're always asked to endure and put up with things. I have no idea why. I had a classmate who got hit by a motorbike on the way to school and even when they were bruised and bleeding, they refused to go home and continued to walk to school. Just to get an award for perfect attendance. That obsession to endure everything followed us into working life. You go to work even when you're sick, and on days when you simply can't get out of bed, the dread of skipping a day's work eats at you more than the illness. Honestly, it's common logic that you should rest when you're not well. So why are we like this? That's why I hate how keeping up your fighting spirit even when you're unwell or on an IV drip has become so much of a thing that there's even a phrase for it.'

'You're right, we're allowing ourselves to be exploited,' said the man who aspired to be a latte dad.

Minjun followed the discussion by reading the pages which the members referenced. There was the story of Lucy, who was happy not working but feeling guilty about how she was disappointing her parents. She confessed, sighing multiple times, that, 'I just – I feel like I should get a job so that I don't feel like I'm letting everybody else down . . .'[9] But she added that she was uncertain if she could do it.

Then, there was Samantha who quit her job as a patent lawyer to work as a part-time waitress at a bar. Minjun read over her words twice, slowly. The last sentence in particular spoke to him.

'It felt like growing up because I was doing things I had consciously chosen to do for the first time.'[10]

It felt like growing up. *That's what work is about, isn't it?* Minjun thought.

The discussion ended on a harmonious note. In his closing remarks, Wooshik expressed hopes for society to progress to a point where people who derive happiness from paid work can do so, and those who don't could find an alternative path. Everyone clapped. It was almost half past ten. As everyone chipped in, they managed to clean up in less than ten minutes. The ten of them, including Minjun, left the bookshop together. At least for today, they would go to bed linked by the same sense of camaraderie and solidarity.

[9]Frayne, *Refusal*, 196.
[10]Frayne, *Refusal*, 198.

Yeongju and Minjun said goodbye at the crossroad. His gaze followed her as she walked towards the main road before he turned into the alleyway. For now, he decided to find answers from books. He planned to finish David Frayne's book before moving on to Erich Fromm's *To Have or To Be?* which Frayne mentioned.

Later, having fallen in love with Fromm's writing, Minjun would go on to read all his works in chronological order. Even though he was still feeling conflicted, he had a clearer sense of direction. He now thought about how he should live in the present moment. And this was a thought which hadn't crossed his mind until then.

## Finding Its Place

Like any other day, Jungsuh was busy knitting a scarf. Mincheol stared at her busy hands from across the table, chin propped in palm, as if he was gazing at the vast ocean. Beside him, Yeongju was absentmindedly following bits of their conversation as she looked through what she'd written on her notepad.

'Imo, is knitting interesting?'

'Of course. But I do it for the sense of satisfaction.'

'Sense of satisfaction?'

'The pride of completing something. If I was looking for fun, I'd play video games. I loved gaming when I was younger. Are you good at it?'

'So-so.'

Pausing at his indifference, Jungsuh suddenly looked up. 'Oh you! Such is the ignorance of what torture a life devoid of satisfaction is like. The emptiness of working yourself to the bones. No, there's something left – a life of exhaustion!'

At her theatrical tone, Mincheol burst out laughing. She chuckled, before returning to her usual self.

'I worked so hard, so intensely, but at the end of the day, time just passed me by. I hated that feeling. I hope you'll never experience that. Go for satisfaction instead.'

'. . . Okay.'

Yeongju was still half-listening to their banter as she organised the reflections she'd put on paper over the past few days. She'd been mulling over 'what it means for the bookshop to find its place.' When her mind drew a blank, she did what she always did when writing – search for the definition. The following came up: to settle down in a place; to find stability in life. Stability in life. *That's right. To have stability, the bookshop needs to bring in the bread*, she thought. But she hated the idea of equating stability with cold hard cash. What if she shifted her thinking a little? To find stability, she first needed to reach out to more customers.

Her thoughts drifted to the residents in the neighbourhood. While there were several regulars among them, the majority had only come in out of curiosity when the bookshop first opened. She'd also heard many complaints about how hard it was to be a consistent reader. It was only after running her bookshop that she realised how difficult it was for people to get back into the habit of reading, particularly for those who hadn't read for a long time. Telling them 'Books are great for you, you should read' wasn't the least bit helpful. Instead, she wanted to bring the bookshop – as a space – closer to them. She wanted to make more space available to more people.

Having made a decision, the immediate task at hand was to clear the area beside the café, which they had been using as a storage of sorts. In between their usual tasks, Yeongju and Minjun cleared out the rubbish bit by bit; items which still had a use were given a new lease of life elsewhere in the bookshop. The newly emptied area was renamed the 'Book Club Room'. She planned to actively recruit more members to form three book clubs – plainly named Book Clubs 1, 2 and 3 for now. The naming could be left to the members later. She would put up the announcement online via the blog and Instagram the next day, as well as on the signboards at the bookshop. She'd already secured the leaders of the book clubs: Wooshik, Mincheol's mother, and Sangsu, a regular customer who easily outread Yeongju by a mile.

When she had put the finishing touches to the recruitment post, Yeongju finally looked up at the other two. As she'd spent the whole time buried in her notepad, her sudden movement caused them to stare back.

'Can I take up some of your time?' Yeongju asked.

She led them to the middle of the book club room and explained her plans to furnish the place.

'We're holding book club meetings here and on weekends, this is where we'll host the book talks, too. Where you're standing, there'll be a big table. Ten chairs should be sufficient . . . And I suppose we'll need an air-con unit. I can't make up my mind on the colour of the walls, though. What do you think?'

At Yeongju's instructions, the two of them paced the room to get a feel for the space. It was small, but cosy. She was right. The big table and chairs would already fill up the room. Nevertheless, the space didn't feel cramped. Small, but not claustrophobic. Just the right amount of space for people to pay attention to one another.

'No windows, but with a door to the backyard, it shouldn't be stuffy. I guess a few pretty frames on the wall would be nice . . . I hope people will be eager to join the book clubs, even if it's because they want to enjoy this space . . . Do you think that'll happen?' Yeongju muttered as she circled the room.

'I would think so?' Jungsuh said, tapping the wall lightly. 'I was excited the first time I came to the bookshop.'

Yeongju turned to look at her.

'I've gone almost everywhere in the neighbourhood – from the big franchises to the hole-in-the-wall cafés – to look for the best place. I like it here the most, so I made myself at home. The music's great, not too loud. I love the lighting too. And how nobody paid me special attention. The comforting vibes drew me here, again and again. Whenever I take a break from knitting and look up, I feel at ease. Then I realise it's the sense of security of being in a space surrounded by books.'

Out of the corner of her eye, Yeongju watched Mincheol exit to the backyard.

'Sense of security?' she asked.

'I didn't expect to feel this way either. It's the comfort of knowing that as long as I mind my manners, nobody here would ever step all over me. It was exactly what I needed back then. That's why I kept returning, even if I'm not here to read. I've become a permanent fixture here.'

Yeongju recalled how Jungsuh had asked her how often she needed to order a new coffee in order not to be a nuisance to the bookshop. So that was her trying her best to mind her manners. Was it because she thought good manners was the optimal way to obtain the greatest freedom without inconveniencing others? Yeongju's gaze followed Jungsuh as she walked around the room. Just as she was about to say something, Mincheol came back.

'I think it's okay to leave this wall grey,' he said.

Jungsuh murmured an agreement. 'Yeah. Maybe just touch up the paint where there are scuff marks?'

'Is that enough to make the space look inviting?'

'Put more effort into the lighting, like you did for the main area,' said Jungsuh, solving the problem with a single stroke.

When she was back in her seat, Yeongju added 'grey walls' to her notes. The preparation for the book clubs was on track and, starting next month, she planned to have movie screenings on alternate Thursdays, alongside late-night book shopping. Juggling the increase in night-time events wouldn't be easy, but she decided to give it a go first. The question of how long she could sustain the pace could come later. Maintaining a work-life balance was already difficult as it was, but now she had to add profits to the equation too.

In the past two years, Yeongju had seen independent bookshops shut down one by one. Some of them faded away after a quiet run, while others jerked to a halt. Among them were bookshops that collapsed when their funds dried up, while others managed to eke out a living but lacked the stamina to operate at the same intensity in the long run. Given how there were also several well-known names among them, it seemed like running a bookshop on adrenaline and organising a lot of events wasn't sufficient to bring in the revenue.

Running an independent bookshop was like roaming a stretch of land without roads. There was no tried-and-tested business model. Bookshop owners live day by day, hesitant to plan too far ahead. This was why Yeongju had told Minjun that his job might expire after two years. At that time, as with now, she'd had no idea where the book-shop was heading.

Despite the bleak outlook, independent bookshops continued to sprout up in the neighbourhoods. A thought crossed her mind. Perhaps the business model of an independent bookshop was one built on dreams – whether it was a dream of the past or the future. Those who start a bookshop probably dreamt of doing so at some point in their lives. And when they woke up from the dream a year or two later, they would close that chapter in their lives. As more and more bookshops sprouted up, so did the number of dreamers. Bookshops that were ten, twenty years old were rare. But ten, twenty years later, independent book-shops would still exist.

*Perhaps it's almost impossible for independent book-shops to find their place in our country,* Yeongju thought. If so, whatever ideas she had were bound to fail. No, she corrected herself. Exceptions exist in everything. And there's meaning in the act of trying (it's important to ascribe meaning to things!). If the process is enjoyable (albeit diffi-cult!), results shouldn't be the focus. Most importantly, right now, Yeongju enjoyed giving it her best at running the bookshop. Surely that was enough, wasn't it?

Reining in her thoughts, Yeongju returned to the tasks at hand. The next thing was to send out invitations to secure the speakers for the two series of seminars she planned to hold on Saturdays. Seeing a growing inter-est in writing, she was thinking that the two series could cover different aspects of writing. She'd already decided to approach the authors Lee Ahreum and Hyun Seungwoo to headline one each. The emails were drafted and ready to be sent out.

'This should do,' she murmured.

As if waiting for the moment, Mincheol looked up at her. Closing her laptop, she said, 'Sorry for looking so busy.'

Mincheol shook his head.

She smiled. 'It's the holidays. Any plans?'

'Just normal stuff. Attend supplementary classes, go home. Rinse and repeat. Eat, bathroom, sleep.'

'Nothing particularly interesting going on?' She thought she already knew the answer. It wasn't as if she had anything particularly interesting going on for her back in high school. She remembered those days feeling like a persistent bout of indigestion.

'Nothing.'

'Ah, I see.'

'But . . . does everyone really need something interesting? Why can't I live a mundane life?'

'Well, it's true that forcing yourself to find something would be tough,' she mused.

'My mum is the same . . . I don't get why people see a mundane life as a bad thing. Sometimes I'd rather she forced me to study, instead of trying to make me look for something *interesting*. Isn't life just about going through the motions of living? We live because we were born.'

Yeongju didn't reply immediately. Instead, she looked around the bookshop first, to make sure there weren't any customers who needed assistance, before she returned her gaze to the child who'd already concluded that life was nothing to shout about.

'You have a point. But having something you're interested in clears the airway.'

Next to Mincheol, Jungsuh nodded in agreement. A frown creased Mincheol's forehead.

'Clears the airway?'

'It makes breathing easier, and when that happens, life seems much more bearable.'

Mincheol looked as if he was deep in thought. It occurred to Yeongju that she'd never made this face at his age. She had been a simple child. Like him, her time was spent shuttling in between school and home, but she was always fretting over studies – no, the competition – and her future.

Because she hated worrying about her studies, she worked even harder; because she hated competition, she obsessed over coming out top; because she hated stressing about her future, she spent more time living for her future. Looking at the child across from her, Yeongju was envious, but at the same time, happy for him. Mincheol might not understand it yet, but she thought he was living his life well.

'Fatigue. Monotony. Emptiness. Hopelessness. Once you fall into any one of those, it's hard to get out. Like plummeting down a well and crumpling at the bottom. You feel like you're the most unnecessary person existing in the world, the only one suffering.'

Eyes fixed on her yarn, Jungsuh expelled a deep, heavy breath though her nose. For a while, Yeongju watched Jungsuh's hands.

'That's why I turn to reading,' she said, her expression softening. 'Sorry, is it dull when I bring up books?'

'Not at all,' he replied.

'If there's something I learnt from reading, it's that all writers were once there. At the bottom of the well. Some only just climbed out, others did a long time ago. But everyone says the same thing – I'll end up inside again.'

'Why, then, do we have to listen to their stories? Since they'd fallen, and will fall again?' Mincheol was perturbed.

'Hmm . . . it's easy. Knowing that we're not alone in our misery gives us strength. It's like I'd thought I was the only miserable soul, but now I think, Oh, everyone's the same. The pain remains, but somehow, it feels lighter. Has there ever been a person who has never fallen into the well once in their life? I thought about it and my answer is no, there hasn't.'

Mincheol wore a solemn look as he listened to her. She smiled.

'Then I tell myself, it's time to get out of this lethargy. Instead of curling up at the bottom of the well, I stretch my limbs and get up. Hey! This well isn't as deep as I imagined it to be. I laugh at myself, at how I've been living in the dark all this time. Then, thirty-five degrees to my right, a light breeze caresses my face. That moment, I'm so thankful to be alive. The wind feels good.'

'I'm not sure if I'm following. I'm sorry.' The crease in his forehead deepened as he blinked back the confusion.

'Oh, my bad. I was too self-absorbed.'

'Yeongju imo.'

'Yeah?'

'Is this related to what you were saying just now, about clearing the airway?'

'Yup.'

'How so?'

'The wind.'

'The wind?'

She nodded, her face easing into a smile.

'Sometimes I think about how lucky it is that I enjoy the wind. When the evening breeze blows, I thank it for clearing up the stuffiness in me and letting me breathe easier. They say hell hath no wind, so thank goodness where I am now must not be hell. If I could capture a moment like this every day, I'll be strong enough to keep going. Humans are complex, but sometimes, we can be so simple. We can be content with having some time – whether ten minutes, or an hour – where I can feel, Ah, I'm so glad I'm alive, so glad to seize and enjoy this moment.'

'Right, right,' Jungsuh murmured.

Mincheol glanced at her before returning his solemn gaze to Yeongju.

'I see . . . Does my mum also think that I need to have such a time?'

'Well, I don't know what your mum thinks.'

'Then, imo, what do you think?'

'Me?'

'Yeah.'

'Well . . .'

Yeongju flashed him a bright smile.

'I think it's good to try getting out of that dry well. Nobody knows what'll happen next, so why not try it once? Aren't you curious? About what will happen once you climb out?'

## I Wanted to Say No

These days, he would reach home at about six in the evenings. By the time Seungwoo finished showering, preparing dinner, eating, resting, and doing the dishes, the clock struck eight. This was when he turned into a completely different person. As he shrugged off the cloak of an ordinary company employee, it was as if he, too, put aside the responsibilities of his title, erased the pre-programmed thoughts and actions, and peeled off the façade of indifference. From this moment, every second belonged completely to him. Time was real.

For the past few years, the hours before bedtime were when he could be truly himself, diving deep into some-thing that captivated his interest – the Korean language. He'd spent the past ten years immersed in programming languages, but he was no longer a programmer. Right now, he was just another ordinary company employee, dutifully checking in and out of the office every day.

Immersing himself in the Korean language was tiring, but fun. He enjoyed having something to focus on whole-heartedly, devoting himself to studying something he liked. The energy expended at work, he recharged at home. He had even started a blog to share what he learnt. Once he grew more confident, he began to apply his knowledge to examine other people's writing. Gradually, he gained more followers and started to see himself as a blogger. A company employee by day, blogger by night. It had been five years since he'd adopted this dual identity.

He never failed to be amazed by how his followers – who didn't even know his face – supported him wholeheartedly by leaving comments on his blog, promoting his book, and sharing his posts. They were generously spending time on someone whom they'd never met. It seemed like people had a favourable impression of him because he was teaching himself the Korean language, writing on his own initiative and sharing his knowledge generously on the blog without expecting something in return. Some told him they were motivated by his attitude to life. He was surprised, given that he'd never mentioned anything about his private life. Is the written word a reflection of the writer's life? It reminded him of Yeongju's question.

*How similar are you to your writing?*

Yeongju's face swam in front of him again, but now, he just let her be. Several times, he'd been flustered by how she'd remained crystal clear in his mind long after the book talk. He had no idea what it was about her that lingered in his thoughts. Was it the sparkle in her eyes when she looked at him? The calmness in her words? Or was it the melancholy within her writing that was at odds with her bright and cheery attitude? (He'd read the bookshop's blog before meeting her.) Was it the way her intelligence shone through when she spoke? Her humour and wit? Perhaps it was everything about her.

If he simply left her there each time her face flashed in his mind, surely, at some point, he would stop thinking of her. After all, there was no reason for them to cross paths again. But a few days ago he'd received an email from her. His immediate reaction was to send a polite rejection, but until this moment, he had yet to click on the reply button. From the perspective of the sender, it was probably unacceptable not to have received a response after a whole week. It looked like he could no longer put off the reply. Clicking on the email, he reread it.

*Dear Mr Hyun Seungwoo,*

*I'm Lee Yeongju from Hyunam-dong Bookshop. You haven't forgotten me, right? :) We have many customers coming in to look for your book. Once again, thank you for writing such a good book.*

*I'd like to ask if you are interested in conducting a series of seminars about writing. We're planning to hold a two-hour seminar every Saturday for eight weeks. Should you be keen, I'm thinking that the series could be called 'How to Edit Sentences'.*

*These seminars are not meant to teach writing but editing. I was thinking that you could refer to your book when preparing the materials. What do you think?*

*Since* How to Write Well *is divided into sixteen chapters, perhaps you could go through two chapters per session. In this way, you wouldn't need to do much extra work.*

*I'd love your thoughts on this. Are you available on Saturdays?*

*It'd be more polite for me to give you a call, but that might add undue pressure, so I decided to write to you instead.*

*I'll give you a call when I receive your reply.*

*I look forward to hearing from you.*

*Sincerely,*

*Lee Yeongju*

A straightforward email, but he kept reading it over and over. Each time, it was easy to conjure the most appropriate response in his head: *I am sorry. I do not think I have the sufficient expertise to be conducting seminars. Thank you for the invitation, but I would have to say no. Have a good day.* The problem was he couldn't bring himself to type it out. He lifted his hands as if to mentally prepare himself for a challenging task and positioned his fingers on the keyboard. The next step was to type out a few sentences: *I am sorry . . .*

He wanted to say no. Or rather, he should say no. Since his book launch, he'd been doing a book talk almost every week. His editor told him, in a tone that clearly meant 'Hey! You should be happy about it!', that it was rare for a new writer to receive so many book talk invitations, especially for a debut work. But he couldn't get his spirits up. Each talk felt like it ate away the entire day, after which he spent even more time trying to recall if he'd said something out of place. By then, it was time to fret over his next book talk, not to mention the hours spent fielding his editor's frequent calls and the interview requests from newspapers. In other words, releasing a book had cost Seungwoo plenty of his personal time. With everything added up, he no longer had bandwidth for the things he really wanted to do. He was desperate to return to life before the book, his simple-as-elementary-arithmetic life.

That was why he couldn't – shouldn't – agree to do the seminars. How could he conduct seminars? What more, it was not a one-time event, but a commitment of eight weeks. The only right thing to do was to reject. He strengthened his resolve, ready to press down on the 'I' key with his right middle finger, when he suddenly paused. A wave of curiosity passed through him. The fluster that had gripped him for the past weeks ebbed; what was left was curiosity.

Seriously, what was it about Yeongju that had disrupted the balance in his life? He hadn't felt this way for a long time – a zing through his chest whenever he thought of her. It was a feeling long forgotten. A feeling he'd never thought he would experience again.

Should he follow his heart? He was not one to run away from his feelings. He was curious, too. The type who would want to seek an answer. What would happen after the answer? He would think of it when it came.

Having decided, he let his heart lead and typed out seven lines.

*Dear Ms Lee Yeongju,*
*Thank you for your proposal.*
   *I will do the seminars.*
   *However, I can only make it in the evening on Saturdays.*
   *Have a good day.*
*Sincerely,*
*Hyun Seungwoo*

Without checking what he'd written, he hit the send button.

## The Feeling of Being Accepted

One evening, Jungsuh found herself stepping into Yeongju's apartment after Jimi. Initially, her plan was to go home once she'd wrapped up her knitting, but before she knew it, it was almost closing time at the bookshop. She ended up leaving together with Yeongju, when they bumped into Jimi outside the door. As if it was the most natural thing to do, Jimi took her arm and half-dragged her along, telling her how she loved the crochet scrubby and wanted to do something nice for her in return.

Jungsuh took an immediate liking to Yeongju's apartment. With only a desk as the centrepiece, the living room looked somewhat bare, but the calmness exuding from the minimalism more than made up for it. Yeongju's home felt like an extension of her – somewhat lonely, but a reassuring presence nevertheless. Instead of the ceiling lights, Yeongju switched on one of her floor lamps while Jimi, shaking her head, groaned, 'So dark. Too dark!'

'I love your place,' Jungsuh said as she came out of the bathroom, having washed her hands.

'Stop being polite. I can't believe a house like this exists.'
Jimi raised her voice over the running water as she washed
her hands.

'It's not pleasantries. I think it's perfect for meditating
and knitting. Right there, in front of the wall.'

The two eonnies turned to where she was pointing. It was
the wall across from the desk, where they would usually lie
down.

'Alright. That spot's yours.'

Jungsuh brought herself down to a meditative pose on
the cushion Yeongju had passed to her. Instead of focusing
on her breathing, she observed the two eonnies. They were
completely in tune, like best friends who hung out together
frequently after school. While Yeongju took out the cutlery
from the top cabinet, Jimi rummaged in the fridge for
snacks that would go down well with the alcohol, and be
filling enough. She ended up with three 350ml cans of beer,
an assortment of cheese, dried fruit chips, smoked salmon,
radish sprouts, and a bottle of delicious-looking sauce that
seemed like it would go excellently with the salmon and
sprouts. She set the spread on the floor. At first, Jungsuh
thought Yeongju didn't have a low table, but she quickly
spotted the folded table by the sink. *Ah, guess these eonnies
just love a picnic.*

'Cheers!'

The beer went down easily. Yeongju took a piece of cheese,
Jimi a sauce-dipped salmon slice, and Jungsuh mandarin
orange chips to wash down with the beer. *Delicious*, Jungsuh
thought. It was her first sip of alcohol since quitting her job.

She relaxed her pose, stretching out her legs to lean
against the wall as she sipped the beer and listened to their
conversations. Yeongju and Jimi were lying on the floor

like two sides of an equilateral triangle. Jungsuh imagined that they must occasionally fall asleep in this position. At times, they would suddenly sit up to take a bite, along with a swig of the beer. Most of the time, they would lie down again, but sometimes, they would turn to her to propose a random toast. Jungsuh thought the beer tasted particularly delicious today as she gulped it down greedily.

Despite her not making head or tail of the conversations, the two eonnies would turn to her occasionally, giving her the 'You think so too, right?' look, or asking for her opinion. No matter what she said, they would nod in satisfaction at her reactions. Jungsuh was enjoying herself so much that after half past ten, she stopped checking the clock.

'Minjun told me this,' Jimi said quietly. 'So, I think I'll rein myself in for now.'

'What do you mean?'

'I need some time to think. In the meantime, I'll stop yelling at him. I'll stop nagging too. Don't be too disappointed when you don't hear me complaining about how I had to scream at him.'

'Why would I be disappointed?'

'And don't worry either.'

'What's there to worry about?'

'I'll be fine.'

'Eonnie, I'm definitely not worried.'

Jungsuh got up, casting a glance at the two eonnies who were on their backs, now staring silently at the ceiling. She strode to the full-length window overlooking the neighbourhood, marvelling at the beautiful scenery. The streetlight by the road stood with poise, adding a nice touch to the landscape. Behind was a row of short houses, speckled with light from the windows. Seeing the lights – which seemed to be within an arm's reach – go out made her happy, somehow. Engrossed in the moment, she didn't notice that Yeongju had slid up to her quietly.

'Pretty, isn't it?' Her tone was friendly as usual.

'Yes, it is,' Jungsuh replied softly. A curious feeling swept over her. The feeling of being accepted. She was strongly reminded of the moment she'd walked into Hyunam-dong Bookshop for the first time. Why? That the same feeling, that precious feeling, had come back to her, right here in Yeongju's apartment, was both unexpected and sad. A beautiful melancholy. She finally realised the crux of the issue.

'When did you start meditating? Has it been a long time?'

The two of them stirred from their thoughts and turned around. Jimi was rearranging the leftovers on a single plate as she put the extra plates away. When Jungsuh didn't reply, Jimi peered at her, carrying a stack of plates in her hands.

'I'm just curious why people meditate.' She paused. 'If it helps, I want to try it too.'

# The Ability to Tame Anger

To get to why she started meditating, Jungsuh needed to begin with why she'd quit her job.

'I left my job because I was so, so angry.'

Leaning against the wall, she swallowed hard and told her story. She had quit earlier this year, during her eighth spring in the workforce. She was frustrated by the directionless anger that consumed her every day. The anger would overwhelm her suddenly – whether it was on the way to work, while eating, or in front of the TV – fuelling a burning desire to destroy everything in her line of sight. She got herself checked at the hospital; the doctor only told her to go easy on the stress.

Jungsuh had started out as a contract worker, and at the end of her eight-year career, she was still not permanent. She'd wholeheartedly believed her team leader's assurance that if she worked hard enough, she would be converted to a permanent employee. And so, she put in her very best. She worked as hard as the permanents. Like them, she poured her soul into the company, working late into the night and bringing home the undone work. The permanents saw her efforts and encouraged her. 'You'll have no problem getting promoted.' However, that didn't happen. The team leader only said sorry and told her she'd definitely make it next time.

'At that time, he said something about being a flexible workforce and what not. I didn't pay much attention to it then. But two years later, when I failed to become a permanent for the second time, I recalled what he said. I searched online and found many articles. What they call "flexible workforce" is basically companies having free rein to fire workers anytime they want. According to those articles, companies can only survive the fierce competition in the market by firing workers to reduce the payroll. At first, I thought it was just part and parcel of life. After all, I remember when I was a kid, my dad used to say, "Companies must survive for the people to live. Only when companies do well will the people make a good living." By this logic, for companies to survive, I must remain a contract worker. And how dare I complain, even when I get fired and chased out of the company? At that time, I thought – what the hell? Is this how life is supposed to be?'

Jungsuh paused to look at the two eonnies who were listening with rapt attention. For a moment, she thought she'd overshared, but the alcohol was nudging her to go on. Luckily, there wasn't a hint of boredom in their eyes. Jungsuh stretched forward for the beer and looked at the two eonnies in turn. They held up their cans and knocked a toast. She gulped down some beer before continuing.

'It felt like a slap, but at that time, I didn't quite know what was right. So, I just let it slide. Then, two years ago, a friend of mine who was a nurse left for Australia on a working holiday. Nursing is a professional occupation, right? But she told me she decided to leave for Australia because she hated her job. I asked her why, and she confessed that she was contract staff. The job was tough, but the added disappointment of being a non-permanent took the passion right out of it. There wasn't a single night she had slept well in the past few years. If life was going to be tough anyway, her logic was to go somewhere with at least a slither of hope. In fact, she told me there are many non-permanents at the hospital. The ajumma cleaners, the ajusshis in the facilities department, the young security guards. Even the doctors! It hit me at that moment. All this bullshit about workforce flexibility was a lie. It doesn't make sense to claim that companies hire contract workers for jobs that might be made obsolete, in order to make it easier to fire them in the future. Does this mean we won't need cleaners, facilities managers, security guards, nurses, and doctors anymore? What's this nonsense about hiring them on a contract basis because their jobs are unstable? Eonnies, this is my eighth year working in content development. Throughout the eight years, I was a non-permanent. Does it make sense that because of this *flexible workforce*, a content creation company hires content developers on a contract basis? That's just bullying and undercutting our worth.'

The two eonnies nodded.

'So, I moved to another company in the industry. I refused to stay in a place that wasn't going to convert me. That said, I was still hired as a non-permanent at the new company. According to them, it was a *permanent contract* position. Huh. If it's a contract job, call it that. Why tag on the word *permanent*? That's just wordplay. At the new company, they continued to dangle permanency like a carrot. They made me work overtime, do extra events, and dumped their work on me. All the while telling me that if I worked hard enough, I could become a permanent. I had to make a living, so I pretended to buy into the spiel and worked late, worked extra, and worked at home. It got to a point where I started hating everything. But I still had to force myself to do it, and it made me perpetually angry.'

Being a permanent didn't grant them the entitlement to delegate the lesser tasks. Even though they had a personalised employee pass hanging from their neck, whereas Jungsuh only got a general access pass, the permanents, like her, also clocked in every morning and walked on eggshells around the bosses as they left the office. Yet, something was clearly different between them. She was familiar with the oft-quoted saying that workers are like spare parts of a machine – usually cogs – stuck in a never-changing routine. Easily replaceable, too. However, contract workers couldn't even be cogs in the machine. At best, they were like the oil helping the cogs turn. A part of parts. The company, too, treated them as separate entities. Like oil and water.

'After that incident, I just hated it all. Work. Humans. You know what happened? The director called me over for a chat one day. There was a new project and he told me to give it my best shot. He said that it was the perfect project to showcase my abilities and what I was made of. In my mind, I wasn't really thinking *If this goes well, maybe . . .* That said, I still worked very hard because I loved having full control over the project. For two months, I poured in my sweat and blood. It'd been a long time since I enjoyed work this much. At the end of the two months, I submitted my work to the director. You know what that scumbag did? He took my name out and replaced it with this fool of an assistant manager. The guy was infamous for his lack of brains! And you know what the director told me? He offered an insincere apology and told me to be understanding. He said, *Jungsuh, you can't be promoted anyway, so take it as doing a good deed.*'

It was an uncivil society, and that toxic behaviour filtered downwards. Many colleagues put up a kind front while stepping on others to climb upwards. Those who weren't part of it looked on indifferently from the sidelines. Beneath their indifference was fear. What if someday I take a misstep, would I end up like that person? And to the permanents, Jungsuh was 'that person'.

The hardest thing for her was that she developed an intense hatred for people. Her blood boiled to hear the director's voice laced with mock friendliness, and she felt nothing but contempt at the sight of that moron assistant manager. Whenever she saw them laughing and chatting in the hallway, she couldn't help but think: *These bastards aren't better than me. They are where they are only because of sheer luck, and now they're doing all this shit because they're scared shitless of losing their jobs.* It made her miserable to be full of contempt and disgust for people, which in turn fuelled her anger. She couldn't concentrate at work. Work was a chore. She hated everything.

'I no longer recognised myself. The anger destroyed my body. I couldn't sleep even though I was so exhausted. There were many nights where I lay in bed, eyes wide open, yet I had to go straight to the office in the morning. So, I quit. Well, if it's just a contract job, I'm sure I can find something else again. When I told my friends I was going to quit, they told me to go on a vacation instead. I refused. If it was an anger that could be put out by spending a few days overseas, it wouldn't have materialised in the first place. At some point, I'll have to work again. And the anger will return. I can't keep going on summer and winter vacations. What I needed was peace in my life, the ability to tame my anger. I thought about what I could do and came up with an answer: meditation.'

Yeongju thought she knew where the story was heading. Jungsuh sitting at the café with a cup of coffee was her attempting to meditate, but because she couldn't get into it, she ended up crocheting instead. Having discovered the joy of making things, she moved on to knitting. The moments in between when she closed her eyes were an attempt to empty her mind.

'The tangled mess in my head didn't disappear with meditation. And the anger remained. Even when I tried to close my eyes and focus on my breathing, the face of that bastard director and that lazy prick of an asshole assistant manager – now the asshole manager – kept swimming in front of me. I read somewhere that keeping your hands busy would make those distractions disappear. I tried it. The thoughts didn't disappear, but they appeared to disappear because my focus was elsewhere. There're two great things about returning to reality after a couple of hours of knitting. First, I made something. Second, I feel refreshed. At the very least, I wasn't angry while I knitted.'

The two eonnies listened to her until the very end. Then, they lay down again and urged her to do the same. Jungsuh stretched out against the length of the wall. She felt the dark clouds within her disperse the same way they did when she was knitting. Everything became a little blurred around the edges, as if she'd crossed into another realm. Sleep beckoned to her, and her eyelids fluttered to a close. She thought sleepily, *If I can fall asleep like this, I'll probably wake up in a good mood.*

# The Writing Seminars Start

Dressed in a thick sweater and carrying a backpack, Seungwoo made his way to the bookshop. He could have driven, but he wanted to experience, at least once, the walk from the subway station to the bookshop. He'd noticed it during his previous visit, but walking the route now made him even more certain that Hyunam-dong Bookshop was not a place you would stumble upon on the way to else-where. Unless you lived nearby, you had to deliberately make your way there. *What was she thinking – and why – when she decided to open a bookshop here?* he wondered.

It was a serene neighbourhood. Just ten minutes ago, he was on a bustling street but now, he felt like an actor retreat-ing backstage at the end of a show. He imagined residents here going around carrying shopping baskets instead of plas-tic bags, and it felt as if people brushing past each other in alleyways would exchange silent nods of greeting, or at least recognise each other. Perhaps the charm of the bookshop, and what drew the customers, was its location in this quaint neighbourhood at the crossroads of the past and present.

A twenty-five-minute walk later, Seungwoo finally reached the bookshop. He paused in front of the signboard outside.

*At last! Hyunam-dong Bookshop is launching a series of seminars on writing. Every Saturday, come and learn about the art of writing with Lee Ahreum, author of I READ EVERY DAY, and Hyun Seungwoo, author of HOW TO WRITE WELL. ^^*

Having yet to get used to his new identity as an author – a published one, too – Seungwoo's cheeks flushed at the sight of the words. Just a few years ago, he wouldn't have imagined that he would one day write and publish a book. Indeed, no one can predict the future.

Stepping in, he was once again serenaded by melodious guitar chords as his eyes took in the warm, friendly glow of the elegant lights. Though it was his second visit, he surveyed the shop as if he was new to the place. Silently, he counted the number of people leisurely browsing the shelves, leafing through a book, or simply running their fingers across the covers. He slowly turned his head, his gaze fixed somewhere. In his line of sight was the back of a customer who was making a purchase at the counter. Seungwoo stood in silence, waiting for the customer to move. The melodious music and the friendly glow of the lights slowly faded from his senses. The spot he was gazing at was where Yeongju stood.

She was wearing a pea-green round-neck t-shirt, which she'd layered under a khaki cardigan reaching her hips. She matched her top with cropped jeans, completing the look with a comfortable pair of white sneakers. Her eyes followed the customer as he made his way out, before landing on Seungwoo. A smile lit up her face. Calmly, he walked towards her but inside, he was frantically trying to come up with an appropriate greeting. As he started to question if there was ever such a thing, his brain seemed to calm down again. Of course, his expression remained inscrutable as usual.

Yeongju came out from behind the counter.

'You're early. Smooth traffic?'

He had an appropriate response for that.

'Oh. I took the subway here, so it was fine.'

'Didn't you drive last time?'

'Yes, I did.'

A smooth answer to an easy question.

Looking into her eyes, he wondered if they were the reason why he was so nervous right now. Of course, there was also the (not insignificant) possibility that he was simply jittery about the seminar. An engineer by training, Seungwoo rarely had a need to speak in front of a crowd. He'd participated in technical seminars, but all the speakers had to do was drone on while the audience listened impassively. There wasn't a need to make the talks interesting, so long as they were factual and lucid. Would that be enough for today's seminar? He wasn't quite sure which side of himself he would be showing today.

*Probably just making a fool of myself.*

The thought made him less nervous. Over the next couple of hours, he was bound to be flustered – whether because of her, or the talk. He was certain that he would sound awkward, look awkward. He couldn't even be his normal self, much less perform at his very best. In that case, he might as well do away with the greed of wanting to do well. As long as he wasn't bothered by how others might view him, he had already successfully avoided the worst-case scenario.

The room she guided him to was small and cosy. He could faintly hear the music seeping in from the main area, which was much more welcome than an oppressive silence. Yeongju turned on the laptop and switched on a projector with a remote control. At the same time, the screen installed next to the door rolled down slowly. He sat down on the table while she called up the materials he'd emailed her ahead of time. Hunched forward, Yeongju typed away at the keyboard, telling him that she would be printing out the materials and that he was free to conduct the seminars in any way he wanted. If he needed a drink, he could order it at the café counter.

Once she was done with the setup, she sat down across from Seungwoo, smiling.

'Are you nervous?'

Was it showing on his face?

'Yes, a little.'

'The speaker for the afternoon seminars told me that the atmosphere was better than expected,' she said, peering at him from across the table. 'The audience came with an open mind, and they took in everything she said positively.'

*She's clearly saying this to ease my nerv*es, he thought.

'Ah, I see.'

'The participants had to fill in a survey form when they signed up for the seminars. Out of the eight participants, six owned a copy of your book, two are your blog followers, and three of them have read your column. Speaking from experience of hosting book talks, the mood is always great when the participants are familiar with the author's writing. I'm sure it'll be the same today.'

While his anxiety wouldn't fade just because of her words, he listened to her quietly. Perhaps it was the contrast between the Yeongju as he knew her now and the one he'd glimpsed from her writing. Her writing was like a calm river with deep waters, and he'd thought that the person writing it must be poised and dignified. When he met her in person, he thought of her as a leaf more than a river. A healthy green leaf, dancing in the wind and going where the flow takes her. Where she landed, she would murmur softly, her eyes twinkling with refined manners and rapt attention. It was this contrast that'd stirred his curiosity.

Done with the preparations, he looked up and their gazes locked. He'd felt it previously, too, that Yeongju seemed to have no qualms about looking people in the eye. If there was any awkwardness, it was on the part of Seungwoo and it was up to him to break the silence. He tried to think of something but soon gave up. Seungwoo almost laughed at himself. Why was he so nervous and stiff? She was just sitting there, her eyes shining with excitement.

As they held each other's gaze, his nerves seemed to melt away. This moment, sitting face to face, seemed to ease into a natural rhythm, and everything else – his anxiety over the past few weeks, his hesitation to send a reply, the fluster of his thoughts constantly straying to her – was irrelevant. His heart settled and he regained his usual composure. Breaking the eye contact, he said, 'Honestly, I hesitated for a long time before agreeing. To the seminars, I mean.'

Yeongju smiled, as if she'd already guessed as much.

'I thought so. I didn't receive a reply for some time, so I got a little worried thinking that I'd put forth an unreasonable request. When I thought of organising the seminars, your face just flashed across my mind.'

Seungwoo leaned back against the chair.

'Why did you immediately think of me?'

'Didn't I tell you? I'm your fan. I love your writing. That's why on the day of your book launch, I acted quickly, and hey! I succeeded in being the first person to invite you for a book talk,' Yeongju gushed as if she was recounting an amazing incident.

'I thought it would make sense for the seminars to be headed by a strong writer, so I was over the moon when you agreed. I'm so glad I own a bookshop. You don't know how thrilled I am to invite my favourite authors to my space. From when I was young, I've always been so—'

Yeongju grinned sheepishly at her overenthusiasm.

'I'm talking too much about myself.'

'Not at all.' He shook his head. 'I'm just not used to sitting face to face with someone who says she's my fan.'

Ah. Her mouth was slightly agape.

'I'll restrain myself.'

He smiled softly.

'I enjoyed the walk from the station.'

'That's quite a distance. You walked?'

'Yes. I was quite surprised when I first visited. I wondered why you chose to open a bookshop deep within a neighbourhood, and why people come all this way. I think I found the answer on the way here.'

'And what do you think the reason is?'

He looked at her for a moment.

'It's like taking a walk down the streets when you're overseas. You look curiously left and right, peeking around the corner of a turn. The excitement of the unknown, of the unfamiliar. It's what makes travel so alluring. On the walk here, it occurred to me that perhaps Hyunam-dong Bookshop is that kind of destination for many.'

Yeongju let out a soft gasp as if moved by his words.

'I'm always thankful for people who travel here when it's not an easy place to get to. If they truly felt the way you described, I'd be absolutely delighted.'

'I did feel that way.'

Wearing a bright smile and with a playful glint in her eyes, she leant forward slightly.

'Can I ask you something?'

'What is it?'

'What made you say yes?'

How should he answer? He had yet to find the appropriate words to describe his feelings but at the same time, he hated to lie. Pausing a beat, Seungwoo answered, 'Because I was curious.'

'About?'

'The bookshop.'

'The bookshop?'

'Something about this place draws you in, and I'm curious what that is.'

For a moment, Yeongju chewed over his words. Then, a look of understanding dawned on her face. Was it what Jungsuh had said about the vibes of the bookshop, which made her a regular? Did that mean that the bookshop had a good chance of surviving? Was she on the right track? She felt good. Checking the time, she stood up.

'I'll keep these words close to my heart. It's what I've always hoped for, that the bookshop gets closer to the people. Thank you for the encouragement.'

Noting that it was time for the courier to arrive, Yeongju stepped out and closed the door behind her. Seungwoo finally had the chance to look around the small and cosy space. He'd tried to carefully conceal the truth without resorting to lies, but thinking back to his answer, what he said was the truth, too. Something about the bookshop had captivated him. He liked it here. No matter how the seminar turned out later, Seungwoo thought he'd already avoided the worst scenario today.

# I'll Be Rooting for You

Seungwoo had no hand in landing Yeongju her own newspaper column, although it was through him that the journalist met her. Despite having worked together for quite some time, he'd met the journalist only once, solely because he kept politely rejecting her invitations. It wasn't that she was particularly keen to meet, but as the person in charge of his column, she had the responsibility to check in on him from time to time. However, Seungwoo didn't like meeting for the sake of formalities, neither was he fond of the inconvenience – to both parties – of having to pretend to bond over small talk.

She had understood his personality in the early days of their working relationship, and she liked that about him. She had less to do, knowing full well that if she didn't reach out to him, there was no way he would initiate a meetup. His essays always came in on time every fortnight and the drafts were clean. There was no need for fact-checking either, no controversial topics that'd attract a bunch of nasty keyboard warriors. Seungwoo had a strong command of the Korean language, so she barely needed to touch up the sentences. His column was like a vessel sailing peacefully along the tailwind.

That said, she couldn't completely cut off contact, so occasionally she would look up his name on the Internet for any updates, and that was how she discovered, from a bookshop's blog, that he was running writing seminars. What more, the seminars were scheduled for a second run. The Seungwoo she knew was not one to accept such gigs. He would think it terribly troublesome. Why? Hyunam-dong Bookshop? Was it famous? Brimming with curiosity, she followed the blog and checked it out from time to time. That was how she came across Yeongju's writing. It was perfect timing, too. She'd been on the lookout for someone to take on a book column and having seen an increasing number of booksellers who wrote, she thought she would jump on the trend too. While their writing tended to be more subjective and personal, with a little help editing, she thought she could discover a good columnist.

That was how the journalist and Yeongju ended up meeting on a Sunday morning. It had taken several calls for Yeongju to change her mind, so in order to allay her concerns, as well as to put faces to the names, they decided to meet up. Surprisingly, Seungwoo joined them. When they'd spoken on the phone a couple of days ago, the journalist had mentioned to Seungwoo that Yeongju was likely to do a column for the newspaper. Giving him the backstory, she told him it was thanks to him that she'd discovered Yeongju and her writing. He didn't seem surprised. When she told him about their upcoming meeting on Sunday, he murmured a polite acknowledgement. However, right before they hung up, Seungwoo, in his usual collected manner, asked if he could come along, adding that they could take the opportunity to discuss a contract extension.

That moment, she thought she could hazard a good guess as to why he'd taken on the seminars.

'I was under the impression you wouldn't be extending the contract. What changed your mind?'

The journalist was about to head off after the Sunday morning meeting when she suddenly turned to him. She wanted to fluster Seungwoo, who always seemed unflappable, and it seemed like a golden opportunity. She flashed him a knowing smile as she held her gaze steady. Sensing the peculiar mood, Yeongju glanced curiously at him from the side. The journalist had picked up a scent, Seungwoo realised, but he didn't let it show on his face. Keeping his expression neutral and his tone even, Seungwoo replied, 'Because I think writing is going to be more enjoyable from now on.'

The journalist let out a short laugh and stood up. The answer was just enough not to reveal his feelings while clearly telling her *I know you know*. It was such a well-poised response that she no longer wanted to tease him further. Quipping that working mothers are busier on weekends, the journalist bade them goodbye and thanked them for their time.

Left alone, Yeongju and Seungwoo lapsed into silence. A while later, Seungwoo asked, 'Shall we get lunch?'

A piping hot pollock stew was set in the middle of the table, surrounded by an assortment of side dishes. Professing her love for fish, Yeongju had brought him to a restaurant specialising in pollock stew. Seungwoo was neutral towards pollock. He ate it occasionally with friends when they craved it, enough to remember that there was such a fish in the world.

As he stared at the assortment of side dishes that came with the stew, he thought it didn't look like a place where people would simply debone the fish and eat it. Observing the way Yeongju ate strengthened his conviction. In her left hand, she held a piece of seasoned gim, which she placed some rice on top of. With her chopsticks, she pinched out a bite-sized piece of pollack flesh, dipped it into the sauce, and set it on the rice alongside a few strands of beansprouts. She proceeded to roll the dried seaweed before putting it into her mouth, chewing happily with her mouth full. Laughing silently, Seungwoo picked up some rice with his chopsticks.

'Is it common to eat this way? Putting the fish on top of the gim?'

She swallowed the last bite before replying.

'Hmm. This is also my first time eating it this way.'

Seungwoo reached for the beansprouts this time.

'But you are a natural at this. I thought it's how you usually eat pollock stew.'

Seeing how Seungwoo was picking at his rice and side dishes but not touching the stew, she placed a piece of gim in his hand.

'How difficult can this be that it's possible to eat it unnaturally?' Yeongju laughed as she took a piece of gim for herself.

'Try making a wrap with this. It's delicious.'

Following what she did, he first added the rice, then the pollack meat and the beansprouts to the gim, before rolling it up and stuffing it into his mouth. The more he chewed, the stronger the umami taste, and it was indeed, as she said, delicious. She made another wrap for herself and waited for him to swallow.

'How is it?'

'Good.'

Seungwoo poured a cup of water and offered it to Yeongju.

'But a little spicy.'

'I thought so too.'

It was not even noon when they left the restaurant. From where they were, it would only take them five minutes to walk to Sangsu subway station on Line 6. Without saying anything, they automatically headed in that direction.

'You must be afraid of the cold,' Seungwoo said as he looked at Yeongju hugging herself tight.

'Not really. Honestly, I don't know. Sometimes I'm good at enduring the cold but on other days, it really seeps into my bones. I guess it all depends on my mood.'

'So how do you feel right now?'

'Now?'

'Yes. Now that you're on your way home after a delicious meal of pollock stew. Is it colder than you expected, or not as bad?'

'Hmm . . . you see that person over there?' Yeongju pointed to a man walking ahead. A man in his thirties was hurrying ahead with his arms folded, as if he couldn't take the cold anymore.

'Look at the thickness of his scarf. Don't you think it looks like the scarf is swallowing his head? I don't think I feel as cold as he does. Perhaps just the kind of cold that could be dispelled with a cup of hot tea? Is this a good enough answer?'

Seungwoo stopped.

'In that case, shall we get some hot tea?'

The traditional teahouse that Seungwoo found on the Internet was a ten-minute walk away. They chatted about how it'd been some time since their last visit to a teahouse and soon arrived at the place. Peering at the menu, Yeongju picked the quince tea, and Seungwoo said he would have the same. On the first sip, they both recognised the familiar taste, a taste long forgotten.

He took another sip before speaking.

'Once, I was on a work trip.'

'Where?'

'The United States. Atlanta.'

'Oh. I've been curious about the work you do, but I didn't dare to ask.'

'Why so?'

'Because I don't want to chip away at your mysterious aura?'

At her teasing, Seungwoo chuckled softly. His blog followers had also told him how he seemed to be veiled in mystery.

'These days, not talking about yourself would make you appear mysterious. I'm only an ordinary company employee, shuttling between work and home. We're living in a world where everyone reveals too much of themselves.'

Yeongju nodded.

'You're right. But I – I thought that you might not answer if I asked you something you're uncomfortable with. I'm like this, too. If there's something I don't want to talk about and someone asks me about it, I'll bristle.'

'I won't bristle. Promise.'

Seungwoo gazed at Yeongju, his expression more relaxed than usual.

'I was previously a programmer.'

'Ah! An engineer by training! How about now?'

'I switched departments. I'm now doing quality control.'

'Why the switch?'

'I got tired.'

'Tired?'

'Yes. Exhausted. But, hmm, that was not what I wanted to talk about.'

'Oh, right.'

'I was going to say that the business trip brought me to the States for two months. There was just so much to do I barely got any rest. One day, I was out on a field test when I chanced upon a Korean restaurant. Instead of water, they served jasmine tea. I drink it occasionally in Korea, so at the time, I didn't think too much about it. But when I returned home from the trip, the scent of the tea lingered in my mind. From then on, I started to drink jasmine tea at home.'

'Did you recreate the exact same taste you had in the States?'

'No.'

'Oh.'

'I couldn't recreate the taste, but drinking jasmine tea brought back memories of the trip.'

'What kind of memories?'

Seungwoo touched the cup lightly with his fingertips as he gazed into Yeongju's rounded eyes.

'I was having a hard time then. Almost every day, I thought about giving up everything and returning home. The restaurant I chanced upon gave me comfort. I'm not sure why – maybe the mood, or the friendly owner – but the place gave me strength and thanks to that, I managed to pull through.'

'A place to be grateful for indeed.'

'That's right. The reason I mentioned this is . . .'

'. . .'

'I'll remember this teahouse for a long, long time. I'll probably think back to this place many times in the future.'

'Are you going through a very difficult time now?'

Seungwoo burst out laughing. Yeongju stared in fascination at the man laughing heartily. Anyone could laugh like this, but somehow Yeongju was transfixed, perhaps because it was a side of him that was hard to imagine, or maybe laughing out loud suited him better than she'd thought. The Seungwoo in front of her was like a different person.

Looking at him smile, she said, 'I thought of something too.'

'What is it?'

'It was back in the days when I worked for a company.'

'Did you work for a company for a long time?'

'More than ten years.'

'When did you quit?'

'About three years ago.'

'Did you start the bookshop right after you left?'

'Yes, right away.'

'Was it something you'd planned before quitting?'

'Nope.'

'Then, when did you start thinking of opening a bookshop?'

'Seungwoo.'

'Yes?'

'I'm going to bristle,' she said, cutting him off with a smile. He backed off immediately. 'Okay, got it.'

'One night, I finished work at about eleven at night.'

'Did you work late often?'

'Yes. Too often.'

'No surprise you would want to quit.'

'Right . . . That night, I really craved a beer after work.'

'A beer . . .'

'Not just any beer, but beer at a standing bar.'

'Standing bar?'

'Yes. The fatigue would slip away if I sat down, and I hated that. I wanted to gulp down the beer at the peak of my fatigue. I was curious how or if it would taste different.'

Seungwoo looked at her, bemused.

'So, how did the beer taste?'

'Like honey.'

'This means you managed to find a standing bar?'

'I did. It was crowded too, and I took the last spot. It was pure bliss to down a beer standing up.'

'Happiness is never too far away.'

'That's what I wanted to say.'

'About happiness?'

'Yes, I wanted to say happiness is never beyond reach. It's not in the distant past, nor on the horizon of the future. It's right in front of me. Like that day's beer, and today's quince tea.'

She smiled brightly at him.

'In that case, if you're looking for happiness, you can simply drink a beer!'

She laughed out loud.

'Bingo!'

'And for that extra dose of happiness, you can make yourself very tired and drink it standing up.'

'Very true.' She laughed heartily.

'I . . .' Suddenly, she quietened down and in a subdued voice, she said, 'I think life becomes easier knowing that happiness is not that far out of reach.'

Seeing Yeongju's change of mood in a split second, Seungwoo had an urge to ask: what's making your life difficult? Those who waxed lyrical about how life was getting easier were more often than not the ones who were having a hard time. Because they were suffering, they spent time thinking about how to make life easier, how to keep their chin up, and how to keep moving forward.

For Seungwoo, the hardest part of a conversation was calibrating how much he could probe, and when to stop. How does one pinpoint the fine line between curiosity and rudeness? From his experience, once he started having doubts when asking a question, it was time to stop. Once he started wondering if the question was appropriate, it was a signal not to ask it. When he didn't know what to say, it was time to listen. If he kept to these rules, at the very least he wouldn't come across as ill-mannered.

'When do you feel happy?'

Just as he decided to listen quietly, Yeongju tossed him a question. Happiness. He'd never thought about it. While humans naturally chase happiness, Seungwoo was neutral about it. Instead of happiness, he spent more time thinking about productivity. To him, a happy life was perhaps a life where he used his time well.

'It's a tough question, given that I don't know what exactly it means to be happy. You said you derive happiness from drinking beer. I think I can understand the feeling. If you're feeling happy in that moment, then that's happiness for you. Everyone has a different definition of happiness, and out there, there's probably something that'll fit me. But it's a challenging question. What is happiness to me? Is there a one-size-fits-all definition?'

'There're many schools of thought on what happiness is. According to Ari—oh, never mind.'

Yeongju chastened herself internally. *Again! Not again!* Ever since she started the bookshop, she liked to quote from authors or books in conversations – a habit she'd come to adopt as she worked hard to find the best recommendation for customers looking for stories that could help them navigate their way in life. The habit became more deeply rooted when she started writing about books. Whenever a thought flashed across her mind, it was usually accompanied by a related book. When she spoke, she naturally referenced a quote, an author's name, or a particular theory, which sometimes bored the other party. She didn't find it boring at all, but she was aware that it could make the listener uncomfortable.

'What were you going to say?'

'Nothing.'

'What is it?'

'Nothing.'

'Ari – mmm, did you mean to say Aristotle?'

Yeongju wrapped her hands around the cup, pretending she didn't know what he was saying.

'Is it *The Nicomachean Ethics*? I've heard of it but haven't read it. I know Aristotle talks about happiness in his work. So, what does he say about happiness?'

Yeongju was a little embarrassed at having her thoughts read, so instead of answering, she took several sips of the lukewarm tea. Stopping halfway through a sentence felt silly, just like how being flustered now was also silly. She sneaked a glance at Seungwoo, who was calmly looking at her, waiting for an answer. Somehow, it felt like he was willing to listen to everything she said, no matter how boring it might be. She decided to carry on.

'So, Ari – what's his name again? He posits that happiness is separate from pleasure. Happiness, to him, refers to the achievements over a person's lifetime. If someone wanted to become a painter, he would have to strive hard to become one. Should he succeed in becoming a renowned painter years later, he would be seen as having lived a happy life. In the past, I used to subscribe to his view. Our mood changes all the time, so the same situation that makes us happy tonight may make us miserable the next day. Take this quince tea, for example. You're happy drinking it today, but there's a chance that tomorrow, no matter how much quince tea you drink, you'll be miserable. Such fleeting moments of happiness are not attractive. So, I thought if our life's achievements determine our level of happiness, it was worth giving it my all. I was confident pulling out all the stops. At least that was how I felt back then.'

'Whoever hears this would be so envious.'

'What did I say?'

'That you have the confidence of putting in the effort.'

'And why would that cause envy?'

'Well . . . it is often said that being able to put in effort is also an ability in itself.'

'Oh.'

'Why did you change your mind? Why did you start to dislike the happiness this Ari person put forth?'

'Because I wasn't happy.' Her face was slightly flushed. 'Accomplishments over a lifetime of hard work are amazing. But I grew to understand that what Ari-what's-his-name said is, basically, to work for your whole life so as to earn the final few moments of happiness. To achieve happiness at the end of life, you have to be miserable for a lifetime. When I think of it this way, happiness becomes horrible. It's such an empty feeling, to stake everything on a single accomplishment in life. So, I changed my mind and decided to chase after pleasure – the feeling of happiness – instead.'

'Do you feel happy right now?'

She nodded slightly.

'More than before.'

'Then it's great you changed your thinking.'

Yeongju stared at Seungwoo uncertainly, as if she didn't quite know if it was, after all, a good thing.

'I'll be rooting for you.'

Her eyes widened. 'For me?'

Seungwoo looked at her tenderly.

'Yes. I'll be rooting for you to find your happiness. I hope there'll be lots of joy in your life.'

Yeongju blinked several times and took a sip of her tea. It'd been a long while since anyone had said such encouraging words to her, and she liked how it enveloped her with strength. Setting down the cup, she smiled at him.

'Thank you. For the encouragement.'

It was almost five in the evening. They were surprised at how fast time had passed. Walking out of the teahouse, they naturally headed for the subway station. At the station exit, they stood facing each other.

'I had a good time,' said Yeongju, just as Seungwoo held out a bottle of quince tea concentrate he'd bought while she was in the bathroom. Smiling brightly, she took the bottle, marvelling at his thoughtful gesture.

'Be happy every time you drink it.'

'I will.'

He nodded in goodbye and turned around. Her eyes followed his back as he huddled forward a little when a sudden gust of wind blew. Putting the bottle in her bag, she turned and headed down the stairs to the station, thinking what a happy thing it was to meet a person on the same wavelength.

## The Book Club of Mums

Once she'd figured out when her son would usually appear at the bookshop, Mincheol's mother came in only on early weekday afternoons or Saturdays, but when the book club started, she started dropping by every other day to consult Yeongju and seek her advice.

Today, Mincheol's mother shared a table with Jungsuh. The two ladies had only exchanged silent greetings thus far, but when Mincheol's mother spotted a couple looking for an empty table, she went up to Jungsuh and asked if it was okay if she moved to sit with her instead. Jungsuh, who was busy knitting a twisted scarf, startled at the sudden question. She looked around before shifting to the side, a silent agreement to the suggestion. The two women sat side by side, chatting occasionally as they each did their own work.

'Mincheol told me he could spend an hour watching you knit. Now I understand why.' She stroked the half-completed red scarf on the table.

'I also enjoy how hours can pass while I'm knitting.'

Mincheol's mother chuckled.

Looking up, Jungsuh asked, 'May I ask what you're working on?'

Her hands paused as she peered at the laptop in front of Mincheol's mother.

'Oh. This?' She looked slightly abashed. 'I'm the leader of a book club. To do my job properly, I thought I first needed to organise my thoughts. I'm trying to write them down now, but it's not going well. I must do it. If not, I'll trip over my words.'

Mincheol's mother hadn't given it much thought before agreeing to take up the role. After all, what could be so difficult about a group of ajummas from the neighbourhood coming together to chat about books? She had gathered a group of five other mums she met at the cultural centre classes, who went there to pass time, and encouraged them to join 'Book Club 1' (later renamed as 'The Book Club of Mums'). Their first book, Yeongju's pick, was Park Wan-suh's *The Evening's Chance Encounter*[11].

The nerves kicked in at the very beginning of their first meeting. She wanted to speak, but her mind drew a blank as her heart thumped wildly and her hands trembled. At a loss for what to do, she got the members to introduce themselves while she fled the room. At the café counter, she asked Minjun for a glass of iced water. She downed it in one, grabbing Yeongju's hands, wailing that she was a goner as she stamped her feet. Practically in tears, Mincheol's mother moaned that she couldn't find the words, as if someone had skewered her mouth shut like a sanjeok. Yeongju gave her hands a firm squeeze, saying that she would be fine, to just go slowly according to the order of proceedings; everyone would understand that the first time is always the most challenging.

[11] Park Wan-suh, 저녁의 해후 *Jeonyeogui Haehu* (Munhakdongne, 1999)

Taking a deep breath, Mincheol's mother pushed the door to the book club room open. She returned to her seat, quickly flipping through her notes. As she read out the order of proceedings, her heart settled into its rhythm again. Thinking back to what Yeongju had said – that it wasn't possible to be perfect from the beginning, that people would understand – she forced back the tears that threatened to spill. The other members, having completed a round of introductions, stared at her. Their familiar faces looked alien. She laced her fingers tightly under the table and summoned the effort to speak.

'Er . . . everyone. I mean . . . Let's start with a real introduction.'

The rest of them blinked and stared in incomprehension. Hadn't they just finished the introductions? Taking a deep breath, she continued, her voice growing steadier.

'Hi everyone. My name is Jeon Heejoo. All of you here, even though you've known me for some time, find it awkward to call me by name, right? During our book club meetings, I'd like to suggest that everyone be on a first-name basis. I don't want to be addressed as Mincheol's mother. I want to be called by my name – Heejoo. Let's do another round of introductions, not as someone's wife or someone's mother, but with our names. Minjeong, Hayeong, Sunmi, Yeongsoon, Jiyoung, what's on your mind recently?'

Something else happened during the first meeting. At first, the members were shy, waving their hands in refusal to speak, but later, everyone jostled for airtime all at once. These ladies, who normally talked only about their husbands and children during a get-together, were fascinated that they suddenly had two whole hours to talk about themselves. They laughed, cried, hitting each other on the arm at the same time as they pulled out tissues and hugged one another. There was empathy, and a healthy dose of chastising, as they shared about their lives – somewhat gruffly, but with raw honesty. That night, still feeling the lingering intensity of the atmosphere, Heejoo didn't sleep well. In the wee hours of the morning, she found herself thinking about buying a laptop. She wanted to be better prepared for their next meeting.

The Book Club of Mums would be holding their fourth meeting soon. This time, they would be reading another Park Wan-suh title. Everyone in the book club had become a huge fan of the famed author and wanted to challenge themselves to finish her whole bibliography. This time, Heejoo picked the book. She'd read the synopsis online and when she showed it to them, everyone responded enthusiastically. The title was *A Standing Woman*[12]. Heejoo had read it once and she was typing out her thoughts on her laptop as she read it a second time. Suddenly, she stopped typing and turned to Jungsuh.

'Did Mincheol mention anything about being neglected by his mother recently? I haven't been paying much attention to him. Now that I am busy with my own things, I spend less time thinking about him. Of course, I'm not completely ignoring him. But it does seem like running a book club helps when raising a child who doesn't listen to you. It diverts my attention, which is much welcomed. I've been going crazy because of him.'

The two ladies had been sitting side by side for the past few hours, one knitting, the other writing. Out of the corner of her eye, Heejoo saw a man walking into the book club room. *Is there a meeting today?* she wondered. Oh, right. The seminars. The man who walked into the room must be

---

[12] Park Wan-suh, 서 있는 여자 *Seo Inneun Yeoja* (Seygesa, 2003)

an author. A short while later, he came out to order a drink from Minjun and then walked towards Yeongju. He had a worn-out look about him, like what she imagined an author to look like. She thought authors were usually fastidious but looking at the way he kept nodding at Yeongju's words, he didn't seem to fit the type. From afar, just from the set of his lips, he looked like he was the quiet, talented type. A tired face, a petite frame; good with words, good at conversations. Hmm. An author. Heejoo looked at the two of them and smiled. She simply smiled.

# Can I Make a Living with a Bookshop?

One month after she started the column, Yeongju was contacted by a newspaper journalist who wanted to interview her in her capacity as an independent bookshop owner. She hesitated, but eventually decided to accept, thinking that it could be good publicity for the bookshop.

After the article came out, something about the customers changed. They nodded their heads in greeting at her, with some even coming up to speak to her as if she was a long-time friend. As the number of customers grew, so did the sales. It surprised her how a one-off interview could bring about such changes. While the impact wasn't as immediate or obvious, there were also people who came to visit because they'd read her newspaper column. In the past, people who spoke to her at the bookshop usually asked her about her social media posts, but these days, they mostly came up to her because of her book column, either saying they enjoyed it, or asking her to continue recommending more good reads. There were also nearby residents who came in for the first time after reading her column. A lady, who looked to be in her thirties, told Yeongju that she went around bragging to her friends that the columnist owned the bookshop in her neighbourhood. She promised to drop by often, and indeed, Yeongju started to see her every few days. The lady seemed particularly interested in the world of tomorrow, seeing how she mostly bought books about AI or about the future of humanity.

Yeongju also received commissions for essays. Over the phone, the unfamiliar voices of her prospective clients would at times ask for ambitious topics, like *The Future of Independent Bookshops*, *The Death of the Reader*, or *Properties of Books and Their Influence on Reading Habits*. She rejected topics which had never crossed her mind. But topics she was keen to explore, like the properties of books and their influence on reading, she gladly accepted. She took care and pride in writing each piece, even though it felt like she had to squeeze out every last bit of her brain juices. She thought these commissioned pieces were a good opportunity for more people to know about the bookshop. Like books, bookshops need to make their existence known in order to have a chance of survival.

Thanks to social media, Hyunam-dong Bookshop was known to book-lovers, or bookshop lovers, but these days, Yeongju knew that it was reaching a bigger crowd. While it was excellent news for the bookshop, she could feel the mounting strain. The increase in footfall also meant that Yeongju needed to spend more time interacting with customers. There were also the new programmes she'd started on top of what she already had to do on a daily, weekly, or monthly basis. She was beginning to lose her rhythm. *Ah, at this rate, I'm going to screw everything up.* When the thought hit her, she knew she couldn't continue like this.

It was then that she received an unexpected proposal from the most unexpected person. The sharp-eyed Sangsu, having accurately observed that Yeongju was the bottleneck in the bookshop's operations, approached her one day.

'What are the busiest hours for the bookshop?'

Sangsu, who led one of the book clubs, was a few notches above Yeongju when it came to reading. Finishing two books in a day was no big deal to him.

'Huh?'

'I'm asking which part of the day you feel the most flustered?' Sangsu was his usual taciturn self, his short spiky hair complementing his gruff voice.

'I don't k—'

'Think.'

She really gave it some thought.

'Uhm . . . maybe the three hours before closing?'

'Alright. I'll help out during those three hours.'

'What?'

'I'm asking you to hire me as a part-timer. It's a simple solution, why didn't you think of it?'

Sangsu asked for the minimum wage in return for manning the cash register only. He asked Yeongju not to saddle him with additional duties, arguing that a dedicated person at the cash register would already make things a lot easier for her. He told her he would be reading when nobody was at the counter; if she hated that, she could find someone else instead. Yeongju asked for an hour to consider. When the hour was up, she went up to Sangsu, who was reading in a corner.

'Six days a week, three hours a day, three months as a start. What do you think?'

'Deal.'

Sangsu kept to his word. He sat behind the counter and read, but when a customer approached, he would process the payment smoothly, as though he'd done it countless times. Once there were no customers, he would turn his attention back to the book. However, it was his own doing that led him to gradually move beyond the role he'd set for himself. He liked to boast when it came to books. Whenever a customer approached him for a recommendation, he would pretend to grumble, but in fact, he would flaunt his wealth of knowledge, and somehow, the customer would always end up buying an additional couple of books. From then on, among the regulars of the bookshop, Sangsu earned the very long nickname of The-Gruff-Part-Timer-Ajusshi-Who-Knows-A-Lot.

As Hyunam-dong Bookshop became a well-known name beyond the neighbourhood, people who dreamt of opening their own shops started to reach out to Yeongju. Some even came all the way to the bookshop. When it was apparent that there were more than a couple of prospective bookshop owners, she decided to give a talk. Such one-time events were less taxing than an event series; they were also a good way of spreading the bookshop's name in a short time.

Two fellow bookshop owners joined her for the talk at eight o'clock on a Tuesday evening. About ten potential bookshop owners turned up. As expected, bread-and-butter questions were at the top of their list: can I make a living with a bookshop? None of them were expecting to make a pot of gold from selling books. It was their dream, and they would be satisfied with making a modest living doing something they enjoyed. Bookshop A's owner got the ball rolling, shyly saying it was his first time speaking about this topic.

'Understandably, this is what you'd be most curious about. In my case, I barely scrape by. After deducting the shop rent, maintenance fees and more, I'm left with about 1.5 million won a month. And when you factor in my apartment rent, those maintenance fees . . . well, you get the picture. Six months ago, I decided to return to my parents' home. I moved out at the age of twenty, but at the age of thirty-seven, I'm living with my parents again . . . I shall stop here. Please consider carefully: running a bookshop is no romantic dream. But if you're determined to start one, I'd say: do it. You need to do it so that you have no regrets in the future.'

Bookshop B's founder pretended to sob, as if saying this was the story of her life too. What she had to say was slightly more positive.

'First, I'll be honest and say that sometimes I earn more than A, sometimes less. If I think I didn't earn enough the previous month, I'll hold more events the next month to attract footfall. When things get too hectic, I'll scale back for a while to get some rest before gearing up again. Like any other bookshop owner, one of my biggest concerns is how long I can keep the place running. For those here who want to start a bookshop, you'll be worrying about this, and other things too. But if you decide that a bookshop is not for you, and you want to pursue something else instead, it'll come with another set of worries. What I'm trying to say is: whatever you do, you will face challenges. Even if it's not a bookshop, you'll fret over whatever business you're start-ing; if you work for a company, that comes with its own set of worries too. In the end, it boils down to this: what kind of work do I want to do, despite all the worries? For me, I choose to worry as I run a bookshop.'

Next up was Yeongju.

'I'll start by confessing that I still worry about many things. Something I'd like to emphasise is that you need to have enough savings to sustain the bookshop on the assumption that it won't earn anything for six months to a year. I know it's difficult; it's a huge amount of money. But it is important to have the financial buffer while the bookshop takes time to establish its name. Of course, it's not like it is guaranteed to find its footing in a year. It's my third year and I'm still worrying about its stability.'

Bookshop A's founder nodded.

'I'm in my fifth year and it's the same for me. Instead of thinking about whether the bookshop has found its place, my focus is to make it hang in there longer. That said, it doesn't mean that no independent bookshop has ever found its footing.'

Rolling her eyes in thought, B threw out some names – bookshops which maintained decent earnings because of the variety of activities they offered; bookshops seen as a local attraction – which the participants quickly wrote down on their phones or in a notebook. The three of them took turns to share, followed by a Q&A session which ended after ten o'clock.

*

These days, Mincheol appeared automatically at the bookshop twice a week without being nagged. Sometimes, he would go back home to change out of his school uniform first, to avoid standing out among the customers. As Yeongju had her hands full that day, Minjun took over the role of chatting with him. While the bookshop got busier, the number of tables at the café remained unchanged, so there wasn't a huge increase in his workload. He did feel slightly busier, but it wasn't as if all the coffee orders came in at the same time. Mincheol loitered around the café and, spotting a lull in between customers, he walked up to Minjun.

'Is Yeongju imo very busy these days?'

'Yup.'

'Why aren't you helping her, then?'

'I need to make the coffee.'

'Does your contract state that you only make the coffee?'

'Yup. Why? Do I seem unsympathetic?'

'A little. But if it's written into your contract, I can't say anything.'

Minjun chuckled at his honest response.

'Boss has a lot more on her plate now, but that's because she's trying to grow the business. That's why she's a little overwhelmed at the moment.'

'Why is she doing this?'

'It's an experiment, she says.'

'On what?'

'On how far she can go.'

'Hmm . . . Well, being busy is a good thing.'

Minjun gave Mincheol a sideways glance as he brewed the coffee.

'You're saying things you don't believe in. You don't think busy is good, right?'

'Everyone's busy. All of you.'

'But not you.'

'I'm the exception, I guess.'

Minjun nodded absentmindedly.

'Yeah, it's not a bad thing to be the exception.'

'Is that so . . .'

'Alright, quit talking and try this,' Minjun said, tilting the coffee server over a cup.

'I don't like bitter stuff.'

'It's not bitter. Just try it.'

In his free time, Minjun had been practising hand-drip coffee and he usually roped in either Jungsuh or Mincheol to be his taste tester. Having started on coffee in his first year of high school, Mincheol had already developed an immunity to caffeine.

'It seems like I'm not fully developed as a human yet, seeing how I absolutely cannot take bitterness,' Mincheol once jokingly told him.

From that day, Mincheol became his most hard-to-please customer – i.e. the very best. Minjun spent his time experimenting with how to remove the bitterness from the coffee. This time, he seemed to have finally gotten it right.

'It's kind of sweet.'

'Is it good?'

'I don't know what's considered good. But this is kind of nice,' Mincheol said. 'It feels like the coffee is melting in my mouth.'

'What do you mean?'

'Maybe because it's smooth?'

'So, you're saying that it's so smooth that it feels like it's melting?'

Minjun poured some coffee out from the server and sipped it.

'Well, it's really quite good. Hyung, your skills are improving.'

'I've always had the skills,' Minjun retorted as he took another sip.

'No, you haven't.'

'Yes, I have. Just that I couldn't make a coffee you liked. Now I've tamed your taste buds too.'

'Hey. That doesn't sound good.'

Grumbling, Mincheol took another sip of the coffee. Minjun glanced at the boy, who was talking a lot more than before, and suggested a date for their next tasting session.

'The day after tomorrow, same time. Are you free?'

'Okay.'

While Mincheol acted like he was indifferent to everything, he'd never once rejected Minjun's request for help.

'I'll make you an even better cup next time.'

'I'll only be able to tell when I drink it.'

Mincheol gulped down the remaining coffee and set down the cup.

'I'll head off after saying goodbye to Yeongju imo.'

As Minjun cleared away the server and cups, he glanced in the direction of Yeongju.

'Alright, if you can even catch her for a moment.'

Mincheol patiently stood to the side as he waited for Yeongju to finish her call. While she'd put up her hand to signal her apologies, he continued to stand there as if he was planning to wait it out. When she was finally done, she walked up to him and asked him how he'd been. Mincheol answered her questions dutifully.

'It feels like my mum is writing a graduation thesis these days.'

Yeongju burst out laughing as she walked him to the door. He bowed slightly and – perhaps it was too cold – hunched over as he walked out. Watching his back, Yeongju contemplated organising an event for teenagers for a moment, before she caught herself in time. No, she had enough on her plate.

# Barista 'IN' on Monday

*- Barista OUT on Mondays*
*- The coffee menu is unavailable today*
*- Other drinks still available*
   *#baristaworksfivedaysaweek #qualityoflife_barista*
   *#wesupportWLB*

On Mondays – Minjun's day off – the bookshop didn't sell coffee. To avoid any mix-ups, Yeongju would post a notice on the blog and social media every Monday morning. These days, except for first-time customers, nobody would ask for coffee on a Monday. Even on the rare occasion someone tried to order coffee, once she explained the rationale, they were all supportive of the barista's need for work-life balance. You could say this had become part of the bookshop's culture. Hence, Yeongju was exasperated when Minjun was the one who broke it.

When Minjun came in for the first time on a Monday afternoon and asked to stay a couple of hours, Yeongju initially thought that it was alright to make an exception that day. Minjun had explained that he needed someone to taste-test his coffee and it wasn't possible to do so at home. Even when he approached her every half hour with a fresh cup of coffee, she couldn't quite chase him out. Thanks to the caffeine overdose, she didn't sleep a wink that night.

Losing a night's sleep wasn't the issue. The bigger problem was Minjun, who continued to appear at the bookshop on subsequent Mondays. Several people took turns to be his taste testers and it suspiciously looked like they'd made prior appointments. Jungsuh would arrive at the café around the same time as Minjun to drink cup after cup, and if it wasn't her, it would be Heejoo. And if not Heejoo, Mincheol. If not them, Sangsu would be his guinea pig. Minjun would observe their reactions carefully as if examining an X-ray film. A slight shift in their expression would translate into delight or disappointment on his face. *That look in his eyes! As if he's going crazy trying to gauge their reactions! How am I to demand an explanation when he looks like this?* Yeongju thought.

She fretted over the customers' confusion. Those familiar with 'No Barista Mondays' clearly knew that Minjun was the barista in question. Several times, she'd seen customers double-checking their phones to make sure they hadn't gotten their days wrong. Some of them would ask if they could get a coffee, while others simply went ahead and ordered. Yeongju, conflicted that her weekly Monday announcements were being made redundant, decided to think of a solution.

'Boss, I'm making things difficult for you, right? Just let me do this a few more Mondays. I feel like I'm getting the hang of it.'

Minjun had approached her the previous week, having noticed that she was upset. Yeongju had made the decision right then.

'Minjun, shall we try this?'

> - *Barista 'IN' on Monday (today)*
> - *Hand-drip coffee available at Hyunam-dong Bookshop*
> - *50% off from 3 – 7 p.m.*
> - *Non-coffee menu is also available*
>   *#hyunamdongbookshopbarista_evolving*
>   *#handdripcoffee_sincerity #comeandhavecoffee*
>   *#notaweeklypromotion*

After the event started, the bookshop saw another change –
a significant increase in the number of coffee regulars.

# I'll Help You Take a Look

Yeongju lived in anxiety every day as she struggled to handle the sudden increase in workload without making any mistakes. Even when she was smiling, the weariness on her face was obvious. 'Still, thanks to Sangsu, my workload has gotten a lot lighter.' Despite saying so, Yeongju still had too many things on her plate. She was busy writing the introduction for this month's book event when Jungsuh called out to her.

'Eonnie. It's obvious you're struggling to stay afloat.'

Yeongju burst out laughing.

'Really? I thought I hid it well.'

At her flippant manner, Jungsuh turned serious.

'Do you have too much to do? You need to cut yourself some slack, eonnie.'

Yeongju glanced at her.

'It's not that bad,' she said sincerely, switching from her joking tone to indicate that she was grateful for the concern. 'It's just that the tension has gone up a notch. Let's say it was a level six not too long ago – which I'd probably be able to maintain for another six months, or even two years. But these days, it feels like an eight, so I probably can't continue at this intensity. How long do you think humans can hang on at this level of tension? Not too long, right? If you try to sustain this level, your body and mind will crumble. Many people have gone down that path, but . . .'

She took a deep breath as if to recalibrate herself.

'I haven't hit the stage where I'll snap at any moment. You can't ever predict the flow of the customers in a bookshop. Just when you think you're getting more footfall, suddenly people stop coming. Forever. Adios. The busy period will pass soon. There are a few projects I've started, so my plate is full, but in no time, the bookshop will be forgotten by the crowds again. When that time comes, I'll go back to living at a six.'

Hmm. Jungsuh didn't quite know what to say.

'When you put it like this, I can't decide if a six or eight is better. In any case, I'm glad to hear that.'

'Hear what?'

'There's no need to worry about those who know what they are doing. I'm relieved that I don't have to be too worried about you.'

Yeongju squeezed her shoulders, as if assuring her that she was fine.

'There's one thing, though. I haven't been reading these days. I don't have the time. Now that I say it out loud, it really feels like a problem, not being able to read.'

At nine in the evening, as the bookshop wound down for the day, Yeongju closed the front door. She sat down next to Seungwoo, who was editing her essay. She'd gotten used to watching his stoic expression from the side, whereas in the past she used to feel very small next to him.

As the deadline to submit her first piece of writing to the newspaper had drawn closer, Yeongju had been close to a panic attack. She'd finished the essay a couple of days earlier, but she couldn't tell, at all, if it was of a publishable quality for a newspaper. Strange. As a reader, she could easily discern good writing from bad, even if it was a subjective judgement. But when it came to her own writing, she was completely at a loss. She had no clue at all – as if she was illiterate – whether it was a piece that could be published anywhere at all.

She read it once. Twice. Over and over again. Just when she was convinced that it wasn't good enough to appear anywhere in public, she received a text from Seungwoo. *How's the writing going?* It was a short and simple message, but she poured her tangled feelings into a verbose reply. Seungwoo responded with another short message: *I'll help you take a look.* She jumped at the offer.

The next day, Seungwoo came to the bookshop. She handed him her draft in trepidation. Writing was tough; showing it to someone else was worse. Each time she posted something on her blog, her heart thumped wildly. This time, it was an actual newspaper. And look – who was in front of her? The writing expert who'd waged a public war with a publishing CEO. How would he judge her writing? Observing his profile, she couldn't see even a hint in his expression or body language which would clue her in on his thoughts. When he'd finished reading the last sentence, he put down the piece of paper and rummaged in his bag for a ballpoint pen. Only then did he finally speak.

'I'll mark the parts that need to be edited. I'll also include the reason why I marked them.'

She was still clueless, judging from his expression, what he thought of the piece.

'Is my writing . . . okay?' she asked, not realising how defeated she sounded.

'Yes, it is. I know what you're trying to say.'

Was that a normal thing to say if the writing really was passable?

'It's not that good . . . right?'

She felt like ants in a frying pan.

'It's good. I feel the emotions in your writing, and I can almost see the images in my head – the day-to-day operations of a bookshop. I share your anxiety as you wait for the customers to come in.'

She scrutinised his face, trying to discern if he was just being polite or speaking from his heart. As usual, he was unreadable. Or rather, he was just calm. At the very least, looking at his expression, it didn't seem like an excruciatingly embarrassing piece to read. She decided to take it positively.

But when Seungwoo picked up the pen and ruthlessly began highlighting parts of her writing, she started to wonder if she'd been deluded. To her, at least, it looked ruthless. Next to the underlined bits, in his neat penmanship, he wrote a short explanation of each mistake. Ten minutes later – which felt like an hour – he was still at the first paragraph. Several thoughts criss-crossed her mind. The resolve to coolly accept that her writing was terrible was smeared with the disappointment in Seungwoo for nitpicking at everything – but as he reached the fourth paragraph, the conflicting thoughts merged into one: *what made him put so much effort into this?*

For almost a full hour, he focused on her writing in silence. By now, the disappointment had given way to the realisation that for Seungwoo to offer his help meant that he would do so with utmost care and effort. It must have been this tenacity of his that led him to achieve what he did. And his forever-tired face was probably also the result of his intensity. Out of politeness, since he was working hard on her behalf, she sat next to him and did some work too. When she noticed that he was at the last paragraph, she grabbed two bottles of beer from the fridge, uncapped them, and passed one to Seungwoo, who was deep in concentration. He looked up suddenly, surprised to see the beer.

Taking it, he said, 'Sorry to keep you waiting. I'm almost finished.'

When he was finally done, the first thing he told her was not to be upset about the underlined bits. Unless you're a professional writer, this level of edits is to be expected, he said, adding that there were some bits he'd marked out despite them being minor mistakes he could've just passed over. 'The flow is generally logical, so I didn't have to make too many edits on that part,' he said, trying to reassure her. However, he immediately followed the comment with, 'On and off, there were bits that weren't logical. Once they're edited, you'll be fine.' Yeongju was initially confused, but after listening to his explanation, she realised that she only had to rework one sentence to resolve the issue. For the next hour, the two of them huddled together to make the edits. Finally, they reached the last sentence.

'*Sonnim gidaryeojyeotda* – the customers were awaited. The phrasing is awkward.'

'How so?' Yeongju began to ask. 'Oh right . . . passive . . .' Having discovered the mistake, she trailed off.

'That's right.'

Seungwoo explained briefly about passive verbs.

'We use the passive form when the subject undergoes an action. So, *eat* becomes *eaten*. But using the passive form with the verb *to wait* makes it seems like the subject, the customers, was undergoing the action of waiting and this is odd. Hence, it should be edited to *sonnim gidaryeotda* – I waited for the customers.'

'Ah, I see. But . . .'

'Yes?' Seungwoo prompted her encouragingly.

'If I write it this way, it doesn't seem to adequately express my feeling of awaiting the customers.'

'How so?'

'The feeling of waiting without meaning to do so. The subconscious anxiety, and the yearning. It doesn't seem to be conveyed.'

He scrutinised the sentences before looking up again.

'Try reading the essay from the beginning. Your sentences clearly bring across the feelings you hope to express. You're thinking that you have to put the emphasis in this sentence, right? There's no need to. Those emotions have been sufficiently conveyed throughout the text. In fact, it's better to keep this sentence plain.'

She carefully read through the essay from the beginning, focusing on whether her feelings had indeed been captured. Meanwhile, he quietly waited for her as he fiddled with his pen. A while later, she nodded.

'I get what you mean.'

'That's right.'

'Thank you so much. If I had known that it would take up so much of your time, I wouldn't have asked for your help.'

'No worries. I had fun too.'

'When are you free? I must buy you a meal for your trouble.'

'You don't have to,' Seungwoo said as he put down the pen. 'Instead, let me edit your writing a few more times.'

Yeongju raised her eyebrows. Wasn't that more beneficial for her?

'If we look through your writing together a few more times, you'll learn how to edit your own writing. Then, you won't feel as anxious, or cast doubt on your sentences.'

'Since you're busy, why don't I work on it myself the next time. If I remain as anx—'

Thinking that she'd taken too much of his time, she tried to decline his offer, but he gently cut her off in the middle of the sentence.

'I'm not busy, so don't feel like you're a burden. Once you're done with the next piece, don't fret over it on your own; just send it to me immediately.'

Not giving her the time to react, he added, 'Got it?'

'Alright then. Thank you.'

Yeongju quickly sent out the edited version to the journalist. If she couldn't make it better than it was right now, she might as well get it out of sight, out of mind. Seungwoo declined to drink as he had driven, so they chatted while she finished the beers. Circling back to the topic of waiting, they decided to each share the thing they'd been waiting for most earnestly in life. 'Customers,' said Yeongju emphatically, the acute yearning of the past few years captured in the three syllables. Seungwoo, after some thought, replied, 'I can't think of anything,' causing Yeongju to immediately brand him a cheater. From the time they browsed the bookshop till they turned off the lights, locked the door and stepped outside, not once did their conversation break off.

A few weeks later, they found themselves leaving the bookshop together again. Bidding each other goodbye, they headed off in opposite directions, but a few steps later, Seungwoo stopped. Noticing it, Yeongju looked over her shoulder just as he turned around to face her. Surprised, she stopped in her tracks and turned around too.

'Do you remember when we talked about waiting?' he asked. She nodded. 'I'm curious about something,' Seungwoo said. Yeongju's eyes widened.

'You answered "customers", right? Leaving them aside, I was wondering if there's something else, in this moment, that you're waiting for?'

She couldn't think of anything else, so she replied no.

'That day, I told you I couldn't think of anything either. The truth is, I vaguely know what I am waiting for. But I felt like I shouldn't reveal my feelings in haste. Instead, I should slowly figure out what exactly I want.'

Yeongju stared at Seungwoo, her expression clearly clueless about what was going on. He kept his gaze steady.

'Right now, what I'm yearning for . . .'

The two of them stood face to face, four steps apart.

'. . . is someone's heart.'

Seungwoo smiled softly as Yeongju stared right at him, trying to comprehend what he'd just said.

'That day, you accused me of being a cheater. Even though it's late, I'd like to get rid of that label. Hence, I'm telling you now. Get home safely, alright?'

For a long moment, Yeongju watched his back, before she turned in the direction of home. *Someone's heart. What does he mean? Why is he telling me this?* The memory of Seungwoo passing her the quince tea flitted into her mind. And him saying that he would be rooting for her happiness. Why did these images dance into her mind? She didn't know. Pausing, she turned back to gaze at his retreating figure before she walked on ahead, deep in thought. She put on the fur hat she'd been holding in her hand.

# With Honesty and Sincerity

Yeongju was chatting with Mincheol when Seungwoo stepped into the bookshop after work one evening. When she got up from her seat, the two men ended up sharing the table. She'd introduced Seungwoo as 'an author' and Mincheol as 'a nephew next door'. Not too concerned about sharing tables, Seungwoo made himself comfortable and started to go through her writing. However, when he realised that the boy across from him wasn't doing anything else, he started to become a little self-conscious. What's more, the child was staring straight at him.

'You like to sit around doing nothing?'

Feeling an obligation to speak to the boy who was just staring right at him, Seungwoo threw out a question.

'Yes.'

'Well, go watch YouTube or something.'

'I can do that at home.'

Hearing that, he gave the boy a slight nod and returned to his work, as if indicating that he wouldn't mind him any further. This time, it was Mincheol who attempted a conversation.

'Do you enjoy writing?'

Actually, Mincheol wasn't staring at Seungwoo for nothing; he was trying to find the best timing to start a conversation. He'd been agonising over a writing assignment – the newest condition he'd agreed to. A few weeks ago, Heejoo declared that unless he did a piece of writing every two weeks, he'd have to attend after-school classes and study till midnight. He tried to rebel by threatening to stop visiting the bookshop. Sure, she said, not batting an eyelid. She knew that her son had grown to look forward to the bookshop visits. Since cram schools were as bad as school, he'd no choice but to agree to do the essays. Heejoo tagged on another requirement in a this-is-final kind of voice. He needed to 'write properly'.

'No,' Seungwoo replied without looking up.

'That's still amazing. Writing is super difficult for me, yet you do it as a job.'

Seungwoo's eyes remained glued to the sentences as he underlined the text here and there.

'Writing is never my job.'

'Then, what do you work as?'

'Just at a company.'

Mincheol didn't seem put out by Seungwoo's clipped answers and continued to bug him with questions. Suddenly, he asked if Seungwoo was free right now. Puzzled, Seungwoo looked up. Mincheol explained that he had something to ask, but if Seungwoo was busy, he would not disturb him. Mincheol realised that he was somehow bolder and more talkative than usual, perhaps because he was talking to a writer. It felt as if an author would be able to help him resolve his biggest challenge right now, something that he couldn't work on alone.

Seungwoo paused to think for a moment before setting the pen on the table. Seeing how he leaned back in the chair,

Mincheol smiled and immediately launched into another question.

'What do you do at the company?'

'Just normal work.'

'Uhm . . .' Mincheol hesitated a moment, looking more solemn than before.

'Between writing and doing normal work at a company, which one do you enjoy more? And which one are you better at?'

This time, it was Seungwoo who went, 'Hmm.' What was it that he wanted to know? Why was this child staring at him so intensely? At this rate, the conversation looked like it would drag on. He stared into Mincheol's intelligent eyes.

'Can I ask why you're asking me this?'

'It's related to something that I've been agonising over,' said Mincheol. Should he pursue something he liked, or something he was good at? He wanted to find the answer. This was the essay question his mum had set him; at the same time, it was something he wanted to find out himself too.

Some time back, his one and only favourite teacher at school, who taught the Korean period, told the class that 'To find happiness, do what you enjoy. All of you should find something you enjoy doing, something that makes you excited. Instead of pursuing what is recognised and valued by society, do what you like. If you can find it, you'll not waver easily, no matter what others think. Be brave.'

According to Mincheol, many of his classmates were touched by the words. One of them was enraptured by their boldness. Bold and risky, because the teacher had acknowledged that kids have their own thoughts. Raising his voice, he urged the rest of them, 'Come on, think about it. Who else would tell us that? Where else will you find a teacher who'll tell us to do the complete opposite of what our parents want? Those are bold words, indeed. And remember the old saying? Bold words are what we should keep in our hearts!'

His friends were stirred by the teacher's words. Meanwhile, Mincheol became anxious for the first time. *Really? Do I have to do something I like? But I can't think of anything. Nothing I particularly enjoy or get excited about.* To him, everything was just about the same as any other. Sometimes he might find something interesting, but soon, he'd get bored of it. He'd never felt strongly about anything – that he'd die if he didn't get to do it – nor was there anything he hated to do so much that he'd rather die. He wasn't particularly good at anything, either. He was simply average, and ordinary, at everything in life. How should he navigate a life in which there was nothing he liked, or was good at? He was lost.

Seungwoo thought he understood what Mincheol was struggling with, and what he was curious about. It wasn't just a teenage worry; many continued to fret over it in their thirties and forties. In fact, just five years earlier, Seungwoo had probably been stewing over the same worry. Despite getting parched lips and puffy eyes, he doggedly held on to his job because he couldn't quite let go. He was doing something he liked, how dare he give it up? Yet, he wasn't happy. At the same time, he fretted about possibly living with regrets if he gave up what he liked.

'I feel so frustrated. Other teachers tell us to do well, and they stop there. They line us up according to our marks and say, "See, this is where you stand!" and embarrass us, telling us to do more, to do better. However, no matter how well we do, we're still stuck in a line. It doesn't make sense. So, I thought I'd ignore what those teachers tell me. But I simply couldn't ignore what my Korean teacher said. Or could I?'

The furrows between his brows deepened, and his head seemed to hang lower.

'I'm not good at anything, nor is there anything I like. I used to have nothing at all, but these days, I've been thinking that coming here isn't too boring – chatting with the aunts, with Minjun hyung, helping to taste the coffee, and watching Jungsuh imo knit.'

'I don't think it's frustration you're feeling. It's anxiety.'

'What?' Mincheol looked up.

'It seems to me that you're getting anxious, thinking that you have to discover quickly what you enjoy or do well.'

'Is it so? Hmm . . . that's true.' Mincheol averted his gaze as he mumbled. He turned back to Seungwoo. 'It feels like I have to find it quickly.'

'Why are you in a rush? You don't have to hurry. If coming here isn't boring, just come over more often. Be who you are right now, and you'll be fine.'

Mincheol lowered his head again as if he was struggling with his thoughts.

'Do you think finding something you enjoy will make you happier?' Seungwoo asked.

Mincheol shook his head slightly. 'I don't know. But if that's what our teacher says, I suppose so.'

'Being happy by doing something you enjoy . . . yes, that's possible. I'm sure there're such people out there. At the same time, there're also people who are happy when doing something they're good at.'

Mincheol frowned. 'Are you saying it's a case-by-case thing?'

'Doing what you like doesn't guarantee happiness. Unless you're also in an excellent environment, then maybe.

Sometimes, it's the environment that's more important. If you're in an ill-suited environment, what you enjoy can become something you want to give up. What I'm saying is, not everyone fits into the mould of finding happiness just by discovering what they like. That's too simplified, not to mention naive.'

Since middle school, Seungwoo had dreamt of becoming a programmer. And he did. He joined a company that produced mobile phones, as a software developer. At first, he was thrilled that he got to spend all his time doing something he enjoyed. He didn't even complain when he had to work late. But in his third year at the company, the exhaustion seeped in. The fact that he enjoyed his work – and was good at it – became shackles. The work wasn't distributed fairly. Those who were good had to take on more. Every other day, he worked late; every other month, he went on business trips. He endured and endured until one day, he threw in the towel. That day, when it struck him that liking the work and being forced to work in an unsupportive environment were completely different matters, he requested to switch departments. Overnight, he gave up what he enjoyed. He stopped coding. He refused to work overtime. And he'd never once regretted his decision.

'Does that mean it's the same with the things you're good at? If you aren't in an environment that allows you to enjoy the work you're good at . . .'

'Yup, the same logic.' Seungwoo nodded.

Mincheol was still frowning.

'That said, you can't just sit there and blame the environment for everything.'

'What should we do then?'

'Nobody can predict the future. To know whether you enjoy the work, you need to give it a try.'

Seungwoo spent five years doing what he liked, and another five in a job doing what he didn't like. If he had to decide which life was better . . . hmm. If he had to pick, he would choose the latter. It wasn't because the job was less complex, or that he could take things easy – doing stuff he didn't like made him feel empty. But he filled the void by immersing himself in the Korean language, which brought him to where he was today. Life is too complicated and expansive to be judged solely by the career you have. You could be unhappy doing something you liked, just as it was possible to do what you didn't like but derive happiness from something entirely different. Life is mysterious and complex. Work plays an important role in life, but it isn't solely responsible for our happiness or misery.

'Are you telling me not to think and just do whatever?'

Frustrated, the words tumbled out of Mincheol without a care.

'That's not a bad thing,' Seungwoo replied. 'Just try something out, and who knows, you might find joy in it. It might be something you stumble upon but end up wanting to do for life. Who knows? Nobody knows what'll happen unless you try. Instead of agonising over what you should do, think about putting effort into whatever you're doing. It's more important to try your best in whatever you do, no matter how small it may seem. All your effort will add up to something.'

Looking at the boy staring at him with widened eyes, Seungwoo let out an 'uhm'. It wasn't easy for adults past their thirties to wrap their heads around it, and even more so for a teenager. He tried to find another way to explain. First, he decided to suggest something tangible that Mincheol could do right away.

'Alright, to sum up what we've spoken about: right now, you have an essay to write. So, don't think about anything else. Just focus on the essay and work on it.'

Mincheol sighed.

'When you start to write, perhaps you'll discover a penchant for writing.'

'I highly doubt it.'

'You won't know until you start. Don't decide the future before it happens.'

Mincheol stared glumly at Seungwoo.

'My head is spinning. There're even more thoughts swirling in my head right now. I'm supposed to write about whether I should do what I like, or what I'm good at. But I have no conclusion.'

'Well, if you don't know, just say so.'

'Is it okay not to have a definite conclusion?'

'By forcing an answer, you risk closing your ears to what your heart is telling you, misinterpreting your feelings or worse, deceiving yourself. Write how you really feel. You're thinking and fretting over it now, right? Say so. Or you can just whine about not having an answer; that's also another solution. What you're doing now is not just writing an essay. You're carefully considering what you want to do in life. In that case, you shouldn't rush into an answer.'

Mincheol scratched his head with a finger.

'I think I'm kind of getting what you are saying.'

'Being relaxed or relieved is not the state that we always have to be in. Sometimes, there's a need to hold on to the frustration of the situation, to the complexity of things as you think and ponder.'

'To hold on to these feelings . . .'

'That's right.'

'Sir, what should I do to "write properly"? My mum told me that I have to write this properly.'

Picking up his pen, Seungwoo replied: 'Didn't I already tell you? Write honestly. Write with effort. With honesty, and sincerity. Then whatever comes out of it will be properly written.'

## To Focus on Coffee When Making Coffee

After yoga class in the morning, Minjun would nip home for a quick shower before heading for Goat Beans. He'd started to learn roasting recently, in the hope that under-standing the process would help him to better bring out the flavours in his brew. He had also taken up the role of making morning coffee for Jimi and her staff, brewing the coffee according to their individual preferences. The roaster was a much more suitable place than the bookshop to practise. He had easy access to a variety of beans, and if something wasn't available, he could coax Jimi into bringing it in.

Everyone at Goat Beans was serious about their coffee; it was what drew Minjun here every day. They would be goofing around the moment before, but once the coffee was served, the mood changed. At each step – taking in the aroma, swirling the dark liquid in their mouths, and swallowing the first mouthful – they would give detailed feedback. The roasters were also learning, through his coffee, how their beans performed, and how their roast-ing techniques could be further honed. Whenever there was something different about his coffee, they made sure to point it out. Patting him on the shoulders, Jimi told him: 'If you can achieve a difference through consistent practice and not sheer luck, you're going to make a pretty decent barista.'

He was going to stay true to his path. He learnt that if he hated the wavering, the uncertainty, all he needed to do was to hold on to something to stay focused. So, he did. He anchored himself with coffee. Emptying himself of distractions, he embraced it wholeheartedly. He wanted to see where it would take him, where he could go with it. A simple thought – so simple it was almost embarrassing – but it gave Minjun strength.

He didn't have a goal in mind as he brewed the coffee. Each time, he just did his best. Even so, he could feel his skills improving; his coffee was getting better. Wasn't it enough? He thought it was sufficient to grow at this pace. Did becoming the best barista in the world matter? Would the glory mean anything, if he had to work himself to the bone for the title? For a moment, he wondered if it was a case of sour grapes, but it wasn't. He would just aim for a more achievable goal, or, in fact, do without one. He would focus on giving his best to the day's work – the best coffee he could make. He decided to only think about his personal best.

He stopped looking too far ahead into the future. To him, the distance between the present and the future was a few pours on the dripper; the future within his control. As the stream of water circled the grounds, he thought about how the coffee would turn out. That was as far as he allowed himself to look into the future.

There were, of course, times he was frustrated that his best effort was put into a future a mere stone's throw away. On those days, he would stretch and stand up, as if trying to prolong the future – to an hour, two hours, or a day. He defined the past, present and future within the boundaries of time in his control. There was no need to think beyond that. Where do I see myself in one year's time? To know this is beyond human capacity.

Once, he shared these thoughts with Jungsuh. Immediately, she understood him and even helped him to take it a step further.

'Like focusing on coffee when making coffee, right?'

'Well . . . I mean . . . yup.'

'That's the basic tenet of a spiritual lifestyle – to exist fully in the moment. It's what you're doing.'

'Spiritual lifestyle?'

'What people mean when they say, "live in the moment". It's easy to say, but what does it really mean to be in the moment? It means to completely engross yourself in what you're doing at that point in time. If you're breathing, it means to focus on inhaling and exhaling; if you're walking, to focus on taking each step forward; and if you're running, focusing on the movements of your arms and legs. To focus on the single action of the moment, and to put aside the past and future.'

'Ah . . .'

'To adopt a mature attitude towards life is to know how to live in the moment.'

'Is that so?'

'Of course.'

Jungsuh glanced at Minjun, who seemed to have fallen deep in thought.

'Seize the day,' she suddenly said in English.

He laughed at her theatrical manner and replied:

'Carpe diem.'

'Just like what Mr Keating told his students: find your own walk, your own way of striving, pacing, direction. Anything you want!'

He was much comforted by Jungsuh that day. Before talking to her, he'd perhaps chosen to focus on the immediate future only because he couldn't quite see beyond it. It was a choice of the last resort. But that day, Jungsuh told him that his attitude towards life was rooted in religious traditions. Like what she said, he was perhaps on his way to becoming a more mature person. Would that mean that his life thus far had not been a futile endeavour? If so, that would be a relief. His efforts had not come to naught.

That day, Jungsuh told him, 'I guess that's why your coffee has become even better.' She was heaping praise on the movie *Dead Poets Society*, which she'd rewatched, when she suddenly changed the topic and told him how happy she was for him. As she took the first sip of his fresh brew, she also told him this:

'If you focus on cleaning when you're spring-cleaning, your house will be sparkly clean. It's the same with coffee. If you're focusing on coffee while making it, your coffee will turn out even more delicious. I keep thinking about how you see a cup of coffee as the distance between now and the future. I like this line. And your coffee is also truly delicious.'

Her words gave him strength and a confidence boost. The reason he was able to stand strong in his conviction was not just because he was anchored by coffee, but because people like Jungsuh, Yeongju, Jimi and the rest appreciated his coffee. The coffee he made was like a collaborative effort with people around him. A flavour unique to him, and the folks at Goat Beans and the bookshop. With good vibes coming together, there was no way the coffee would turn out bad.

From that day on, hand-drip coffee would be added to the regular menu. They decided to start with three brews from different regions. If possible, Minjun wanted to offer different flavours every month, but as Yeonju always said, it was important for things to find their place first. Minjun hoped that word would spread that Hyunam-dong Bookshop made delicious coffee; that his coffee would live up to the expectations of those who came by specially to try it; that the flavours of his coffee would meld into the bookshop's vibes, and the aroma would linger to warm the hearts of its customers.

This was the first time he aspired to achieve something with his coffee. *I did change a little*, he thought.

## Who Was the Man Who Came to Look for Yeongju?

The four of them shared a table. Seungwoo and Mincheol were there first, seated across from each other. A while later, Jungsuh joined them and soon after, Minjun sat down with a cup of coffee. While Seungwoo was editing, Jungsuh was crocheting and giving Minjun feedback on his coffee as he listened attentively. Mincheol, as usual, was staring at Jungsuh's hands, occasionally throwing questions at the three of them in turn.

From time to time, conversations criss-crossed the table. Jungsuh was curious what Seungwoo had received in return for editing Yeongju eonnie's writing; Mincheol bluntly asked Minjun if it was really alright for him to be sitting with them when Yeongju imo was so busy; Seungwoo asked Mincheol to let him take a look at his essay; Minjun wanted to know what was the most obvious note in the coffee that Jungsuh could pick out and whether she liked it or not. Meanwhile, seated behind the counter, Sangsu was leisurely leafing through his newest read in between attending to customers, while over at the bookshelves, Yeongju was checking the sales records and deciding where to shelve the books she'd ordered that day.

It happened then. Just as Minjun placed his palms on the table, ready to get up after receiving satisfactory feedback on his coffee, he saw the front door open, and a man walked in. He appeared to be scanning the bookshop for something when his gaze landed on Yeongju. A look of recognition lit up his eyes, but he kept standing at the entrance and continued to watch her. Judging from the emotions flitting across his brows and the soft set of his lips, he seemed to know her well. Was he a friend of Boss? Minjun turned towards Yeongju, who was busy arranging the books on the shelves. It was only then that she seemed to finally notice the persistent gaze. Slowly, she set down the books in her hands. At the look on her face, Minjun quietly lowered himself back into his seat. Their faces had clearly stiffened at the sight of each other.

When Minjun sat back down, Jungsuh and Mincheol turned to stare at him. Seeing his eyes fixed elsewhere, they twisted their bodies around to follow his gaze. Seungwoo, pen still in hand, was also staring at Yeongju and the stranger. She was saying something to the man, but she looked as though she couldn't decide whether to smile or cry. Slowly, she turned around and headed in their direction. Her expression crumbled immediately, and the fatigue she'd been holding back spilled over, draining her face of colour. There was a smile plastered on her face, but when she spoke to Minjun, the corners of her lips were quivering. Even so, her voice remained calm.

'Minjun, I'm going out for a short while.'

'Alright.'

She was about to walk away when Seungwoo stood up and called out to her.

'Yeongju.'

She turned around.

'Are you alright?'

Seeing the worry on his face, she knew that she'd failed to keep her emotions in check. She put on a faint smile.

'Yes, I'm fine.'

After they stepped out, the four of them silently returned to what they were doing. Who was the man who came to look for Yeongju, and why did she turn so pale? Since none of them had the slightest inkling, they refrained from speculating among themselves. Minjun returned to the café counter. Seungwoo, looking sombre, continued to work on the edits. Meanwhile, Jungsuh was attaching a strap to the eco bag she'd crocheted and Mincheol – chin propped on his right palm – continued to stare at her hands as if he would never tire of seeing her work.

Each time the front door swung open, all of them would look up simultaneously to check if Yeongju was back. She had already been out for two hours. Unable to stand it any longer, Jungsuh went up to Minjun and nudged him to give her a call, but he shook his head and suggested that they wait a little longer. Right then – twenty minutes before closing – Yeongju walked in, wearing the same expression she'd had when she left. Anyone could tell her eyes were slightly swollen. She forced a smile.

'Are you all waiting for me? Thanks very much. Minjun, all's good at the bookshop, right? Jungsuh, have you finished the eco bag already? That's for me, really? And Mincheol, why are you still here? Hurry, go home and get to bed. Seungwoo, I'm sorry. I don't think I can make it today. I'll buy you a meal next time, for sure. I'm really sorry. Thanks, everyone. Alright, I'm going to quickly tidy up the place and head home!'

Murmuring a response, the four of them looked on worriedly. In their own ways, whether they rearranged the books on the messy shelves, shut the windows, or aligned the tables and chairs, they tried to help out discreetly. Yeongju, who'd said she wanted to quickly tidy up the bookshop, was sitting in a daze at her desk, absentmindedly rearranging items. She closed the laptop, put the stationery back in its rightful place and aimlessly flipped through her notepad. Thinking back to what had happened earlier, she stifled a sob, and for a moment, she closed her eyes. Her face stiffened, and she hastily tried to rearrange her expression. As she struggled to hold herself together, Minjun slid up to her and sat down.

'Nothing much happened while you were away,' he told her. 'There was an unreasonable customer, but Sangsu handled it well.'

She nodded. 'Great. Good to hear everything's fine.' In her usual playful tone, she joked, 'I've been nailing myself to the bookshop thinking the place will collapse without me. Guess I'm free to play truant from now on.'

Minjun shook his head. 'We need you here. Would be nice to step out, but don't you think about it.'

Yeongju chuckled softly.

Jungsuh, Mincheol and Sangsu had left quietly while she was sitting in a daze. Only Seungwoo remained at the table, checking the text over and over while stealing occasional glances at her. Once Minjun was done tidying up for the day, he sat back down next to her. As if she'd been waiting, she started to talk.

'I was just thinking back to the day of the bookshop's opening. I've always lived rather chaotically, but that day was a complete whirlwind. The shelves were barely a quarter filled. I'd been so focused on getting the bookshop ready that I hadn't even thought of a name. In a rush, I named it Hyunam-dong Bookshop. At first, I regretted it. It sounded so tacky. But now, I love it. It feels as if the bookshop has lived in the neighbourhood for a long time.'

She paused.

'Back then, all I wanted was to take a break and get back into reading. One or two years is fine . . . I wanted to rest and do something I enjoyed. I thought it was fine even if I wasn't making money.'

'I kind of sensed it, seeing how much you're paying me,' Minjun said as he tried to imagine the bookshop with only a quarter of its current collection. 'But look at you now. You're so busy. I don't think you're getting any rest.'

'Mmm, I can't quite remember exactly when my goals changed, but it was after you arrived. One day, I told myself that I want to keep this bookshop running for a long time. But when I kept fretting over what to do to sustain the business, my anxiety grew, and that was when I started to lose sleep.'

'Did you figure out how to keep this place running?'

'Nope, not yet. And I'm a little scared. The busier I become, the more I revisit the past. I hated my life then, when everything was extremely hectic. I hated it so much that I abandoned everything and escaped. I left everything and everyone behind. I couldn't bear living like that anymore, so I listened to my heart and threw everything away.'

Minjun noticed that her voice was trailing off towards the end. He tilted his head, quietly observing her. Seungwoo slung his backpack on his right shoulder and walked towards them, silently handing Yeongju a piece of paper. Knowing that she would claim to be alright, he didn't ask how she was. She held out her hand for the paper and stood up.

'Thank you. But today, I . . .' Her voice was apologetic.

'You said it just now. Don't worry about it.'

She took a glance at the paper, which was filled with his edits and notes.

'Thank you, truly.'

The conflict on her face deepened, her eyes sad and red-rimmed. Seungwoo thought the look in her eyes was familiar. It was the same melancholy he'd glimpsed from her writing before meeting her in person. At that time, he hadn't been able to match her bubbly personality with the impression he got from her writing. Now he knew. The incident today probably stemmed from the root of her sadness. Who was the man? He wanted to know more, to find out what had happened, and what all this meant to her. But he suppressed his curiosity and simply gazed at her in silence. Inclining his head slightly, he was about to take his leave when Yeongju called out to him.

'Seungwoo.'

There was a hint of determination in her voice. He turned back.

'The man just now. Aren't you curious who he is?'

The wilting look on her face was at odds with her voice.

'I am,' Seungwoo replied, trying to keep his voice neutral.

'He is a friend of my ex-husband.'

He tried not to let the shock in his eyes show as he stared at her.

'He came to convey my ex-husband's regards and to see how I'm doing.'

'Ah . . . I see.'

He lowered his gaze as he tried to process her words.

Yeongju's eyes followed him as he bade her goodbye once more. The moment he pushed open the door and stepped out, she slumped into the chair, as if drained of the last ounce of energy. Next to her, Minjun sat in silence.

## Letting Go of the Past

That night, after a Herculean effort to shower and change, Yeongju lay on the bed. Her body and mind were completely drained. Yet sleep evaded her. In front of her, Chang-in's face flitted in and out in a blur.

Propping herself up, Yeongju reached for the book on her bedside table and went to the living room. She sat down by the window, turning to the page she'd left off. She tried to read, but nothing was going in. She decided to go back to the beginning of the book. She barely managed to run her eyes over a few sentences before she closed the book and drew her knees closer to her. She rested her chin on her hands, placed on her knees, as she gazed out the window. A man and woman – likely friends – were chatting as they walked past. Seeing them reminded her of the conversation with Taewoo that afternoon. As Chang-in's face surfaced from her memories, she tried to put a stop to it, but realised there was no longer a need to. She could now think of him whenever he crossed her mind . . . today, she'd received his permission to do so.

Taewoo was Chang-in's friend. And hers. The two men had been classmates at university before they joined the same company. That was where she first got to know Taewoo. Strictly speaking, he was also the one who introduced Chang-in to her. One day, they were having coffee at the office pantry when Chang-in walked in, so Taewoo made introductions. If Chang-in hadn't taken notice of her that day, he probably wouldn't have approached her when they next met again for a new project. As he slowly got closer to her, he confessed that it was his first time taking the initiative to speak to a girl, to invite her out over the phone for a meal, and to suggest that they date. Yeongju thought it was cute when he clumsily told her all this, so she agreed to date him. A year later, they got married.

They had many things in common. They were similarly inexperienced in matters of the heart, and their failed relationships from the past had largely followed the same track and ended on a similar note. They shared a laugh over how their previous partners had left them because they were sick of playing second fiddle to their careers. They delighted at how, being equally career-oriented and busy, there was no need to be apologetic. When one of them had to cancel a date to return to work, the other person never got angry. They couldn't, not when they'd have done the same, too. After a comfortable courtship, they naturally walked into marriage. There was no one else who would understand them as well, they both thought.

While they were equally career-minded, they didn't compete on who was faster; they chased after success hand in hand. The times they bumped into each other in the company cafeteria far exceeded the times they saw each other in the kitchen at home. While they were clueless about what the other was thinking in life, they were familiar with the projects that the other had worked on, how successful the projects were, and the roles they played. Their conversations were sparse, but the trust strong. At work, they held each other in high regard. Outside of work, they liked and respected each other as partners. No one would ever think that they would break up. Until the day Yeongju started to change.

Yeongju hated to dramatise what had happened to her. Company employees who suffered from burnout were a dime a dozen. Anyone could wake up one day and, out of the blue, dread going to the office. She was sure she wasn't the only one who'd experienced it. One day, in the middle of a meeting, she felt as though her heart was being squeezed. She wanted to say something, but her mind was shrouded in fog, and her legs turned into a puddle. The symptoms showed up again several times, and once, she felt so breathless – as if someone's hands were on her throat – that she fled from the office building.

Thinking that she was stressed out because of the project she was working on, that the symptoms were a manifestation of her fatigue, she continued to put up with the discomfort for several more months. One day, just as she was about to head out for work, she suddenly broke down and cried. There was no way she could make it to the office. Chang-in was startled at her outburst, but after telling her to get herself checked out at the hospital if she was unwell, he left for the office. For the first time in a long while, she took a day off that day and headed for the hospital. The doctor asked her when she had last gone on a vacation. She replied that she didn't remember. Subconsciously, she didn't want to tell him that she'd worked during her last vacation, too.

The doctor prescribed her some anxiety-relieving pills and said he would monitor her progress. Surveying her with kind eyes, he told her that she'd been living with anxiety for a long time, but because she hadn't realised it, her body was sending her these signals. He suggested that she take a break, even if it was only for a few days. Her shoulders crumpled and she broke down in front of him. It wasn't because of what he said. It was the kindness in his eyes. How long had it been since she had experienced such tender concern?

From Chang-in's perspective, it must have been baffling to see the 180-degree change in her. He must have been shocked to see the once brilliantly confident Yeongju reduced to a lost child overnight. She asked that he stay by her side, forcing him to sit down and listen to her. She wanted to talk about what was happening to her. She needed a listening ear. However, Chang-in was busy. He could only apologise, saying that he would make time for her later. She could see things from his perspective. Yet, she resented him for it. He cared for her, but he was never affectionate. It was the same for her. Their marriage was not built on affection.

Because he was never available, she had no choice but to work through it herself and make her own decisions. She reduced her workload and, where possible, she used up her annual leave. Now that she had more time, she started to think back to the past. As the doctor told her, she'd been living with anxiety. When had it all started? Perhaps the first year of high school. Yeongju grew up loving books and playtime with her friends, but things changed when she entered high school. While it was partly because her parents' business had crumbled overnight, the bigger reason was that she had been absorbing her parents' anxiety in the three years they spent trying to rebuild their company. Her parents always seemed to hover around looking strained and ashen-faced as they despaired over their failure. She soaked up their anxiety, and as a teenager, she was always teetering on the edge. At the thought of how she might also fail with a single misstep, she nailed herself to the study desk. Even then, she trembled with anxiety.

Yeongju thought back to her high school days, the times she was excitedly heading to her friends' homes only to suddenly stop, turn back and make a beeline for the study room, seized with panic. It was the same in university. She had very few memories of having fun with her friends. While people approached her because of her bright personality, they gradually distanced themselves when they found out that she could never make time for them.

She was always trying to be ahead of the curve. It wasn't as if she had to deliberately push herself to do it. Even without conscious effort, she still studied and worked hard. She lived like a robot who didn't know rest.

When Chang-in was at work, she spent her time at home thinking about how to live her life from then on. First, she would quit her job. When she informed Chang-in of her decision a few days later, he was surprised, but he accepted it. However, it wasn't enough for her. She wanted him to leave his job, too. If his life continued on the same trajectory, she felt as if she would be living with her past self; whenever she looked at him, it was as if she could feel her throat constricting, and her heart squeezed as the tears flowed. He should quit, for her sake. He shot down her request, of course. For several months, they clashed over their difference of opinion, until one day, she suggested that they end their relationship.

Everyone who knew the couple berated her. No husband in the world would agree to such a ridiculous request! It would be better that she quit on her own and go on a trip somewhere. She could understand why everyone took his side. Even she herself felt like the bad guy, both to herself, and to Chang-in.

The strongest opposition came from her mother. She started coming over every day and was careful to tread lightly around her son-in-law. She fussed over preparing a hearty breakfast for him, but she spewed curses at Yeongju which she had never once heard her use. Her mother, telling her to get a grip on herself, criticised Yeongju for being the only woman who would want to break up with a husband for working hard. If she was going to continue acting up, she wouldn't see her anymore. You can come to me after you've changed your mind, her mother told her. These were her mother's last words to her, because from then on, Yeongju stopped contacting her.

The divorce proceeded without much fanfare. She settled everything on behalf of the ever-busy Chang-in. He wrote what she told him to, stamped his seal on the documents as she instructed, and showed up when he was asked to. Even as they were heading for their final visit to the court, he still couldn't wrap his head around what was happening. Right till the end, he felt like a bystander observing everything unfold. Only after the divorce was finalised did he stare at her, his eyes empty.

'So, you're leaving me so that you can find happiness. Fine. Be happy then. You must be happy, because I'll be the miserable one. I never knew that anyone could suffer so much living with me. And that I was the source of your misery. Forget about me, then. Forget me, and all the memories we shared. Don't you ever think about me again. Don't you dare remember our times together, and all the moments we shared. I'll never forget you. I'll live my life resenting you. I'll remember you as the woman who brought me suffering. Don't you dare appear in front of me again. Let's never see each other for the rest of our lives.'

Tears streamed down his face. It was as if the weight of everything had hit him in that instant.

Now, for the first time since that day, she thought back to their final conversation. As if a dam had opened, she bawled at the top of her lungs. She had felt so sorry for Chang-in that she couldn't cry properly all this while. It was as if she didn't allow herself to fully let go, and only burst into tears when she could no longer hold them in. She thought she had to force herself to forget because he told her to. She was sorry for not being able to tell him she was sorry; she had done so much wrong that she couldn't even say that she was in the wrong. Today, Chang-in had sent Taewoo in his place to tell her that it was now alright to remember, alright to cry as much as she wanted.

'I chanced upon your newspaper column,' Taewoo told her. They had gone to a café near the bookshop.

'I told Chang-in to read it, and he did so without saying anything. After the divorce, he used to fly into a rage if I mentioned anything about you. It seemed that he read your column from time to time, as well as everything on your blog and social media. Looks like he has calmed down and has let go of the past. A few days ago, he told me to look for you and convey his words. He wanted to tell you that he, too, was at fault for many things. After the divorce, he reflected on himself and realised that he'd never asked you why you were having a hard time. He simply thought you would be fine in no time. He confessed that he was irritated because you didn't go to work, and threw away all the projects you were working on. The people in the office said some nasty things to him, too. He thought that by not passing on the stress he was receiving at work, he was already showing care and concern for you. But he realised it wasn't the case.'

'I would have done the same if I were in his shoes,' Yeongju said as she fiddled with the cup. 'It all happened so suddenly. If Chang-in acted the way I did, I would also be irritated. It was my fault. He didn't do anything wrong. Please tell him that.'

'You wouldn't know if you would have done the same. Maybe you wouldn't,' said Taewoo with a smile. 'Chang-in said you write well.'

Taewoo picked up his cup and took a sip of the coffee before setting it down. He looked her in the eye.

'He saw sadness in your writing. You should be happy doing what you enjoy, but your writing is sad. He said he would hate it if he was the reason that the ambitious and confident Yeongju had disappeared. That's why he thought he should let you know that he's living better than he thought he would. He still resents you sometimes, but he's not miserable. I don't know if I should tell you this . . .'

He hesitated, taking another gulp of coffee.

'He said that you and him made great partners. But partners can only stay together when their goals are the same. Because you two shared the same goals, you stayed by each other's side. But once someone swerves in a different direction, there's no choice but to disband. That was how he put it. Disband. He said that if he really loved you, he would have done what you wanted. But he couldn't, and he was sorry for that. But since you left him so readily, you probably didn't love him that much, either. The disbandment was possible because both of you thought of each other as partners. He wanted me to tell you this.'

She didn't react to his words.

'He said you'd cut off contact with everyone in the past when you left. But you don't have to now. He said that we should continue to keep in touch, too. When I heard that, I was so pissed off. I can think for myself. Who does he think he is? And you. Who are you two to decide on your own whether we should be seeing each other or not.'

Yeongju smiled wanly.

'Yeongju.'

'Yeah?'

'I'm sorry.'

Yeongju looked at him, her eyes red.

'I was too hard on you. I thought you'd abandoned Chang-in too easily and I was very angry. A married couple should work through all issues together. That was what I thought. But later on, I realised that I was thinking more about Chang-in than about you. I hadn't considered how badly hurt you were back then. Even though this apology comes too late, I'm sorry.'

She wiped away the tears, looking down.

'Chang-in said he would like to meet you again in three years. That's about the time he will return from the US office. He's doing very well at work, as usual. He said he was born to work. After you left him so abruptly, he started to do regular health check-ups. He's in the pink of health, physically and mentally. Oh. He says there's no need to meet in three years, if either of you are married or have a new lover. Because it would be rude to the new person in your lives. Most importantly, if both of you are still single, don't ever consider the possibility of getting back together. He said that he has no such feelings at all. He can never fully get over how you treated him towards the end.'

She smiled. She remembered how he used to build a wall around him when it came to women.

On her end, she told Taweoo about how she ended up opening a bookshop and how she had run the place over the years.

'It was my childhood dream to own a bookshop,' she said. 'And after the divorce, I couldn't think of anything except opening one.'

She was desperate to return to the bright and cheery middle-school kid who loved books more than anything else. She wanted to start from there again. That was all she could think about.

Right after their divorce, Yeongju started to look for a location for the bookshop. She settled on Hyunam-dong because of the character hyu 휴, which came from the hanja 休 for rest. Once she heard that, her heart was set. She'd never been here before, but it felt like a place where there were many people she'd known for a long time. Originally, her plan was to take things slow. But once she had a goal, it was like stepping on the accelerator. She diligently visited estate agents to look for available properties and it took her only a few days to find her current location. She was told that it was a single-floor residential unit, but the previous owner had opened a café there, which later went bust. The space was left empty for a few years. The moment she set her eyes on it, she knew it was the one. There was much refurbishment work to be done as it had been derelict for years, but it meant that she could customise every corner. Just like rebuilding her life, she was determined to give this place a new lease of life.

The next day, she signed the contract, and at the same time, she secured an officetel unit nearby with a great view. She had the means to do so because she'd been working almost without any rest since graduation, and there was also the money they'd split when they sold their marital home. The renovation only took two months. Yeongju was hands-on for the entire process, from hiring the contractor and discussing the design to choosing the materials. On the opening day of the bookshop, she sat on a chair and looked out the window. That moment, the weight of everything that had happened crashed upon her and she broke down. Every day, in between fresh tears, she ordered the stock, handled the customers, and made the coffee. When she finally regained some of her senses, the bookshop was seeing more customers and she was back to reading daily like in her middle-school days. It was as if she'd been at the mercy of tumultuous waves, knocking her into a daze as they pushed and pulled her in different directions until, luckily, she landed in a place she really loved.

She grew stronger at the bookshop, but at the same time, the guilt she felt towards Chang-in continued to expand. The guilt of one-sidedly cutting off their relationship, the guilt of not getting to make a proper apology, the guilt of not giving him time, the guilt of not seeking him out after the divorce. He'd told her never to see him again, yet she struggled over whether she should apologise to him in person. Today, Chang-in had sent her a message loud and clear – I've apologised to you, so it's okay for you to apologise, too. And this would be the extent of their relationship.

From now on, she could think of him as much as she wished to. Her thoughts returned to the past, unpacking all the memories and feelings she'd been suppressing. Images and memories stabbed through her heart, but she thought she was now strong enough for it. She'd expended too much energy bottling things up; they lodged deep inside her. From now on, she could let go. Even if the tears returned, it was something she had to see through. To learn to let go. When the time came for her to be able to recollect the past without tears, she would finally be able to put her hand up and happily hold on to the present. And to cherish it dearly.

## As if Everything Was Fine

Despite the incident the day before, the atmosphere at the bookshop remained the same. There was a slight frenzy during the peak hours, but when all was quiet, it was time to enjoy slices of fruit. In between, there were a couple of minor episodes. When Yeongju was there alone at noon to get the bookshop ready for the day, Heejoo stepped in. She'd never come before opening.

Surprised, Yeongju asked if something had happened, but Heejoo simply looked at her with narrowed eyes and said nothing. Heejoo had seen her through the difficult times when the bookshop first opened. It looked like she was here to check on her again, as if afraid that she would rebound to her old self. Yeongju looked back into her watchful eyes and laughed heartily. Seemingly relieved, Heejoo gave her a few suggestions for the book club before taking her leave. At the door, she paused. 'Call me if you need anything,' she said.

In the afternoon, Jungsuh popped by with two slices of Yeongju's favourite cheesecake. 'What's with the cheese-cake?' she asked. Jungsuh, in her unique silvery voice, told her to eat them when she craved a nibble. 'Thank you,' Yeongju said. With a bright smile, Jungsuh waved goodbye.

In fact, the person who was the most help to Yeongju – which she probably didn't realise – was Sangsu. In his own roundabout way, he helped to ease her burden. Upon seeing a customer trying to approach her, he would stare at them persistently until their eyes met. When that happened, the customer would usually end up going to Sangsu instead, and, sucked into his particular brand of literary colloquialism, they would end up leaving the bookshop with at least a book or two.

Thanks to Sangsu holding the fort, Yeongju could focus on the list of questions for the upcoming book talk in a few days' time. They would be screening a movie for the first time. The plan was to watch it together from half past seven to nine, before moving on to a discussion of the movie, as well as the novel, until ten at night. As they'd invited a movie critic to lead the discussion, she would be able to participate mostly as a listener this time.

She'd spoken on the phone with the critic once and their conversation had boosted her confidence about experimenting with a new format. He sounded cheery and well-spoken. Most importantly, he seemed to be the type who enjoyed speaking about topics he was passionate about.

In any case, she had prepared a couple of questions based on the novel. Later, when she watched the movie, she would include a few more questions comparing the two mediums. Muttering the questions under her breath, she edited them with a ballpoint pen. Out of nowhere, Minjun came up to her and peered down at her list. Startled, he asked:

'Is this the list of questions for the upcoming book talk?'

'Oh? Yeah, it is.'

She looked up at his abrupt question.

'Is the title *After the Storm*?'

'That's right,' she laughed, realising why he was shocked.

'The screenwriter is coming?' Minjun's eyes widened in disbelief.

'Nope. Our bookshop is not at that level yet.'

'Then who's coming?'

Minjun followed Yeongju to her desk as they talked.

'A movie critic is hosting the talk.'

'Ah, I see. Right. How could Director Kore-eda be coming?'

He sat down next to her and furtively examined her face.

'You've watched his movies?' Yeongju asked as she called up a Word document on the computer, oblivious to his stare.

Her eyes were a little swollen, but she looked much better, and the colour had returned. The swelling wasn't as bad as yesterday. Looking relieved, he replied:

'Of course, I'm a fan. I've watched almost all of his films.'

'Just by reading his books, I don't quite understand why his work is deemed a masterpiece.' She shrugged as she clicked on a sentence to edit.

'You've not watched anything by Director Kore-eda?'

She shook her head. 'I guess you've watched this movie?'

'I did, last year.'

'How was it?'

'Well. How should I put this? It's the kind of movie that makes me think and reflect. It made me ponder whether I've become the adult I wanted to be, and what it means to live a life chasing after dreams.'

'And your conclusion is?'

She was methodically typing in the sentences she'd edited on paper.

'. . . If I remember correctly, the mother of the male protagonist said that only by giving up something can happiness be within your grasp. For the longest time, he couldn't write a novel, right?'

She nodded.

'Even though he wasn't writing, he was still chasing after the dream of completing a novel, and it made him miserable. No wonder his mother came to that conclusion. Because of this wretched dream of his, my son is unhappy. Watching that scene, I found myself agreeing with the mother rather than feeling sorry for the guy. It's true. Dreams can make you miserable.'

Yeongju paused, her fingers resting on the keyboard.

'But his mother also said this: if you're chasing after an impossible dream, you can't enjoy everyday life. She's right. But if you feel happy chasing the dream, then that's also a type of happiness, isn't it?'

She glanced at him for a moment before her fingers continued dancing across the keyboard.

'I think everyone's different,' Minjun said. 'It depends on what they value. There are people who would give everything to achieve their dreams. Although there are many more who can't.'

'Minjun, which side do you stand on?'

Minjun thought back to the last few years of his life.

'The latter, I think. While I might be happy chasing a dream, it seems like I have a better chance at happiness after abandoning it. I just want to enjoy living.'

'Is that why we're on the same wavelength?' Yeongju rested her hands on the laptop and smiled at him.

'But Boss, you've achieved your dreams.'

'That's true. And I'm enjoying what I have now.'

'Then, the conclusion is that we aren't on the same page,' he quipped, drawing a line between them. She shrugged her shoulders, laughing.

'I don't think much of dreams that are stripped bare of pleasure. Dreams, or pleasure? If I have to choose one, I'll take the latter. That said, my heart still flutters at the word *dream*. A life without dreams is as dry as a life without tears. There's a line in Hermann Hesse's *Demian* that goes: "But no dream lasts forever, each dream is followed by another, and one should not cling to any particular dream."'

'Hearing this makes me hope that this kind of life can also be accepted,' said Minjun, getting up slowly.

Yeongju looked up. 'What kind of life?'

'First, to cruise alongside what life has to offer. Then, to live it chasing dreams. And for the last shot in life, to live the life that I was better suited for, and to enjoy it as much as I can.'

'That'll be nice. Oh, Minjun.'

Minjun's eyes were trailing a customer who was heading for the café counter with his eyes glued to his phone. When Yeongju called out to him, Minjun turned back towards her.

'The movie critic who is coming is from the same university as you. Same faculty, and same cohort.'

His eyes went round.

'Really? What's his name?'

'Yoon Sungchul.'

Minjun couldn't quite believe his ears, but the next moment, everything seemed to make sense.

'Wait. How would you know the university he graduated from, much less the year?'

'He was the one who approached me to propose a book talk based on Director Hirokazu Kore-eda's work. And he included those details in his proposal.'

'What? He sure wrote all kinds of random things in the proposal,' Minjun laughed in disbelief.

'Yeah. Definitely TMI.'

Yeongju had chuckled when she read the proposal, wondering who in the world would include so much detail about themselves. Immediately, she sent a reply to thank him for the wonderful idea and to work on finding a suitable date. Even though she'd only just learnt his name, she somehow trusted him. She could tell, from the way his proposal was written, that he had a strong passion for and knowledge of the director's work. More importantly, just by reading a few lines of his proposal, she knew that he had put effort into writing it. If he'd spent so much effort on a proposal, he was likely the type she could trust and entrust responsibility to.

'Do you know him well?' Yeongju asked.

'Yes, very much so,' he replied, hurrying towards the customer who was almost at the café counter.

## Let's Like Each Other

Yeongju brought the A-type stand in from outside the book-shop and closed the door. She cast a glance at Seungwoo, who stood in front of a shelf of novels, and walked up to him. He showed her the book he'd just pulled out – Nikos Kazantzakis's *Zorba the Greek*, the author she'd referenced on their first meeting – before slotting it back to its position.

'When you mentioned Kazantzakis during our book talk, I went home that night and reread this book. Honestly, the first time I read it, I wasn't particularly touched. I only finished it because everyone else said it was good,' he said, scanning the books on the shelf before turning to her.

'I enjoyed it a lot more this time, perhaps because of the person who brought me back to the book. I can understand why people love Zorba. Come to think of it, I was never a Zorba in my life, not even for a moment. It's probably people like me who end up admiring Zorba.'

Their eyes met.

'Aren't you one of us, too?' he asked as he walked past her and headed for the two-seater sofa.

She sat down next to him. Under the lights, they nestled comfortably into the sofa. That moment, Seungwoo felt as if his worries from the past few days were swept away with a single stroke.

'I became curious as I read the book. Did you change because of Zorba, and if so, in what way? Or did you simply admire him?'

Yeongju thought she knew the reason for his question. He seemed to have caught on that she'd once been carefree and happy, but somehow, she'd imprisoned herself in the cage she built. He must be hoping that she would break free from the cage and live as carefree as Zorba. A different life from the one she had. A life that wasn't an imprisonment. A life not held captive by her own thoughts. A life not shackled to the past. She replied a little tartly.

'Zorba, to me, is just one of the many freedoms out there in the world. I love the freedom he represents, but I never wanted to live like him. In fact, the thought never crossed my mind. I was born to be like the narrator of the story, as someone who admires Zorba. That's me.'

Nodding, Seungwoo said, 'But if you admire someone, wouldn't you look up to them? And aspire to be like them, hopefully, even if it's just a little?'

'That's also true. I did try to be like him. I think you would have also enjoyed that particular scene in the novel.'

Seungwoo turned towards her.

'The dance?'

'Yes. When I was reading, I thought: *let me live like this, too. Dance, even in disappointment. Dance, even in failure. Let go. Laugh, and keep laughing.*'

'So, were you successful?'

'Half successful. But I'm not born to be like Zorba. Sometimes, tears follow my laughter. Halfway through the dance, I may fall. But I'll get up again to dance, and to laugh. I'm trying to live like this.'

'That'll be a pretty cool life.'

'Is that so?'

'Sounds like it.'

Looking at him, she chuckled.

'Why? Does it look like my life is very frustrating? Like I'm trapped in the past?'

He shook his head.

'That's not it. We're all shackled to our pasts. I just wanted to steer your thoughts in a direction that'll benefit me.'

There was a short silence.

'How?'

'Like Zorba.'

'What do you mean?'

'To love effortlessly.'

'Love? Effortless?' she retorted, laughing, but he didn't laugh along.

'Only towards me. I'm being greedy.'

Silence came in between them.

'I have a question for you. May I?' Seungwoo asked.

Yeongju nodded, looking as if she could already guess his question.

'That friend of your ex-husband's. He didn't try to harass you or anything, did he?'

She had suspected that he was going to ask about her ex-husband, but this wasn't what she had expected at all. She laughed out loud.

'No, he's a good person. Also, my friend.'

'Alright, I'm glad to hear that. You looked really upset that day.'

'I can understand why you thought that,' she replied, trying to keep her voice bright.

Seungwoo said nothing and leaned back on the sofa. A moment later, he sat up again.

'There's something else I'm curious about.'

'Uhm. Do I have to answer this too?'

Her voice was still as cheery. He couldn't tell if she was hiding her feelings beneath the façade.

'Why did you tell me who that man was?'

Their eyes met. Her eyes were quickly morphing into the look she wore when telling him about the existence of her ex-husband. Sad. Conflicted. She was definitely masking her feelings. He was sure now.

'Because I didn't want to lie.' Her voice remained calm.

'What do you mean?'

'Keeping silent can also be a form of lying. Sometimes, not saying anything makes no difference. But sometimes, it becomes a problem.'

'When is that?' he replied evenly.

'When the other person has special feelings.'

At her words, Seungwoo leaned back into the sofa and echoed what she said.

'Special feelings.'

Silence. And again, Seungwoo was the one who broke it.

'I read your writing before meeting you.'

She turned her head and stared, as if asking, *really*?

'While reading it, I was curious about the person you are. When we met, you were different from what I imagined you to be. Remember that day you asked me if I was similar to my writing?'

Seungwoo continued, his gaze locked on hers. 'I wanted to return the same question. What about you? The way I see it, I don't think it's the same, but I wanted to know how you feel.'

'You should've asked.'

'I didn't want to make you flustered, because I would have said that I don't think you're similar to your writing.

I would hate to see you flustered. I guess I was already carrying those special feelings back then.'

In silence, Yeongju glanced at him before averting her eyes to look straight ahead. Meanwhile, Seungwoo continued to gaze at her.

'But,' he said, 'I changed my mind. I think you might be like your writing. No, scratch that. I'm sure. You are very much like your writing. A little wilted.'

'A little wilted,' she repeated, laughing softly.

'A little wilted because it's sad. Yet you have a smile on your face. I can't tell what you're thinking on the inside and that's made me even more curious.'

The cold had melted away. Even the lightest winter coat was too warm. Most people wore their thinnest jacket or held it in their hands. The season of wearing t-shirts had returned. On the other side of the window behind the sofa, the people passing by were dressed lightly. They were probably on their way home after a long day outside. As they walked past the bookshop, they cast a casual glance in their direction.

Seungwoo spoke her name.

'Yeongju.'

'Yes?'

'I'll keep on liking you.'

Yeongju spun her head and stared at him.

'I know why you told me about your ex-husband. You're telling me to stay away.'

'What do you mean, stay away? That's not my intention.'

Yeongju was flustered.

'Yeongju.'

Seungwoo called out to her more firmly, his gaze steady.

'How long were you married?'

This time, Yeongju looked at him in surprise.

'I had a girlfriend of six years. That was my longest relationship. We were just short of getting the certificate.'

'That's not what I'm saying.'

She didn't try to hide her conflicted feelings as she spoke.

'I told you about my ex-husband . . . to make it easier for you to move on.'

'I'm not going to move on. So what if you were married?' Seungwoo spoke calmly.

'It's not because I was once married that I think we can't be together . . . You're right. There's nothing wrong with being a divorcee. Divorce is no big deal. But, Seungwoo—'

He continued to gaze at her with the same calmness.

'It's not the fact that I was divorced, but the reason for the divorce that is more important. Why I got the divorce.'

At his silence, Yeongju's face flushed as the words came tumbling out in a rush.

'I'm the one who called it off. I hurt my ex-husband a lot. I ended the relationship selfishly in line with my wishes. I loved him. I definitely did, in my own way. But at some point in time, I started to put myself ahead of him. Instead of giving up my way of life to love him, I gave up on him to pursue my life. I put myself first, and I want to maintain the life I have now. I'm the kind of person who may throw someone away again for my own sake, for my own life. I'm not the person you will want to keep close to you.'

She flushed a dull crimson while he continued to gaze at her quietly.

Yeongju seemed to think that she held full responsibility for the divorce. She had branded herself a very selfish and self-centred person and that was why she thought she might possibly hurt another person again. This was why she didn't want to love ever again. But Seungwoo had never once met anyone who hadn't hurt someone else, nor had he met a completely selfless person who places others above themselves. He was no different. In his past relationships, he had hurt the other party and was told how selfish he had been. At the same time, he was also hurt and he, too, thought the other person was selfish. No one was any different and, deep down, Yeongju was probably aware of the fact, too.

Yet, it seemed like she couldn't get over it; she couldn't forget the fact that she had abandoned someone, and that person was hurt because of her actions. Or perhaps she was miserable because she realised what kind of a person she was. Seungwoo thought he could understand how she felt. If the same thing happened to him, perhaps he would also have acted the way Yeongju did.

'Alright. I know what you're trying to tell me,' Seungwoo said, holding back what was really on the tip of his tongue.

'Thank you for understanding.' Yeongju tried not to let her feelings show.

'Did I . . . upset you by having feelings for you?'

He looked at her tenderly. She shook her head.

'Of course not. But . . .'

'Let's leave it there for today.'

Without looking at her, Seungwoo got up and headed for the door. She followed behind. At the door, he paused and turned around. He liked even just looking at her. And it hurt to realise it. He had an urge to pull her into his arms and pat her back softly. He wanted to tell her that everyone lives their lives hurting people and getting hurt. In life, people get together, and sometimes, they break up. Yeongju was just going through what was part and parcel of life, and she probably knew it, too. However, he kept those words and feelings to himself as he replied evenly:

'I'd like to continue with the seminars. Or would you prefer that I don't?'

Yeongju shook her head.

'No, of course not. But it's just, I—'

She looked at him, as if asking if he would really be okay.

'I'm sorry,' he said.

Yeongju looked at him, not understanding why he was apologising.

'I feel like I've put you in a difficult position.'

She didn't know what to say, so she simply gazed at him. For a long moment, they held each other's gaze. Finally, he spoke.

'Yeongju. I'm not asking you to marry me. I'm just saying, let's like each other.'

Having said what he wanted, he dipped his head in farewell and pushed the door open. The lights outside the bookshop lit up the path. As for Yeongju, she stood by the door for a long time.

## A Life Surrounded by Good People

Minjun had never seen this side of Jimi – clapping her hands and throwing her head back, roaring with laughter. Across from Yeongju and her, Sungchul continued talking animatedly, as if invigorated by their reactions. Minjun tried to recall if Sungchul had been as loquacious in the past, but he shrugged. There was no point in reading into it. If he was, Minjun would think that leopards don't change their spots; if not, he would probably think that, as expected, people change over time.

An hour ago, Jimi had stepped into the bookshop, saying that she wasn't going to work today. Because she had nowhere else to go and she didn't want to return home, she decided to come here. When she said this, she seemed to be her usual self. Hence, when she made her announcement, Minjun felt as if someone had delivered a sharp blow to his head.

'I'm going to get a divorce.'

After she said that, she calmly took a sip of the coffee, and then another, praising it for its rich flavour. Meanwhile, Minjun was still stumped. He didn't quite know how he should react, so he simply stood still, his face awkwardly stiffening as if in anger. Jimi glanced up at him before taking another sip.

'This expression is perfect. You don't know how you're supposed to react, right? Me too. I don't know how I should feel. That's why I decided not to feel anything now.'

Minjun couldn't find a response to that. Instead, he carefully refilled her cup, and she murmured a thanks. Like her expression, her voice was no different from usual. It was impossible to tell that something had happened to her. Not when she was laughing next to Yeongju.

*

The movie had started. The thirty participants of the book talk sat down together for a screening of Director Hirokazu Kore-eda's *After the Storm*. Once he was done tidying up at the café, Minjun joined them right at the back. Throughout the movie, the male lead Ryota was a good-for-nothing. When the credits rolled, it was as if the audience had been thrown a question: have we become the person we wanted to be?

Despite watching it for the second time, it still struck him that Ryota was really bad at life. He sighed at the typical portrayal of a man living alone in a huge mess, but because it was part of the setup of Ryota being bad at life in general, it didn't feel too much like a stereotype. Ryota was bad at even the one thing that was precious to him in life – writing a novel.

After the movie, Yeongju and Sungchul moved in front of the audience to get ready for the discussion. Meanwhile, Minjun's thoughts continued to linger on the movie and the reason Ryota was so bad at navigating life. It was his first life. His first time dreaming of becoming a novelist, his first time abandoned by the wife he loved, his first time becoming a father to his beloved son. That was why his behaviour was clumsy, and his speech bumbling. That was why he looked so woebegone.

Looking at Sungchul answering the questions Yeongju posed to him, it struck Minjun that this, too, was his first life. Sometimes, movies made him see what should have been plainly obvious. He felt a course of electricity run through him. Because it's our first life, worries are aplenty, and anxiety, too. Because it's our first life, it's precious. Because it's our first life, nobody knows what'll happen even in five minutes.

Sungchul spoke smoothly, as if he was a news anchor reading off the prompter. He was articulate as he explained to the audience how the director's philosophy of life was reflected in his work. Looking at his shining eyes, Minjun felt a zing in his chest. Seeing a person enjoying what they love to do warms your heart. And because that person was a friend, his heart was positively swelling with happiness.

Minjun met up with Sungchul the same day Yeongju mentioned Sungchul's name to him. He called Sungchul immediately on his way home, smoothly looking up his number and pressing the call button as if they'd only last spoken yesterday. When Sungchul answered with 'Hey! Where are you?', both of them burst out laughing. Right away, Sungchul came to find him.

That night, they stayed at Minjun's place and chatted until daybreak, pouring shots for each other from the bottles of soju Sungchul had bought, washing down the awkwardness and distance of time.

'It's a good thing I didn't manage to find a corporate job,' Sungchul said as he explained how he ended up becoming a movie critic.

'You aren't even affiliated with any organisation. How can you call yourself a movie critic?' Minjun scoffed, to which Sungchul replied nonchalantly, 'I critique movies. Of course I'm a movie critic.' He went on to explain in what Minjun liked to call his 'warped logic':

'Look. There's no difference in the way I write and that of some other critic who claims to be acknowledged by so and so.'

'And?'

'Those people are just playing Go Stop by their own rules.'

'So?'

'Is a movie critic working for some established movie magazine better than me at watching movies? Do they write better than I do? There's no guarantee. People only think their writing is good because it's published in a magazine, and if there are a few people who go, "Oh, this guy writes well," then the person will be, more often than not, deemed a good writer. Do you know how common it is for impressions to form this way?'

'Isn't this the same tune you sang the other time? How is it that you haven't made any progress all these years! Still stuck at the logic about how a movie becomes a ten-million hit because of three million moviegoers.'

'What I'm saying is, there's no absolute yardstick in this world. Of course, there are those who are obviously good, and also obviously bad ones. But when two people are about the same, then it boils down to who has a shinier business card. Look at my writing. This is good writing.'

'Who says so?'

'Me! I, the one who has read countless movie reviews, say so! This is the gold standard of writing. You wait. Once I become famous, people are going to say that my writing went up a notch.'

'Hey, why are we so hung up on this?'

'Well, in short, I'm a movie critic who writes movie reviews. I don't need anyone to bestow the title on me. If I say so, then I am. That's enough, and isn't this what life is about?'

Sungchul paused and, as if tickled by something, he started to laugh.

Hitting Minjun on the arm, he exclaimed, 'Do you know how much I missed bantering with you? How have you been? Are you really going to stay a barista?'

'I think so.' Minjun downed his shot.

'Is it something you wanted to do?'

'No?'

'And you're okay with that?'

'Is there anything I wanted besides finding a job? I wanted to get into a good company, live a stable life with a decent salary. But it didn't work out. I shouldn't keep holding on to the hope.'

'Is it because you think it's too late?'

For a moment, Minjun was lost in thought.

'Maybe? I don't know. But I came to dislike wanting to find a job. I'm having fun now. That's enough and isn't this what life is about?'

Thumping Sungchul on the arm, he continued:

'Making coffee is an art. It's creative work. The same batch of beans can yield a different flavour today and tomorrow. It depends on the temperature, the humidity, my mood, and the atmosphere at the bookshop. And it makes me happy to find the right balance among them.'

'All hail the wise man.'

'Shut up.'

Sungchul stared at Minjun. It had been a long while, indeed.

'. . . Wasn't it tough?'

'It wasn't easy, but I acted like I was okay. Even though the moment I had been waiting for didn't come, I don't think that my life is a failure because of that.'

'You're not a failure.'

Minjun burst out laughing.

'Back then, I told myself not to jump to conclusions to figure out what things mean. I decided not to think too deeply about life. Instead, I spent time eating well, watching movies, doing yoga and making coffee. I started to have an interest in other things besides myself and when I turned back to reflect, I realised that my life wasn't a failure after all.'

'That's right.'

'Now that I think about it, I received a lot of help from others.'

'Who?'

Leaning against the wall, Minjun looked at Sungchul.

'People around me. When I was trying to be indifferent, they did the same for me. Even though I didn't say anything, they seemed to sense my feelings, so none of them tried to make a fuss to comfort me or worry about me. I felt like I was being accepted for who I am. I never had to struggle to explain myself, or to reject who I was. And now that I'm older, I'm starting to think like this . . .'

Sungchul snorted and laughed at the same time.

'Why are you behaving like a wise old man? Alright, I'll ask you. So, what were you thinking?'

'A life surrounded by good people is a successful life. It might not be success as defined by society, but thanks to the people around you, each day is a successful day.'

'Woah . . .' Sungchul exclaimed. 'I like this line. If you see me use it in my writing next time, don't complain.'

'Please, you have such a bad memory you'll forget this in no time.'

'Hey hey . . . This is why it's no good meeting Kim Minjun. You know me too well.'

Laughing, Sungchul raised a toast to Minjun.

'So, do you think we're a good person to each other?' Minjun asked as they clinked glasses.

'You're the problem. I'm already a good person.'

'Then there's no problem. I was born a good person.'

Looking at him now, there was not a trace of the Sungchul who had been drunk a few days earlier, slurring his words. All his sentences were simple, clear and concise. He looked relaxed and happy. For the first time, Minjun thought his friend was good-looking. Not because he was handsome, but because he was glowing.

Turning away from Sungchul, Minjun looked at Yeongju, who was next to him, and Jimi, who sat in the audience. They chuckled when Sungchul said something interesting and nodded their heads in agreement when he was earnestly explaining something. Their smiles seemed to draw out the eloquence in him. They were the same smiles that gave Minjun the gift of time. Time to slowly accept life, and to believe that he could keep moving forward even as he stumbled and made mistakes along the way.

Minjun wanted to send the same smiles to these two women who were now acting like everything was okay. He wanted to do so for the people around him. He had been in a very good mood for the past few days. It was as if a thought that was sprouting had come to full bloom on its own. As if the Minjun of the past and the Minjun of the present had finally come together for the first time in a long while. The Minjun of the past accepted him for who he was, and the Minjun of the present accepted who he had been. Life felt as though it had come full circle.

The morning after they stayed up almost the whole night chatting, Sungchul, who had woken up earlier, shook him awake. When he opened his eyes blearily, Sungchul said, 'I want to ask you something before I go.'

Minjun propped himself up.

'What?'

'What happened to the holes?'

'The holes?'

'Yeah. You said you made the buttons but were stuck because there were no holes. How is it now?'

Minjun shook his head, trying to chase away the sleepiness. He stared up at his friend, a thoughtful look on his face.

'Easy. I changed my shirt. This time I cut the holes first before I made the buttons that fit. Now, the shirt is buttoned up nicely.'

'What? That's it?'

'Somewhere in the world, there'll be people who cut big holes and wait for people to come help them make the buttons that'll fit the holes. I can tell what you're thinking. You're thinking that the system remains as it is and what's the point if a few kind people help each other out? You're right. But like I said yesterday, I need time.'

'What do you mean, time?'

'Time to rest, time to think, time to do what I like, time to reflect.'

Sungchul nodded in understanding. He got up and headed for the door. This time, Minjun was the one with a question.

'How about you? How did you do that?'

'Do what?'

'You had good grades too. But how did you manage to watch so many movies? How is it that you were able to still find time to do things you liked when you were so busy?'

'You're really a fool,' Sungchul said as he tapped his fingers on the sink. 'Obviously, it's because I liked doing it. What other reason can there be?'

'That's it?' Minjun replied, still lying on the blankets. Laughing, Sungchul waved goodbye. When he'd put on his shoes, Sungchul turned back to look at Minjun, who was still stretched out with his eyes closed.

'I'll drop by the bookshop after work. It's going to be my hideout from now on.'

Without opening his eyes, Minjun waved goodbye.

# A Test of Feelings

One day, when Minjun walked into Goat Beans earlier than usual, he saw Jimi sitting by herself and fiddling with coffee beans. Seeing him, she reached for the ground coffee on the table. 'Use this for today's brew.' Like a tame puppy, Minjun did what he was told. Jimi savoured the coffee slowly and, in silence, she set the cup on the table. Minjun drank his coffee quietly while observing what Jimi was up to. She was mixing the beans, and although it didn't seem like she had a purpose, it also didn't look like she was doing it out of the blue.

'If I keep mixing these randomly . . . maybe one day, I'll be able to discover a coffee that's more delicious than anything I've ever tasted,' Jimi muttered under her breath, not looking up.

Noticing that Minjun was even quieter than usual, Jimi said, 'If you've got something to say, say it.'

'It's nothing.'

'Just spit it out.'

'Is it because of me . . .'

Jimi gave him a sidelong glance.

'What are you on about?'

'Is it because of what I said to you that day?'

'Oho.'

She shook her head in disbelief.

'Is that why you have this shrivelled-up look to you? Right now, and the other day, too.'

Feeling sorry again, Minjun felt his face stiffen.

'I want to tell you this. Thanks to you, I was able to look at my married life objectively. I'm thankful. Because of you, I was able to end the relationship that had dragged on painfully for so long.'

Despite her words, he was still tense.

'It was a mistake trying to embrace something that couldn't work out at all. This episode made me realise that being able to end things that don't work is a way of living well. There're so many instances of people not being able to put an end to things because of fear, of others' judgement and of the possibility of regretting it in the future. I was the same. But now, I feel so relieved.'

Turning to Minjun, Jimi leaned her left side against the back of the chair and smiled. It was no different from her usual smile. Taking a deep breath, she exhaled and started her story.

'After you talked to me, I realised I needed time. Time to re-evaluate my relationship with my husband. Hence, I stopped swearing and nagging him. I stopped complaining about him all the time. I welcomed him back home with a smile even though he came back at three in the morning, and I smiled as if nothing had happened when his clothes reeked of an unfamiliar perfume. The next day, I continued to smile, even after he made a pigsty of our house. I decided to observe him, to look at our relationship in an objective manner. That's all I did, but that man started to change. He stopped coming in past midnight, and he swore that he was never once unfaithful. And when I came home after work, the house was all tidied up. I didn't know what to make of it. For the next few evenings, I awkwardly ate the dinner he cooked, and I started to wonder if that was how life would be for us. If I didn't ask him that question, we would probably have continued to live like this.'

Jimi paused. Turning her head, she looked past the roasting machines and out the window. Her favourite season was in full bloom. Spring.

'While eating the dinner that man made, I asked him: why have you been treating me so well recently? He told me it was because I was nice to him, so he treated me the same way. Then, I asked: you were acting that way because I didn't treat you nicely in the past? He replied, yes. I asked him again. Did you deliberately act that way because I treated you badly? He hesitated for a while and admitted it. I asked him when he'd started putting on this show and why that was the only way he could think of. He told me it was because I had stomped on his pride. I had told him point-blank that he was a lazy person who wasn't good at anything. He was angry and wanted to rebel by becoming an even worse version of himself. That moment sealed it. I decided to get a divorce. Everything ended in that instant.'

Jimi downed the last of the lukewarm coffee. Her eyes were red.

'I told you before that I wanted to stay single, right? When I was young, each time there was a family gathering, all my aunts complained about their husbands. Basically, they grumbled about how they bent over backwards cleaning up after their husbands. After marriage, a once cool man became a man-child overnight. A kid that their wives needed to pacify and accommodate, with all their whims and fancies. They told me how their husbands' egos were so big that if their wives said something that they didn't want to hear, they would either shrivel up or get angry. My aunts were all sick of that behaviour. But the older people around them would say that there aren't any men who aren't like this. Everyone's husband is the same. Just be more accommodating and live with it. But I hated that. Why do I have to get married to a person who's like a son? Why do I always have to be the one who accommodates? So, I resolved to stay single. But I met that man and fell in love with him. I told you before, right? I was the one who cajoled him into marriage. That evening, I realised something. I, too, married a son who I thought was a husband. I was living with a man-child. The truth became clear to me. I was so, so, so miserable living with that man. I was suffering because of him. A burning pain in my heart. When I found out that it was all an act, there was no way I could continue living with him. The next morning, I told him: let's get a divorce.'

Jimi looked at Minjun, her face more at peace now.

'When I was swearing about him in front of you, I hadn't realised that I was doing the exact same thing my aunts did to me when I was young. I'm sorry, Minjun. I hope you're not going to be turned off by marriage because of me, right?'

He shook his head.

'You didn't only say bad things about him. In between all the swearing, you also told me that he wasn't a bad person,' Minjun said calmly.

Jimi's face flushed deeper.

'That's what my aunts did too. They cussed and swore at the husbands, but in the end, they said there was no one like their husband.'

The two of them chuckled quietly.

'Thanks for listening to me all the time and never showing a hint of impatience.'

'I'll always be here. If you need a listening ear, call me.' Minjun made a calling gesture with his hand to lighten the mood, and Jimi responded with an okay sign.

When Yeongju reached her apartment, the two ladies were crouching by her door. Looking at the bags in their hands, Jimi seemed to have bought the snacks while Jungsuh was in charge of the beer. Inside her apartment, they automatically started to unpack the food and drinks and laid out the plates. And as if on cue, they lay down on the floor at the same time, stretching out their limbs with their eyes closed.

'This feels good,' Yeongju murmured.

'Absolutely.'

'For sure.'

After recharging on the floor for a while, they sat up and attacked the snacks.

Dipping her spoon into the yuzu pudding, Jimi looked at Jungsuh.

'I heard it's difficult to catch you these days. Been busy?'

Jungsuh took a bite of her vanilla pudding.

'I've been going to job interviews.'

Yeongju's eyes went round as she tore off the plastic cover of her cheese pudding.

'Interviews? You're going back to work?'

'Of course, I have to,' Jungsuh replied in a matter-of-fact tone as she blinked. 'Money. Money. Money is the problem!' she exclaimed, leaning her head against the wall.

'It's always the money,' said Jimi.

'Have you rested enough?' Yeongju asked.

Jungsuh was digging into the pudding as if she'd lost her soul. But when she sat up properly, her eyes were bright and focused again. She nodded.

'Of course. And I learnt how to control my feelings. No matter what happens, I think I'll be able to get over it.'

'Ooh, that's great. Tell us more.' Jimi waved her spoon, encouraging Jungsuh to go on.

'Even if I'm angry, I think I won't feel as miserable. I can always knit or meditate. It'll still be tough but I'm sure I can get over it. There's bound to be shitty people in the workplace. I'll be a contract worker again and there'll still be people who belittle me at work. But those people are not important to me at all. Inner peace. I'll find my own peace. I'll keep the hobbies I enjoy, and I'll continue to meet good people like you two. I'll try to fight and win against this harsh world.'

The two eonnies clapped and cheered. The conversation turned to their stress-relieving routines. Yeongju said she would go for a walk or read; Jimi would chat with someone or sleep the day away. Jungsuh chimed in, saying that she was a very good singer and would visit the noraebang often to sing her stress away. Jungsuh's jaw dropped when she heard that Yeongju had last visited a noraebang more than ten years ago, and immediately cajoled them into a noraebang visit that weekend. Alright, let's hang out again during the weekend, they cheered as they clinked glasses.

'What's going on between you and that author?' Jungsuh asked as she put her beer can on the floor. Blinking, Yeongju pretended she had no idea what Jungsuh was talking about. Or rather, she was surprised at how Jungsuh could have known about *that*. Perhaps her mind was playing tricks on her, she thought, and decided to feign ignorance. Not noticing her deliberate silence, Jungsuh continued:

'Eonnie, doesn't that author like you?'

Yeongju was stunned. This time, it was Jimi who chimed in.

'Who? Which author? So many authors weave in and out of that bookshop of hers. Which one is it? That person says he likes Yeongju?'

'Looks like it. The other day when Yeongju eonnie came back looking so pale, the author lost even more colour.'

Scrutinising Yeongju, Jimi asked, 'Was it that day when your ex-husband's friend came?'

Yeongju caressed the beer can in silence, keeping her eyes on the floor. Seeing how Yeongju's face was a little pale, Jungsuh and Jimi glanced at each other and silently agreed to stop pursuing the topic.

To lighten the mood, Jungsuh told them about her job interview the previous week. She had remained unflappable when questioned about the one-year gap in her résumé as she told the interviewer that she spent the year knitting and meditating. Her imitation of the interviewer's slack-jawed expression sent the two eonnies into peals of laughter. Having eaten their fill, the three of them lay down comfortably on the floor. Suddenly, Jimi stretched out her arm to nudge Yeongju's hand.

'Thanks for today. I know you asked to meet to make me feel better. If either of you are having a hard time, tell me. I'll come running over.'

Yeongju squeezed her hand lightly.

'You are welcome here every day. You can sleep over tonight.'

'I have lots of time too,' Jungsuh chimed in as she looked up the ceiling.

'Uhm. And. About that author.' Yeongju paused, glancing at Jimi. 'I can't believe I'm saying this, but I hope that he'll meet a better woman than me. Hence, nothing's happening between us.'

'What?' Jimi sprang up, pulling Yeongju to a sitting position. 'I can't believe that I'm hearing someone say this. Even dramas stopped using such an old-fashioned line. You hope he meets a better person than you? What makes you think this way? Wasn't he already aware of your situation when he said he liked you?'

'I'm not a good person to be in a relationship with,' Yeongju replied lightly and tried to lie back down again, but Jimi grabbed hold of her.

'Why aren't you a good person to be in a relationship with? You're smart, good at jokes. You know how to make people feel at ease, and you're good at being a know-it-all. That's way more charming than those people who keep saying, "I don't know!"'

Yeongju held Jimi's hand for a moment before letting go. 'I'm not sure how I feel.'

She thought back to a few Saturdays ago when Seungwoo, just about to leave after the weekly seminar, had passed her a book – Kent Haruf's *Our Souls at Night*. 'I was thinking about something like this kind of relationship,' he told her. That night, Yeongju hesitated for a while before flipping open the slim, elegant book, and read it until daybreak in one sitting. The novel was about the loneliness of the twilight years of life, and the bittersweet love that sprouted between a man and a woman. At first, she was surprised. Why did Seungwoo give her a book about old age? But as she read the sentences he'd underlined, she understood his message.

He liked spending time with her, and he enjoyed talking to her. So, don't fear falling in love. When you're lonely, and when you hate being alone, come to me. If you come, my door will always be open for you.

Seungwoo was telling her that he would wait.

Jimi tapped the floor as she murmured, 'Hmm, unsure of your feelings . . .'

Seeing how Jimi didn't have an answer, Jungsuh chimed in.

'This calls for a test, no? If you don't know how you feel, then you should test your feelings.'

'How?' Jimi asked.

'Eonnie. Think about this. That day, would you rather his face turn pale because of you, or that he acts as if it was none of his business? When you feel like crying, do you want him to be sad with you, or be nonchalant? If something good happens to you, would you want him to cheer you on, or not? Try to think about it. If you prefer that he doesn't act like it's none of his concern, then you also have feelings for him.'

Finding her idea cute, the corners of Yeongju's lips tugged up into a smile. Immediately, Jimi smacked her on the arm, as if this was not the time to be smiling.

'I like that you're a logical person. But sometimes logic doesn't make great people, because you'll always place logic above your heart. And you'll claim to not know your feelings when, in fact, you do.'

Yeongju was still smiling. *Do I really know my heart?* She thought back to the look in Seungwoo's eyes when he'd confessed his feelings to her. And when he said to like each other. Was she happy to hear it? Did her heart flutter? Perhaps Jimi was right. She already knew the answer; she knew her heart. *Is that important? Is my heart important?* She couldn't give him an answer. What should she do? What could she do? Yeongju had no idea.

# A Place that Makes Me a Better Person

Minjun, remember what I said to you on the day we first met? I told you I didn't know if I could keep the bookshop running beyond two years. I said that, right at the start, because I thought that it'd help you to plan for the future. But look, we've spent almost two years together.

I have no idea how time passed in the first year, when I started the bookshop. Hyunam-dong Bookshop without you was a mess. Luckily, even though I made mistakes time and again, it wasn't that obvious. Or rather, there weren't many customers to notice my mistakes. If you want to know how things were back then, ask Mincheol's mother. There's nothing she doesn't know about the bookshop.

For the first few months, I didn't even bother trying to woo more customers. It felt like I was the customer, awkwardly hanging out at the bookshop every day. Every day, I opened and closed the bookshop on the dot; in between, I sat down to think and to read. Rinse and repeat. I spent each day picking up the things I'd lost along the way – one or two at a time. I was an empty shell when the bookshop first opened, but slowly, about six months in, that emptiness dissipated.

I started to look at the bookshop through the eye of a business owner. Part of me wanted to run the bookshop like a dream come true; it was, indeed, a time and place for my dreams. Yet, I realised that I needed to view the bookshop from another lens. Even if I had no idea how long I could keep it running – two years, maybe three – I wanted to keep going, and therefore I needed to keep the 'exchanges' active. A bookshop is a space where an exchange of books, and everything related to them, with money takes place. It's the job of the bookshop owner to ensure that such exchanges flourish. I reminded myself every day, as if writing a diary. I started promoting the bookshop actively. I worked hard to ensure that the bookshop's unique characteristics were not lost. And in the future, I'll continue to work hard.

When you started working here, the bookshop welcomed a new type of exchange – the exchange of your labour with my money. This sounds a little stiff, right? As if I'm putting a distance between us. Of course not! It's through this exchange that we became bonded by fate; we spent time together and made an impact on each other's lives. With these exchanges happening simultaneously at the book-shop, my responsibilities grew. I had to work harder to earn more money and pay more wages. As we worked together, I seeded a hope. I hope that through your labour, my efforts will be recognised and valued. In the future, I'll work harder to earn more money, and work harder to pay you more. Have you caught on to why I keep saying *in the future*?

I'm grateful to have someone working for me. Without you, Hyunam-dong Bookshop wouldn't be where it is right now. There wouldn't be customers who initially came in to read, only to be enticed by the aroma of the coffee, nor would there be regulars who come in just for your coffee. The quality of our coffee isn't the only thing that changed because of you. Have I ever told you how your diligence is a role model for me? It's true. Seeing a colleague in the same workspace so focused on his work is a huge motivation. Observing the way you worked for a couple of days, I trusted you completely. In this dangerous (!) world, to be able to trust someone else other than yourself is something to rejoice about. I'm sure you would agree, right?

I'm thankful you're working for me. At the same time, I keep thinking how great it would be if you're also working for yourself. This way, you'll find meaning in the work you do. My experience taught me that even if I'm working for someone else, I need to work for myself. Working for myself means that I'll try my best in what I do. More importantly, never lose myself, no matter if it's at work or outside. There's something else you shouldn't forget. If you're unhappy or unsatisfied with your work life, and each day is spent in meaningless misery, it's time to look for something else. Why? Because we only get one shot in life, and we're living it now. Minjun, what kind of life are you leading as you spend your time here at the bookshop? You aren't losing yourself, right? I'm a little worried about that.

You should be able to guess why I feel this way. Because I was someone who continued to work despite losing myself. It's a huge regret of mine – not having a healthy work life. I had thought of work as stairs. Stairs to climb to reach the top. Now, I see work as food. Food that you need every day. Food that makes a difference to my body, my heart, my mental health, and my soul. There is food you just shove down your throat, and food that you eat with care and sincerity. I want to be one who takes great care in eating simple food. Not for anyone, but for myself.

I've become a better person at the bookshop. I tried to put into practice things I've learnt through books, and not merely leave them to be stories within pages. I'm selfish. I have a long way to go to become a great person, but working here, I've learnt to share and to give. Yes, I'm someone who has to resolve to share and give. It'd be nice to be born with a generous heart, but unfortunately, I wasn't. In the future, I'll strive to be a better person. Good things in books shouldn't just stay in ink and on paper. I want things happening around me to be good stories that can be shared with others. Hence, I'd like to ask you for a favour.

I want to take back my words from our first meeting. I want to try running the bookshop for a longer time. Until now, I've taken a passive attitude to many things. I was scared that if I worked too hard, I'd be living the way I did in the past. I was scared to see the bookshop as work, and only work. Honestly, there are times I wish I could still come and go freely like a guest, which was what I did in the first six months. Because of such thoughts and feelings, I hesitated. I had second thoughts about keeping this place running. But from now on, I want to stop hesitating. I love this bookshop, the people I've met. I love being here. I want to keep this place alive.

I'll find a balance among these conflicting thoughts and feelings as I run the bookshop. I believe I can do it. The bookshop is part of capitalist society, but it is, at the same time, a place of my dreams. I hope it can go on for a long time. I want to live my life thinking about the bookshop and books. And as I tackle these worries, I hope you'll be by my side. What do you think, Minjun? Shall we work together for a longer time? Would you like to join the bookshop as a permanent employee?

## Let's Meet in Berlin

Minjun quickly accepted Yeongju's proposition. The two of them sat at the table to draw up a new contract. With her hands folded across her chest, Yeongju looked at him sign the document.

'Now you can't quit easily.'

He passed the signed contract to her.

'Aren't you aware? Quitting is the trend among permanents now.'

They laughed.

It was after Taewoo's visit that she began to think about the next steps. Until then, it was almost like a habit to think about the bookshop closing sooner or later. Now, she decided to actively carve out a future for the bookshop.

Once she changed her mindset, she busied herself putting Plans 1, 2, and 3 into action. Plan 1 was to keep those she trusted by her side; Plan 2 was to travel. She would take a month off to visit independent bookshops around the world, in the hope of finding inspiration for Hyunam-dong Bookshop's transformation. She wanted to visit independent bookshops with a long tradition; she wanted to know what kept them going.

Her efforts might come to naught, and she knew it, too. Even if she spent an entire year – not just a month – studying other bookshops, it was possible that Hyunam-dong Bookshop might not even last another year. That said, even if there was only a month left, she decided not to think about how it wouldn't work, but to focus on finding hope in the way forward. The bookshop could only change if the people running the place experienced those changes themselves first. Hence, it was important for changes to start with Yeongju. Hope. She would move in the direction of hope.

A month before her trip, she told Minjun and Sangsu of her plans. They decided to keep June's operations to the bare minimum – Minjun and Sangsu would work full-time for eight hours, five days a week, and they would pause talks, events and seminars. Jungsuh and Wooshik agreed to help out whenever they could. Jungsuh would take charge of the online operations, while Wooshik would drop by after work and help with whatever was needed.

When Yeongju announced her travel plans on Instagram and the blog, along with the bookshop's schedule for June, several customers called to send their regards. She picked out a handful of books, thinking that she could continue doing book reviews during the month-long trip. They were essay collections, or novels set against the backdrop of the cities she planned to visit. It was one of the most effective reading methods: to visit the places in the book and read it there. To spend hours reading about New York, Prague and Berlin in the cities themselves. Was there a more romantic way of reading than this?

In between work, she tried to picture her upcoming trip – bookshop-hopping in unfamiliar cities, guided by Google Maps, discovering the shops' charisma and charms, while dreaming of recreating them in her bookshop. She imagined wandering around the bookshops, taking a break at cafés before heading to her next destination. A whole month doing that. Her main goal was visiting bookshops, but there was something else that made her heart flutter. It was her first solo trip, the first trip that would truly feel like a vacation.

In the limousine bus headed for the airport, the summer of Seoul streaked past in a blur outside the window. Her mother's face flashed across her mind, but she closed her eyes, erasing the image. Yeongju knew why her mother was so angry with her. Her mother was someone who hated failure as much as she feared it. To her, divorce is the biggest defeat a woman could experience. She hated – and was afraid of – the disgrace. Hence, she abandoned her. Her mother was weak in the face of failure; she simply did to her daughter what any weak person would do. To such a mother, Yeongju didn't want to explain that she was wrong, that the world had changed, and above all, that her daughter was no failure. She still didn't want to be the one to reach out first.

Leaning back on the headrest, Yeongju was staring out the window when her phone vibrated. It was Mincheol.

'There's something I really wanted to tell you,' he said, sounding abashed.

Keeping her eyes on the scenery, she asked what it was.

'I've decided not to go to university,' he said.

She paused for a moment.

'You've made up your mind. Good for you. You still have lots of time ahead of you,' she added. 'In the future, you could still go on to pursue whatever you wanted.' *That's what everyone says, but it's also the truth,* she thought.

'Okay,' Mincheol replied. 'Oh, I finished reading *The Catcher in the Rye*,' he added.

Immediately, Yeongju's face lit up, as if he was right in front of her.

'What did you think of the book?' she asked.

'Boring,' he said, chuckling softly.

'What? Did you read it just to tell me that it's indeed boring?'

'No, no.' Over the phone, Mincheol sounded a little nervous. 'I mean, it wasn't interesting. But strangely, I kept thinking that the protagonist is like me, even though we have nothing in common. Not our personalities, not the way we act. Everything is different. Yet, I kept thinking we're similar. Is it because we're sick of the world? Or that we lack interest in everything? It's comforting to know that I'm not the only one who feels this way. At the end of the book, he wanted to be the catcher in the rye, to catch the kids if they start to go over the cliff. Do you remember this part?'

'Yeah.'

'It was that bit that made me come to the decision. That it's okay not to go to university. I can't explain why, but that's how I feel. There's no logic . . . but somehow it felt as if he was telling me that it's okay not to go.'

'I get it.' Yeongju nodded as if she was looking at him.

Mincheol startled. 'Really? You really understand? I can't even understand it myself.'

'Yup, I really do. There have been many times I made a decision while reading a book. I understand how seemingly illogical it feels.'

'Ah . . . I'll be fine, right?'

'About?'

'Making an . . . illogical decision.'

'Of course. Even if it's illogical, it's supported by your heart. That's how I see it.'

'My heart?'

'Yeah.'

'My heart made the decision? For my future?'

'That's right.'

'Ah . . . okay . . . it makes me feel better. That my heart was the one who chose.'

'Yeah. You'll be fine.'

Over the phone, Yeongju could hear him breathing deeply. A short while later, his voice brightened.

'Alright. Have a good trip, Yeongju imo. See you back at the bookshop.'

'Okay. Stay well and healthy.'

'Alright. Also, thank you.'

'Why are you thanking me?'

'It's been very helpful going to the bookshop. I enjoyed talking to you.'

'That's great.'

Yeongju was about to return the phone to her bag when she felt it vibrate again. Thinking that it was Mincheol again, she glanced at the screen. Seungwoo. She stared at the name with mixed feelings. He'd kept quiet when she told him about her plans to travel. As the seminars had come to an end in May, she didn't have to worry about how his schedule would be impacted by her trip. They hadn't seen each other for almost a month. She met him only through his column, and perhaps it was the same for him.

While her thoughts drifted, the call ended. Then her phone vibrated again. Immediately, she picked up. She hadn't heard his voice in a long while.

'This is Hyun Seungwoo.'

'Yes.'

'Are you on the way to the airport?'

'Yes, heading there now.'

For a moment, there was silence. He said her name.

'Yeongju.'

'Yes?'

'Could I ask where you will be in the last week of June?'

'The last week of June?'

'Yes.'

'. . . Germany.'

'Which part of Germany?'

'Berlin.'

'Have you been to Berlin?'

'No.'

'I've stayed in Berlin before for two months. For work.'

'Ah . . . I see.'

'Is it okay if I go to Berlin that week?'

'Huh?'

Her mind went blank.

'I've applied for leave that week. I was thinking I could be your travel partner. How do you feel about that?'

'I . . .'

Hearing the hesitation in her voice, he calmly replied, 'Do you prefer that I'm not there?'

'It's too sudden.'

She tried to hide her nervousness.

'I see . . . I understand. Of course, you might feel this way. But I wanted to at least ask.'

For a long moment, there was silence. Thinking that he should end the call, Seungwoo said, 'In that case, have a good trip. I'll hang up.'

Somehow, Yeongju felt as though it would be the last time she'd hear his voice on the phone. She looked out the window. In the distance, she could make out the lights of the airport.

'Yeongju?'

'Yes.'

'You're so quiet. Are you okay?'

'Yes, I'm fine.'

'Alright. I'll hang up now.'

'Ah. Seungwoo,' she hurriedly called out.

'Yes.'

She didn't want to end the call. For some reason, she felt as though if she let the call end here, she would never be able to see him again. But what should she say? She decided to be honest. Honesty is always the best answer to uncertainty.

'I don't know if it's a good thing for you to come to Berlin. Just the other day, someone told me this: if you don't know your heart, put it to the test. But I don't know how. I don't know what to do right now.'

'Let me help you.'

'How?'

'Imagine this. Right now, imagine that you and I are walking along the streets of Berlin. We're moving from bookshop to bookshop, stopping for meals, clinking beer glasses. Imagine this. For a while, no, thirty seconds. Just imagine it for thirty seconds.'

Yeongju did what she was told. She tried to imagine the scene, focusing on each moment – drinking tea with Seungwoo, chatting over meals, making toasts. Him walking alongside her on the street. Stepping into a bookshop for the first time together, chatting about books and booksellers. Sometimes she would be the one asking questions, other times him. Reading next to each other and discussing the books. He would be writing, and next to him, she'd playfully interrupt him. Him cracking a joke while she was reading, making her laugh. She tried to play out these scenes in her head . . . She would enjoy that. She didn't dislike being with Seungwoo. No. She found herself wanting it. She wanted to be with him, to talk to him.

'How was it? Did you dislike what you see?'

'Not at all,' she replied honestly.

'In that case . . . can I come along?' he asked hesitantly.

'Alright. I'll see you in Berlin.' Her expression was relaxed.

'Okay, I'll be there,' he said, just as the limousine bus turned into the airport.

# What Keeps a Bookshop Alive?

A year later.

Sipping the coffee that Minjun had brewed, Yeongju's eyes were trained on the sentences in the novel. Mincheol, who only knew J. D. Salinger, had picked out the book for the simple reason that it was a slim one. As Yeongju worked her way through *Franny and Zooey*, in her mind, she was grumbling, *Serves you right!* While it was short, it was no easy read. She doubted he would enjoy it very much.

Right now, only Yeongju and Minjun were at work, but in fifteen minutes' time, Sangsu would be coming in. Six months ago, Sangsu had joined Minjun as the second full-time employee of the bookshop. When Yeongju asked that he convert from a part-timer to full-time staff, the first thing he asked was about the hair length. If he had to cut his hair short, he didn't care for being an employee.

Yeongju replied, 'Alright, you're one of us now.'

He was his usual gruff self when he accepted her proposal, but when he came in on his first official day as a permanent employee, his face was flushed. A few days later, Yeongju found out the reason. Sangsu let on that it was his first time being a permanent full-time employee.

The day after Sangsu officially joined the bookshop, a new addition appeared in the shop: a small shelf filled with books he'd read. On top, a sign read: 'Crew-cut Bookworm Sangsu's Reads.' Next to it, in smaller print: 'Please read them and have a discussion with Sangsu.'

Because he was now a full-time staff member, he only had time for one book a day. That said, he continued to stay true to his name and impress the customers with his knowledge of books. Regulars in the bookshop would now naturally go to Sangsu for book recommendations and many were curious about what he was reading. Having noticed that, Yeongju decided to create a little corner for him.

Three months earlier, Mincheol also started working part-time at the bookshop. Once he'd decided not to apply to university, he'd taken a three-month trip to Europe and had only come back last spring. Heejoo was the one who'd suggested the trip; it was the condition for letting Mincheol skip university preparations. She reasoned that it was better for him to experience an unfamiliar world, rather than being holed up in his room the whole time. While Mincheol was away, Heejoo told Yeongju – forlorn and excited in equal parts – that the university tuition fees she'd saved up for him no longer served their use, so the family members had decided to use the money to take turns going on holiday. Once Mincheol was back, Heejoo would travel with her husband, who had taken a leave of absence from work. Right now, they were on a round-the-world trip.

Less than a week after he returned, Mincheol had come to the bookshop to look for Yeongju. Looking more tanned and mature, he had asked her to take him on as a part-timer. She agreed readily, and the next day, he started to work twice a week at the bookshop, for three hours a day. But she had one condition. He had to join the Hyunam-dong

Bookshop employee event, where the four of them would read a book together every month.

The event was also open to anyone who was interested. On the first day of each month, they would announce 'The Book of the Month for Hyunam-dong Bookshop Staff' on Instagram and the blog. On the last Thursday of the month, they would then hold a book club meeting to discuss the book. At first, only a couple of people joined them. But now, the number of people had slowly increased, and last month there were fifteen of them. This month, they were going to discuss Salinger's *Franny and Zooey*.

What was the biggest change in the past year for the bookshop? Yeongju didn't make any immediate changes when she returned from her month-long trip. Instead, she continued to stick to the status quo for two months before she started implementing the plans she'd deliberated over during that time. Hyunam-dong Bookshop's charms would lie in the depth and diversity of its collection, she decided. Her idea was to focus on curating books with depth, even if it might be a little challenging for customers. As for promoting diversity, it was decided that the bookshop would stop carrying bestsellers.

Bestsellers had always been a point of contention for her. Looking at the titles that rose through the ranks of the top sellers, she was often frustrated. Not because the books themselves had any issues. Once a book made the bestseller list, it would continue to stay there for a long time. Gradually, she became convinced that bestsellers were the reason the publishing industry had lost its diversity.

Standing in front of the bestseller section in major bookshops felt like looking at the state of the publishing industry – highly skewed towards a few titles. Whose fault was it? Nobody's. It was simply a reflection of a society which doesn't read. Faced with this reality, what booksellers should do, even if they only played a small role, was to introduce a diverse range of books to customers. To show them the publishing world wasn't made up of only a few bestsellers, or big-shot authors. To impress upon them that there were many more awesome books and authors out there, waiting to be discovered.

For that to happen, she decided to exclude bestsellers from the bookshop. If there was a book that became an overnight hit thanks to a famous person who mentioned it on TV, she would no longer bring in more copies of it after they sold out their existing stock. Not because it wasn't a good book, but to uphold diversity. In such cases, she would seek out books with similar themes and stock them instead. Customers who came in looking for the title would be directed to these books.

She wasn't sure if this fresh approach would work for customers. One thing was certain, Sungchul was completely charmed.

'A book becomes a bestseller because it's a bestseller.'

He told Yeongju that he felt a sense of camaraderie, seeing how their industries were facing the same issues. May more people get to know more good books and good movies, he liked to say. This was Plan 3 she'd made even before the trip: to take away the bestsellers.

The bookshop also welcomed several other changes, big and small, yet in some sense, it didn't change much. Whether it was the past, or now, the bookshop reflected Yeongju's philosophy and perspective. One of the key takeaways from the trip was that independent bookshops overseas had their own distinct personality – a personality that reflected that of their owners. To make the bookshop's personality shine, she needed courage. For her courage to reach the customers, she needed sincerity. Courage. And sincerity.

If she could master the courage to put her thoughts into action without losing sincerity, perhaps Hyunam-dong Bookshop could continue to live on like the bookshops she'd visited. If she could continuously reflect and improve, perhaps the bookshop would have a longer lifespan. Most importantly, she mustn't forget her roots – that she was a book-lover at heart. If she and her employees loved books, wouldn't the love also be passed on? If books were the medium through which the four of them communicated, joked, built friendships and love, wouldn't the customers feel the same way? If people started to believe that there's something in life that only people who read can discover, stories in this world that only people who read can tell, wouldn't more of them be seduced to peel back the pages of a book? Yeongju wanted to live her life reading books and introducing them to others, so that when people walked in seeking a story, she could help them find what they needed.

Today would continue from yesterday. Surrounded by books, Yeongju would spend her day chatting, working and writing about books. In between the hustle and bustle, she would find time to eat, to chat and to ponder over life. Happy times, alongside the low moments. And when closing time came around, she would think, I did quite well today, and step out of the bookshop feeling happy. In the ten minutes it took for her to get home, she'd be on the phone with Seungwoo, perhaps for a little longer after she reached home. Shower. Rest. Perhaps Jimi, who'd moved into the unit above hers, would drop by with Jungsuh tagging behind, and they'd enjoy a beer together for the first time in a while. Or maybe she would be home alone, a little melancholic about losing the great view from her window.

Now that she was responsible for the livelihoods of more employees, she had to settle for an apartment with a lesser view. But as she continued reading the novel from where she left off yesterday, her mood would improve. Closing the book, she lay down on the bed. *A day well spent is a life well lived.* Thinking about the line she'd read somewhere, she would drift off to sleep.

## Author's Note

2018. Summer was around the corner. As usual, I was sitting at my desk, eyes fixed to the white screen. It'd been about six months since I'd become a writer. At that time, I was despairing over how much further I had ahead of me to become a good essayist. Still, thinking that I should at least keep writing, I stuck to my desk every day.

Should I try writing a novel?

I can't remember exactly which month, which day, at what hour and minute the thought came to me, but I remembered starting a fresh document a few days later. I had only three things in mind: a bookshop starting with the character *hyu*, Yeongju, the bookshop owner, and Minjun, the barista. I began to write. Everything else fell in to place as the novel progressed. Whenever a new character stepped in, I gave them a name and fleshed out their personality. If I had no idea what came next, I'd get the new character to chat with the older ones, and somehow, they seemed to guide the story and the next scene would come naturally to me.

Writing a novel was surprisingly enjoyable. I had thought writing was a laborious process that dragged and nailed me to the desk. But this was different. I woke up every morning eager to continue the dialogue where I had left off. At night, my eyes dry and my back stiff, I reluctantly got up from my chair, mindful of my own rule not to do more than a day's work. During the time spent writing the novel, I cared more about the characters and their lives than my own. My life revolved around the stories I told.

While I didn't plan out the plot before starting to write, I knew the atmosphere I wanted to create. I wanted to write a novel evoking the mood of *Kamome Diner* and *Little Forest*. A space we can escape to, a refuge from the intensity of daily life where we can't even pause to take a breather. A space to shelter us from the harsh criticisms whipping us to do more, to go faster. A space to snuggle comfortably for a day. A day without something siphoning our energy, a day to replenish what's lost. A day we begin with anticipation and end with satisfaction. A day where we grow, and from growth sprouts hope. A day spent having meaningful conversations with good people. Most importantly, a day where we feel good, and our heart beats strongly. I wanted to write about such a day, and the people within it.

In other words, I wanted to write what I want to read. Stories of people who find their own pace and direction, of people who believe in others and wait by their side as they go through difficult times, lost in worry. Stories of those who support others, who celebrate small efforts and resolve in a society that puts people – and everything about them – down once they take a fall. Stories that bring comfort, providing a pat on the shoulder for those who've lost the joy in life, having pushed themselves too hard to do well.

I'm not sure if the novel turned out the way I hoped, but many readers told me the book gave them warmth and comfort. Likewise, their generous reviews strengthened me, as if a connection had formed between isolated individuals.

You might not notice right away, but everyone in the novel is taking small steps forward, whether it's learning something new, or making a change to their lives. What they're doing might be far from achieving what society deems as success, but they're growing and changing through their consistent efforts – taking several steps away from where they started off. How others judge where they stand – be it high or low, good or bad – doesn't matter to them. The fact that they've progressed, and are happy where they are, is sufficient. The yardstick to measure one's life lies within oneself. And that's good enough.

Even if it's not every day, or often, there are moments in life where we come to think, *That's good enough.* In that moment, all the anxiety and worries melt away, leaving us with the realisation that we've done our best to get to where we are. We're satisfied, and proud of ourselves. If Hyunam-dong Bookshop is an accumulation of such moments in life, I hope that many more people can create a similar space for themselves.

To you, who are spending the day there, I'm here rooting for you.

January 2022
Hwang Bo-reum

# A NOTE ON THE AUTHOR

HWANG BO-REUM studied computer science and worked as a software engineer. Hwang authored several essay collections: *I Read Every Day*, *I Tried Kickboxing for the First Time* and *The Perfect Distance*. *Welcome to the Hyunam-dong Bookshop* is her first novel.

# A NOTE ON THE TRANSLATOR

SHANNA TAN is a Singaporean translator working from Korean, Chinese and Japanese into English. She was selected for two emerging literary translator mentorships in 2021/22, where she was mentored by Anton Hur and Julia Sanches. Her prose translations have appeared in The Southern Review, The Common, Azalea: Journal of Korean Literature & Culture and more.

# A NOTE ON THE TYPE

The text of this book is set in Minion, a digital typeface designed by Robert Slimbach in 1990 for Adobe Systems. The name comes from the traditional naming system for type sizes, in which minion is between nonpareil and brevier. It is inspired by late Renaissance-era type.